America:
The North Star of Humanity

America: The North Star of Humanity. Copyright © 2022 by Michael Urtnowski.

First Edition

Published by MCS

Edited by Louis Maurici

Cover image: *The Prayer at Valley Forge* by Arnold Friberg. Copyright © Creative Fine Art, Inc. Used with permission.

Cover design by Diane M. Palma at Digho, LLC.

ISBN: 979-8-9873801-0-9 (Softcover)

ISBN: 979-8-9873801-2-3 (Hardcover)

ISBN: 979-8-9873801-1-6 (PDF e-book)

Printed in the United States of America

America:
The North Star of Humanity

Michael Urtnowski

Edited by Louis Maurici

America: The North Star of Humanity is dedicated first to my parents,
Eugene Urtnowski and Mary Ellen McBride Urtnowski,
and to my wife, Valerie P. Urtnowski,
for tireless support and assistance.

America: The North Star of Humanity is also in remembrance of
Michael Chodorcoff and Raymond Gimbut.

Acknowledgments

America: The North Star of Humanity has been in development for many months. First, I want to give thanks to God for His inspiration during the development and completion of this project.

I have received assistance from several people along the way. I want to thank my wife, Valerie, for her tireless support. I also want to thank my editor, Louis Maurici, who has provided indispensable assistance in planning, coordinating, and revising materials for publication.

Additionally, I want to thank the following manuscript readers: Jean Chodorcoff and Ernest Dixon for the time and effort they spent reviewing the manuscript. I also want to thank Creative Fine Art, Inc., for permission to use Arnold Friberg's painting, *The Prayer at Valley Forge*. Thanks also to Diane Palma from Digho, LLC., for her talent and creative design for the cover of *America: The North Star of Humanity*.

I'd like to recognize my family — my five sisters: Jean, Mary Ellen, Betty, Rosie, and Judy; my children: Lisa and her husband, Jason; Mike and his wife, Nicole; Laurie; Rhiannon and her husband, Peter; and my seven grandchildren: Anthony, Logan, Tyler, Justin, Scarlett, Sage, and Christopher. I'd also like to thank my friends Tom and Ginny, and my cousin Major Charles Urtnowski (USMC, Retired) and his wife, Rose, for their support and encouragement.

Table of Contents

Foreword ix

Introduction xi

Part One: Occidental Culture 1

Chapter One. The Promise of America 3

Chapter Two. Western Civilization and the Roots of Democracy 23

Chapter Three. Age of Reason/Enlightenment.................................... 59

Part Two: The World Turned Upside Down 91

Chapter Four. By the Rude Bridge... 93

Chapter Five. When in the Course of Human Events 133

Chapter Six. A New Constellation Appears....................................... 177

Part Three: The Bands of Connection 289

Chapter Seven. A More Perfect Union... 291

Chapter Eight. "A City upon a Hill" 319

Notes.. 343

Foreword by the Editor

Humanity needs you to read this book. Liberty and justice are under scrutiny in America, and there are forces working to replace our national identity with something disconnected from the truth of our proud and providential history. It is existentially important that we denounce the cynical and distorted views on our past, and this book is designed to help all people stay inspired in that good fight and centered in the truth of America.

Ardent historian Michael Urtnowski traces the roots of America's founding values from antiquity to the Enlightenment to show that America was a country born to protect every person's God-given rights. He traces the evolution of America's exceptionalism from colonial times to the Civil War to show America as a country that has always fought against great odds to secure liberty and justice for all. He reveals the insidious forces currently working to undermine our freedoms, and he impresses on us the diligence that is necessary to preserve those freedoms.

It is not the author's intention to portray America as a perfect nation. No person or nation is perfect, but the best among us will always strive to create a better and more just world for ourselves and those around us, and the best among nations will always strive to remedy its ills and fight for liberty and justice for all. It is our responsibility as Americans never to forget our nation's legacy and to make sure we remain a beacon of hope and a safe haven for humanity.

Introduction

It was 1962. I was nine years old, and school had let out for summer vacation. My family, consisting of my three younger sisters along with my mom, had arrived at my grandparents' summer bungalow at Lake Ronkonkoma on Long Island in New York. The small bungalow housed upwards of eight to ten of my cousins along with my grandparents and aunts. The cousins would sleep in an upstairs loft where pillow fights were the manner in which we reveled coming together. Our family bungalow provided a place and time to explore the woods and swim in the lake. The fond memories of our time spent with family in an unplanned atmosphere bring me back to a time and place where life was unhurried and simple. On some summer afternoons, my cousins and I would visit a neighbor who was an elderly WWI Veteran. He loved to tell stories of his exploits as a young soldier in France and the ordeals that his fellow "Doughboys" experienced during the "Great War." This WWI Veteran inspired me with his patriotic stories and love for America. I took his message and his reflections on the meaning of America to my heart, and I embarked on a lifelong quest to understand why my country, our country, America, is a special place with benevolent meaning not just for Americans, but for all the people of the world. You don't have to be an American to appreciate the role the country plays in the dreams and aspirations of people around the world.

My lifelong personal journey of understanding the origins of the American experience and the factors that culminated into what we know as American exceptionalism began in the summer of 1962. In the last sixty years, many Americans' attitudes towards their country have changed. An understanding of the richness of American history and the pivotal role the country has played in establishing a liberal international world order have come to be minimized, undervalued, and even lost.

Today, some Americans view events from the past through the distortion of a contemporary lens that misrepresents the true context and historical perspective required for objective analysis. Going back in time over countless generations to the period prior to the emergence of Western civilization, people have struggled with the mistreatment of others and with social maladies inherent to the human condition. The true achievement of America has been the commitment by enlightened individuals guided by fairness, justice, and a moral compass to overcome those social maladies.

America: The North Star of Humanity is a journey through which you are invited to explore the origins and legacy of the American experience. The book is arranged in three parts: Part one reviews the ascendancy of Western civilization, the rise of democracy, and the lasting impact of the Greco-Roman civilization on contemporary times. Provided is an in-depth perspective of the contributions of the great thinkers of the Enlightenment Period including John Locke, Voltaire, Adam Smith, Thomas Hobbes, Montesquieu, and others, all of whom played important parts in the formation of American ideas on mankind's place in the universe, political and social philosophy, and American jurisprudence.

Part two of this book analyzes the American founding from the time of the first settlement at Jamestown in 1607 to the Revolutionary War. It was through the fire, tumult, and struggles of George Washington and his army that a new American character was born. From the Rude Bridge and the Battles of Lexington and Concord through Yorktown, ordinary citizens voluntarily joined the ranks to defend the principles of self-determination, freedom, liberty, and justice. It was presumptuous for the thirteen American colonies to think they could stand up to the preeminent military power of the age. The American success in defeating Great Britain began a new age in human history. The eight-year ordeal of the Revolutionary War created a unique American spirit of resolve and perseverance that ushered in the birth of a dynamic new nation.

Part three of this book outlines the aftermath of the Revolutionary War and the challenges the country experienced under the Articles of Confederation. The remedy for those difficulties was a new Constitution that memorialized the principles laid out in the Declaration of Independence: the God-given rights and exclusive value of the individual. Under the paternal guidance of George Washington and the genius of James Madison, Gouverneur Morris, Benjamin Franklin, and others, a new and enlightened governing system emerged.

This book concludes with contemporary times and the challenges and dangers that our American Republic is facing from pernicious internal forces. Over the last several decades, despotic and elitist elements have worked to undermine America's traditional concepts of governance and social cohesion. Under the guise of correcting the evils of a corrupt and racist society, the modern Left borrows from the playbook of Karl Marx and his ideas on socialism and communism to sow seeds of disconnection in the greater society. This book pushes back against that narrative and its collaborators.

The intent of this work is to provide a succinct evolutionary journey that traces the origins of the American experience and the value of American exceptionalism not just to Americans but to the world. My sincerest desire is to provide a greater awareness, understanding, and appreciation of the richness and legacy of America's history.

Part One

Occidental Culture

Chapter One

The Promise of America

The North Star beams brightly in the northern night sky. As the earth rotates on its axis, the North Star does not rise or set but remains in very nearly the same position above the northern horizon year-round while the other stars appear, from an earthly perspective, to circle around it. Throughout history, the North Star has been a beacon, guiding travelers who have embarked on quests for ports and places where they could find calm and sanctuary at the end of their journeys. It has always been a welcoming celestial lighthouse of inspiration and hope for humanity.

Mariners and travelers for centuries have followed the North Star toward a particular destination, not just toward a mere compass heading. Their voyages across wind-swept seas were marked by their hopes and prayers for that lauded place of security, a safe haven at the end of their journeys. America has been and continues to be that desired destination for millions of people longing for a safe haven of freedom, liberty, and justice. America, like the North Star, has been to the people of the world an aspirational symbol of how to live life absent of authoritarian interference and oppression. In this place, you, as a free individual, determine your life's path and can set the foundation for a better future for yourself, your family, and your posterity. Here you have a chance to achieve that better life and can rise as far as your talents and willingness to work hard will take you. America does not offer a guarantee of success; what America offers is an opportunity to achieve your dreams. America is the place where man has the best chance of achieving a meaningful and purposeful life with equal opportunity for success. It does not guarantee success; that part of the equation is up to the individual.

America is a great and noble country that has been blessed by providential design. It has benefited from bountiful natural riches and advantages of unparalleled potentials. Americans of all political perspectives recognize that the nation has had great fortune in its inherited land. America has been favored and given riches second to no other nation. Our geography is one gift, separated by two oceans on either side, which allowed the virgin Republic to grow and develop with minimal interference from the traditional powers in Europe during the eighteenth, nineteenth, and twentieth centuries. America is centered in a mostly temperate climate with fertile lands that yield rich harvests of varied food products and livestock, and our oceans are great fisheries that have always fed an ever-growing population. America also has expansive forests for lumber, plentiful natural resources, and great rivers and harbors for the transport of goods and commerce. All of these intrinsic advantages have facilitated a continuous growth and have helped America become the world's preeminent economy. These are America's benevolent fortunes from Providence.

The advantages of America's natural wealth are important and have helped the nation develop, but all of these great riches are not, in and of themselves, what make America's greatness exceptional. What makes America's greatness exceptional is the soul, character, and ingenuity of its people. From its earliest colonial period, America has been settled by a diverse set of adventurous and brave pioneers who were willing to risk everything for their dreams for their futures. The amalgamation of their prayers, visions, and aspirations manifested into the American Dream (to find that better place under the sun to live and raise a family and set a course for yourself and have the life that you choose). America is the place where people live under the protection of a constitution by which the rights of the individual are paramount. In America an individual can thrive in freedom, liberty, and justice under the law. Americans of all nationalities, races, and creeds have worked hard and together to build a society with a firm foundation, and they have faced all challenges with steadfast resolve and determination to overcome the crises of their times. The strength of the American people swells from our love for liberty and freedom, the moral compass of our national institutions, and from our faith.

America is not perfect. Perfection lies in the realm of the Almighty and is not attainable by man and his pursuits. As with all societies, Americans have struggled with discrimination, prejudice, and other injustices. These human shortcomings and frailties are part of man's condition in nature and have plagued all civilizations since the time of the Sumerians, generally recognized as the oldest civilization from more than 6,500 years ago. Man, in his unvarnished natural state void of the mollifying effects of culture, civilization, laws, and morality is a rudimentary and primitive being. The seventeenth-century English philosopher Thomas Hobbes believed that in man's natural state moral ideas do not exist. He defined good simply as that which people desire and evil as that which they avoid, at least in the state of nature.

Robert Burns described "man's inhumanity to man" in his poem titled "Man Was Made to Mourn" (1784), which is a story of the history of cruelty and injustice that has been a part of all civilizations and societies since the beginning. The struggle of man in civilization has always been to calm the primitive instincts of the beast within him and to create a more just, benevolent, and beneficial social order. The ascendancy of Western civilization around 500 BC, the adoption of Greco-Roman ideas on logic, reasoning, law, and governance, and the influence of Judeo-Christian beliefs in God and morality ushered in a new way of thinking about governance throughout European and Western societies. Those societies advanced and developed into nation states over the past 1,500 years. The inherited foundational concepts of Western civilization ultimately led to the development of the American society, beginning in the late sixteenth and early seventeenth centuries with the first English settlements at Roanoke in 1587, which disappeared, and the permanent settlement at

Jamestown, Virginia, in 1607. This foundation facilitated the future growth and development of all the American colonies and ultimately the taming of the virgin North American wilderness and the advancement of all of the people of the continent.

America is different than other societies and great among nations because of its endless quest to correct mankind's destructive behavior and prejudicial nature towards his fellow man. The purpose of America is to create as just a society as man is capable of achieving for all of its people. The Declaration of Independence, the Constitution, the Bill of Rights, the Civil War, and the numerous amendments to the Constitution are examples of the continuous efforts to improve our nation and its institutions. The goal is to bring the nation closer in line to the promise of America: freedom, liberty, and justice for all in that "more perfect union" described in the preamble of the Constitution. This is in keeping with what Madison, Hamilton, and the other founders desired to achieve for all the generations of Americans.

The pillars of America's beginnings are deeply rooted in Judeo/Christian morality and the optimism that springs from the creation of a society based on the ideas of faith in God, justice, and rule of law. The desire was and still is the attainment of justice for all American citizens. The enlightened members of the founding generation realized that their generation of the late eighteenth century was yet incapable of achieving the true promise of America. They, with their great wisdom and foresight, laid out the blueprint for those who would come after to continue the work they started. Since its inception, the country has been on a constant mission to correct and improve this noblest of man's endeavors and experiment in democracy - a democracy grounded in man's God-given rights and liberty for the individual. America's collective intellectual consciousness has always been mindful of human frailties and shortcomings with regards to the application of justice and law. The struggle continues as the people of the nation strive to overcome these divisive and harmful tendencies of human nature.

The Founders were particularly concerned about the potential for abuse of power by those who attained the highest offices of government. That is because the people gave the leaders of the country the special authority to make laws and rule over them. The Founders were mindful that elected leadership was a potentially weak point in the chain and that it could be abused to subvert democracy and the rule of law. It could not always be assumed that all of America's elected leaders, up to and including the president, would conduct themselves morally. That is why Article II, section 4 of the Constitution states that "The President, Vice President and all civil Officers of the United States, shall be removed from Office on Impeachment for, and Conviction of, Treason, Bribery, or high Crimes and Misdemeanors." The idea was to establish that no one, not even the president, was above the law and that in America we are all equal under the law and that the implements of power would never be usurped or used against the interests of the people.

Alexis Charles de Tocqueville, a French Aristocrat, diplomat, and political scientist, toured the United State in 1831 and 1832 with an associate, Gustave de Beaumont. Tocqueville authored a work in two volumes in 1835 and 1840 titled *Democracy in America.* His work analyzed the American penal system, mechanics of American democracy, political interaction, volunteerism within the civil society, and the impact of faith on the nation's communities. He believed that "equality was the great political and social idea of the era, and he thought that the United States offered the most advanced example of equality in action."[1] His work also discussed the roots of greatness in America.

> I sought for the greatness of America in her commodious harbors and her ample rivers, and it was not there. I sought for the greatness and genius of America in her fertile fields and boundless forests, and it was not there. I sought for the greatness of America in her rich minds and her vast world commerce, and it was not there. I sought for the greatness and genius of America in her public school system and her institutions of learning, and it was not there. I sought for the greatness in America in her democratic Congress and her matchless Constitution, and it was not there. Not until I went into the churches of America and heard her pulpits flame with righteousness did I understand the secret of her genius and power. America is great because she is good, and if America ever ceases to be good, she will cease to be great.[2]

Faith, Judeo/Christian values, and the enrichment from a strong belief in God are the foundation of an orderly civil society based in morality, fairness, and justice. As noted in The Heritage

Foundation's March 2016 article titled "Tocqueville on Christianity and American Democracy," Tocqueville concludes that "the preservation of America's traditional religion is one of the most important tasks of democratic statesmanship."[3] Tocqueville goes on to state that religion "should be considered the first" of America's "political institutions" and even that it is necessary for Americans to "maintain Christianity…at all costs."[4] In his overall analysis of the country, Tocqueville believed that faith and religion were vital elements that made America great. He also believed in the value of voluntary social groups, such as churches and civic associations, and the positive effects they have on a community. This was different from governmental involvement where participation was not voluntary but compensatory.

Tocqueville's assessment of mid-eighteenth-century America was an important work for explaining the unique characteristics of American society to Europeans, and it was one of the most important works of political science in the nineteenth century. His assessment, from a Frenchman's perspective of the 1830s, was not long removed from the turmoil of the French Revolution. Tocqueville's family suffered during the French Revolution's "Reign of Terror" of 1793 and 1794 when both of his parents were put in jail. He wrote about the French Revolution in his work titled *The Old Regime and the French Revolution*, in which he put forth the theory of continuity, explaining that even though the French tried to disconnect themselves from the past and the old regime, they eventually reverted to a powerful central government. The lesson from the French Revolutionary period for all democratic Republics, especially in contemporary times, is that always lurking in the shadows are the poisonous ideas of totalitarian rule, often disguised as returning order or providing stability to a society. This is just another illusion perpetuated by autocratic Leftists and statists on the people of many nations since the French Revolution.

In reviewing Tocqueville's ideas on American democracy, one could speculate that he was drawing a compare-and-contrast of the American Revolutionary period and the transition from the Articles of Confederation of 1777 to the new constitutional republic of 1787. The American transitional experience was an orderly conversion from a loose union of state governments under the Articles to a strong central government under the new Constitution. The French Revolution, in contrast, was a bloody event of carnage and vengeance. Thousands of French citizens of all classes and "estates," including King Louie XVI and his wife, Marie Antoinette, met their fates by the guillotine. The chaos and disorder that was unleashed during the French Revolution brought a series of new governments, a social transformation, and dechristianization of French society. It was not until Napoleon Bonaparte came to power through a military coup in 1799 that a semblance of order was restored to the French Republic and society. Upon reflection, Napoleon took power in France under the guise of saving the principles of the Revolution, but historians are mixed as to the lasting contribution of his seizure of power. He did restore order, reforms, and the Catholic Church as the majority church to the nation, but he also became Emperor and imposed his family's dynastic rule over France, which, in the end, was a betrayal of France's Revolutionary principles.

America today is not a religiously monolithic country centered on Protestant and, more specifically, Puritan orthodoxy. America has emerged into a society with a much more diverse set of religious beliefs. New immigrants of other denominations, including Catholics, Jews, and smaller groups of other religious faiths, have added to the nation's prayers. Most of these religions have a basic belief in treating your fellow humans with dignity and respect, notably as in Jesus' Sermon on the Mount, which tells us to "do unto others as you would have them do unto you." Arguably, America in the twenty-first century is not as much of a faith-centric society as it was in the 1830s when Tocqueville toured the country. It does, however, still maintain strong roots of morality that have been implanted in the country's institutions. In keeping Tocqueville's perception of America current, the deep roots of morality and justice in American society continue to refresh the values and calming effects that faith-based institutions bring to a society. The central core of his perception of American greatness is that it is rooted in the civilizing effects that come from a belief in God. Belief in God promotes positive values and constructive behavior among the residents of a society. Generally, religions compel the individual believer's behavior to be based in fidelity to a set of principles. These principles guide people to conduct themselves in a selfless manner with devotion and constraint. Atheists and non-religious people also greatly benefit from living in a moral and faith-based civil society. The first amendment to the Constitution states that "Congress shall make no law respecting an establishment of religion, or prohibiting the free exercise thereof." When individuals in a society conduct themselves within the constraints of religious moral behavior, the overall society benefits.

The importance of faith and religion was not undervalued by America's first two presidents. George Washington stated in his farewell address, "Of all the dispositions and habits, which lead to political prosperity, Religion and Morality are indispensable supports. It is impossible to rightly govern the world without God and the bible."[5] Washington stressed the importance of religion to the preservation of free government. John Adams also supported the concept that morality and religion were important for the support of the Constitution and the American governmental system:

> We have no government armed with power capable of contending with human passions unbridled by morality and religion. Avarice, ambition, revenge, or gallantry, would break the strongest cords of our Constitution as a whale goes through a net. Our Constitution was made only for a moral and religious people. It is wholly inadequate to the government of any other.[6]

Belief in God is the anti-toxin for human doubt and despair. The inspirational belief in Providence is the wellspring of the people, and it strengthens the nation during crises when the preservation of unity and social order hang in the balance. In America's nearly 250 years as a nation, our resolve has been tested time and time again. Our religious faiths, as a united people, have propelled the country past times of peril to a better time and place. The cold winter of 1777-1778 at Valley Forge when all seemed lost; the sacking of Washington; the burning of the White House and the Capitol by British Troops in the War of 1812; the national convulsion of the Civil War; the assassination of President Abraham Lincoln; World War 1; the Great Depression; Pearl Harbor and World War 2; the Korean and Vietnam Wars; the assassinations of President John Kennedy, Dr. Martin Luther King, and Bobby Kennedy; 9/11; the rioting, looting, and insurrection in America's cities; and the COVID-19 pandemic of 2020 are all cataclysmic events when Americans had to rely on their beliefs in each other and faith in God to get them through to the other side.

What does it mean to be an American? This question has been asked before, and the answer has varied depending on the circumstances and events of the time. It seems to mean different things to different people. It is, after all, a personal question that seems to make most people stop and consider an answer. It invokes an inward examination of both mind and heart. The notion of one's country usually does involve both intellectual reflection and emotional fidelity. Some Americans relate their answers to their personal lives, their dreams, aspirations, and disappointments. Others relate their answers to the state of the economy, the political environment of the time, and how events affect them and their families. It also seems that many relate the meaning of America to the great events in history and the role the country has played in those events. Still others think about July 4th celebrations: flags, fireworks, parades, and bands playing John Phillip Sousa's patriotic music on the mall in Washington or down Main Street in one of countless American towns. Others think of backyard barbeques with family and friends and a day off from work. Me? I think of belonging to something greater and more important than myself, the dignity of the human spirit, and the God-given rights of the individual. I think of liberty, freedom, and justice under the law; the great deliberations at the inception of our country; the struggles against tyranny; and the sacrifices made to defend democracy, freedom, self-determination, and the American way of life.

Liberty, freedom, justice under the law, and self-determination – separate words and concepts that are often recited together but without extended reflection. What is the subliminal impact of these words on one's life? How do the meanings of these words affect our lives and the lives of our families? *Oxford Language* defines these words as follows. Liberty: "the state of being free within society from oppressive restrictions imposed by authority on one's way of life, behavior, or political views."

Freedom: "the power or right to act, or speak, or think as one wants without hindrance or restraint." Equal Justice under the Law: "all are equal before the law and entitled without any discrimination to equal protection of the law." Self-determination: "the process by which a person controls their own life." These concepts are all bedrock beliefs of American intellectual thought on governance and the prerogative individuals enjoy while shaping their own pathways forward. As people move through their lives, they often take for granted the umbrella of freedoms they unconsciously enjoy as Americans. Most people might have some difficulty articulating which specific clause in the Constitution or Bill of Rights a certain provision falls under. Experience has shown that if Americans' natural rights are challenged or threatened, they will have an innate reaction, and an overt and determined resistance would be provoked. By nature, most Americans are not constitutional scholars; they know the breadth of their freedoms instinctively through immersion in American life and their embedded perceptions. A good example is the resistance movement against excess regulations and shutdowns in several states during the 2020 COVID-19 pandemic.

Most nations have an identity. What are the elements that make nations different from one another? The obvious candidates are language, religion, racial grouping, customs and culture, geography, and others. Homogenous customs, culture, language, and, in some cases, religion, are codified over time and develop into separate and distinct societies that form the basis for a national identity. For example, in Arthur Schlesinger's book of the 1990s, *The Disuniting of America*, Schlesinger comments on different attributes of national identity between the US and Canada, two countries with somewhat similar cultural lineages.

> One reason why Canada, despite all its advantages, is so vulnerable to schism is that, as Canadians freely admit, their country lacks such a unique national identity. Attracted variously to Britain, France, and the United States, inclined for generous reasons to a policy of official multiculturalism, Canadians have never developed a strong sense of what it is to be a Canadian. As Sir John MacDonald, their first prime minister, put it, Canada has 'too much geography and too little history.'[7]

As Schlesinger went on to note, the United States has plenty of history. From the Revolution on, Americans have had a vigorous sense of national identity, forged in the War for Independence, articulated in the Declaration of Independence and the Constitution, and deepened by the subsequent experiences of self-government. As Schlesinger referenced, J. Hector St. John de Crèvecoeur was a French settler to New York in 1759 and published *Letters from an American Farmer* in which he described the melding of various ethnic groups and how, by their intermarriage, they formed a new American race: "Here individuals of all nations are melted into a race of new men."[8] The power of the national creed accounts for our relative success in converting, as Crèvecoeur noted, a "promiscuous breed" into one people and thereby making a multiethnic society work.

America's success since the beginning has been the ability to assimilate people of different ethnic, religious, and racial groups into one nation. The calling of past allegiances is forsaken here to form, as Crèvecoeur noted, a "new man," and that new man is an American. There are two motivating elements at play here. The first is the idea of the life-enriching principles of freedom, liberty, justice, and self-determination. Humans are motivated by self-interest. This is not necessarily bad or good; it's just a condition of human nature. For people to accept a national doctrine and pledge personal allegiance to a new credo, that doctrine and credo must be consistent with basic human nature. The brilliance and creative thrust of the Constitution is that it outlines the limitations of government under the people. The people are the ultimate power over government; however, to protect and maintain a civil society, necessary limitations on individual's behavior, based on generally accepted laws, were put in place. New immigrants have been attracted to America's life-enriching principles of freedom, liberty, justice, and self-determination — principles they didn't experience in their places of birth. America represents a new beginning where your entry fee is the acceptance of these life-enriching principles and your humanity. The second element is justice and due process under the law. The rights of the individual are sacrosanct and derive their legitimacy directly from God. You do not need to be a person of faith to benefit and appreciate this concept. The important thing is that the Constitution protects all individuals and provides a check against the overreach of government authorities.

It will always be important to the well-being of America that our young people continue to study and understand our country's founding and development. This special place, America, has many strengths that have sustained the nation during trying times, defended the principles of democracy, and advanced the ideas and genius of Western civilization. America does have vulnerabilities: should the elements of subversion from the pernicious Left have their way and succeed in dividing the country along racial and ethnic lines, the result will be catastrophic to the cohesion of American society. The intent from the Left is to separate the country into competing camps of special grievance groups with the intent of instituting a new social order. That, in the end, would facilitate the unraveling of America's historical social continuity. The unique character of America, from the beginning, would be lost, and the foundation on which America built this most successful society of disparate people could be lost forever. This cannot be allowed to happen.

To the American cynic, America has not at all times and places lived up to the lofty principles established at its inception. These cynics will point to America's darkest moments and national ordeals. The nation has collectively struggled with the original sins of slavery; racial discrimination; ethnic, religious, and cultural exclusion; and the minimization of woman and people with nontraditional orientations. However, despite America's history of struggling with these issues, new immigrants still yearn to come to America and make it their home. This basic fact is a validation that people outside this country understand the promise of America far better than the pervasive Leftists and Progressives do. Despite the continuous negative rhetoric voiced by the hate-America contingent, new immigrants continue to see America as "the shining city upon a hill."

There is a deep underpinning in American society to do the right thing. This is reflected in America's willingness to help other countries in times of need. The last century is full of examples. In two world wars America joined with our allies and turned back the evil forces of the Nazis, the militarists in Japan, and the Fascists in Italy. When civilization itself was on the line, America jumped into the breach and saved the world from entering a new dark age where liberty and freedom would be ideas of the past. Through the Marshall Plan, America lifted our former enemies from the ashes of conflict to enter a new brotherhood of free nations. The defeat of Communism and the steadfast resolve during the long Cold War are examples of America's willingness to defend the ideas of Western civilization. The success in these struggles are based in most Americans' deep-seated beliefs in God and faith-based institutions. All nations around the world have benefited from America's leadership against the elements of subversion and authoritarian oppression.

Americans, like all people, are fallible and make mistakes on all levels. Abraham Lincoln, the great sage in American history, when speaking of the coming tumult of the Civil War, spoke of passions, faith, and redemption — inclinations that run deep in America. Lincoln knew this well about the American soul, and he could have just as well been speaking about America's current political climate. He noted:

> We must not be enemies. Though passion may have strained, it must not break our bond of affection. The mystic chords of memory, stretching from every battle field and patriot grave to every living heart and hearthstone ail over this broad land, will yet swell the chorus of the Union, when again touched, as surely they will be, by the better angels of their nature.[9]

From the experience of the Civil War that Lincoln was noting, we as a people learned a bitter lesson and corrected the great injustice of slavery in American history. Over time, America has overcome many other systemic injustices within our very complex society, and most Americans are proud of the progress the nation has made over the last 250 years. America's mission is not complete, and the quest to live up to the promise of America continues in the advancement of that better place under the sun for all people to live in freedom, liberty, and justice.

Chapter Two

Western Civilization and the Roots of Democracy

The beginning of the American experience did not just rise from the soil of America, no matter how fertile and productive that soil had the potential to be. As with most cases in human history, new civilizations rise from the foundation of those societies that came before. This is not unlike the Egyptian mythological bird the phoenix, whose life is regenerated and sustained from the fire and embers of the past. So too the founding of the United States rose from inherited ideas and principles that were developed over centuries and which came to form the roots of Western civilization and democracy.

The majority of American historians hold the Founding generation in high regard for its personal courage, insightful understanding of human progress, and thoughtful vision for the future. The Founders are also recognized for their creativity and organization in providing a system of governance that launched the nation on its path with destiny. To some, separation from England, in and of itself, was not enough to secure the nation and advance democratic republicanism for America and other societies to follow. America and its founding required further validation through the epic struggle for independence. The Revolution consecrated the nation, and independence was confirmed through the toil and blood of thousands of patriots who endured the eight-year-long war with the British king and his military forces and surrogates.

As a result of this historic revolutionary struggle, the Founding generation created and established the mooring documents of the nation: the Declaration and Constitution. They also put in place new government systems based on checks and balances and the separation of powers to guard against a single element of authority acquiring overbearing power. They also established institutions for the effective and equitable delineation of justice so future generations of Americans could thrive and prosper. The Founders were a group of enlightened intellectuals and were well versed in classical history and the inherited roots of Western civilization and democracy. The lessons, concepts, and inspirations of Western civilization that rose up through the centuries were put to the test in the American experiment in governance, democracy, and societal organization. America's connection to the legacy of Western civilization is not just inspirational; it is fundamental, and in many respects the creation and establishment of America is the lasting inheritance and greatest expression of Western concepts and ideals.

It is not an overstatement to say that Western civilization is the cornerstone of the modern world. The West's lasting contribution to the progress of man is undeniable. The West's legacy includes ideas of governance, philosophy, science, medicine, economics, individualism, human rights, and property rights. The relative progress of societies around the modern world can be directly traced to their adoption of Western ideas and concepts. This is true whether by inclusion as an original Western society or not. Modernity itself is a Western concept.

The West is generally recognized as societies that originated in Europe and the Western Hemisphere. It also includes Australia and New Zealand, which have cultural and ethnic ties to European societies. The reality is that the West is not simply a geographic distinction, but more of an acceptance of the ideas of Western culture. The nations and societies of the West have a common lineage with the intellectual philosophy of the Greek and Roman Classical Age beginning around 700 BC in the Greek city-state of Athens. Additionally, Western societies and culture are linked to the religious revelations from the city of Jerusalem. The West is indispensably connected to the rise of Christianity, tenets of the Bible, morality, and the ancestral relationship with Judaism and monotheism. Of great importance to Western culture are the ideas of logic and reasoning, including the Socratic and scientific methods. Over time, these fundamental ideas developed into modern science, medicine, and technology, and they ushered in precepts of governance, including democracy, individualism, human rights, economics, and capitalism.

The foundational concepts of Western civilization developed in the Mediterranean societies of Greece and Rome during the first millennium BC. No other civilizations of the time experienced a similar illumination of intellectual reflection and analytical study of man's relationship with God, nature, and his surroundings. It was an awakening that also examined man's individualism, governance, and place in the universe. Other ancient cultures developed great works of architecture and construction and made achievements in mathematics, astronomy, art, writing, and social organization. Those societies included Egyptians from the Nile; Persians from regions around current day Iran; Assyrians from the Levant and Mesopotamia; Hittites from Anatolia; the Chinese and Indians from the East; and Mesoamerican societies from the Americas. All of those cultures contributed substantive elements toward the advancement of human knowledge and progress; however, with few exceptions, none of them experienced an intellectual awakening in study and analysis that was similar to the West, the Greeks and Romans, and the morality-based religious revelations from Jerusalem.

The origins of the West stand apart from other ancient civilizations due to the systematic innovations incorporated by the Greeks during the Classical period and by the Roman Republic and Empire. Other ancient civilizations relied on proven centuries-old methods for the accomplishment of specific tasks from agriculture to construction to social organization. The key for first the Greeks and later the Romans was the continuation of innovation. The concept was to approach a task from a different perspective and in a whole different way. Utilizing applied methods of study and analysis, one can come up with a more efficient and productive way to complete a task. This revolution in productivity can be applied across the whole society, and over time it can relieve individuals from mundane tasks and rededicate portions of the population to other pursuits within society.

In the ancient world, especially in the Mediterranean culture of Greece before the eighth century BC, nine out of ten people were dedicated to agriculture and the production of food. The Greeks took advantage of the moderate climate and the length of the growing season in the Eastern Mediterranean. They also incorporated innovations in agronomy, which increased the harvest. Over time, Greek farmers experimented with different techniques of irrigation and seasonal crop yields. They also incorporated terrace farming and planted staple crops of wheat and barley to produce bread and soups, olives for oil, grapes for wine, and raisins along with other fruits and vegetables. Their innovations dramatically increased food production, which freed up sections of the population from agriculture and facilitated the rise of the Greek city-states of Athens, Sparta, Corinth, Thebes, and more than a thousand others. The surplus products of olive oil, wine, and other commercial goods were used to advance commerce in the Mediterranean region between the Greek city-states and the other ancient civilizations.

America and its founding have a direct connection with the technological innovations of the origins of Western civilization. At the time of European exploration of the Americas in the fifteenth, sixteenth, and seventeenth centuries, long-practiced agrarian techniques and procedures had been established through Western European societies. The original settlers to both North and South America, including the Spanish, Portuguese, Dutch, French, and English, all brought to the New World Western ideas of innovation in agriculture, construction, societal organization, and politics. All of the colonies in the New World benefited from the inheritance of Western culture.

The Greeks

The Greek writer Homer, who is believed to have lived around the eighth century BC, is recognized for writing the poem *The Iliad*. *The Iliad* is the famed mythical story of the epic conclusion of the Trojan Wars, which are believed to have occurred sometime around the twelfth century BC during the Late Bronze Age. *The Iliad* describes the tale of the various Greek anthropomorphic Gods (mythical deities that demonstrated human traits and emotions such as hate, love, vengeance, lust, vanity, and others) and their plots to compete against each other and take sides with their human champions during the struggle.

The ancient city of Troy is believed to have been located at Hissarlik on the Anatolian Peninsula in current day northwestern Turkey. The root story to *The Iliad* describes the tale of Helen (Helen of Sparta and later of Troy) and her lover, Paris, who abducted her from Sparta and brought her to the city of Troy. As the story goes, Helen was very beautiful, and her husband, Menelaus, wanted her back. Menelaus was the brother of the Greek Mycenaean King Agamemnon, and because of their brotherly connection the Greeks waged war against Troy, setting sail with a thousand ships. Part of the epic struggle between the Greeks and Troy was the fight between Troy's greatest warrior, Hector (the brother of Paris), and the Greek legendary warrior and half God, Achilles. Achilles was victorious and killed Hector. In the end, the Greeks pulled off one of antiquity's great strategic deceptions in the offering of a large wooden horse to the Trojans (the Trojan Horse). A Greek advance guard hid inside the horse, and once they were inside the city, they opened the gates and brought in the rest of the Greek warriors who then sacked the city and defeated the Trojans. Homer also wrote *The Odyssey*, which is a narrative that takes place after the ten-years-long Trojan Wars, and which tells the story of Odysseus' journey across the Aegean Sea to his home in Ithaca on the west coast of Greece. Homer's stories, which are likely part reality and part folktale, are important works at the beginning of Western literature. Later, in the Classical Age of Greece in the fourth century, Homer's writings were held in such high regard that it was comparable to the reverence of the Bible of later periods. It is thought that Alexander the Great carried a copy of *The Iliad* with him in his conquest of the lands to the east in Asia.

From a historical context, it is important to note that the Mycenaean Greek civilization flourished in Greece and across the

Aegean Sea for many hundreds of years starting around 1800 BC. Then, seemingly unexpectedly, the civilization collapsed at the end of the Bronze Age around the twelfth century BC. The Mycenaeans and the majority of the other Bronze Age civilizations of the time, including much of the Egyptian civilization, perished around the same time along with the Greeks. A dark age gripped Greece for nearly 400 years, and civilization, along with writing (the use of the Mycenaean script linear B), stopped. Other symbols of civilization, including art, dramatically decreased. Commerce, interaction between societies, and major construction works ended. Population centers declined, and palaces were abandoned. The inhabitants of the region reverted back to elementary farming and livestock herding. It wasn't until the eighth century, when new Greeks walked on the ruins of the Mycenaeans and Old King Agamemnon's cities, that the Classical Greek period began and the roots of Western civilization were planted.

The collapse of the Late Bronze Age civilizations of the Eastern Mediterranean and Asia Minor and the following dark age are a reminder to the modern Western world that societies, even sophisticated and organized ones, are subject to convulsion and regression. Ruinous political intrigues, whether of internal or external origins, and destructive forces of the natural world can cause civilizations to spiral out of control. This can lay waste to human progress and social order. The specific cause of The Late Bronze Age's collapse is still somewhat of a mystery to historians.

The likely causes were invasion from the "sea people" (aggressive seafaring invaders possibly from Sicily and other regions around the Eastern Mediterranean), earthquakes, drought, and harvest failures. Throughout history, many societies stood on the threshold of continuing progression, but their progress was thwarted as unintended appointments with fate thrust those societies backward into a stifling malaise.

Another cause of the collapse of the Late Bronze Age Mediterranean civilizations most likely included a lack of adaptability to unforeseen challenges to societal cohesion and continuity. The combination of disruptive events that these ancient societies faced overwhelmed their ability to adapt and provide successful countermeasures to address them. Presumably, this also involved a failure of will and resolve to overcome the crises of the moment. During the course of history, many civilizations have risen and attained high achievements only to fall because of decay and external intervention. Current day societies of the West are confronted with many challenges, and this is especially true for the United States. The nations of the West need to remember the collapse of the Late Bronze Age civilizations and the numerous other civilizations that came and went during the course of time. The reasons for their demises need to be studied. The elements of decline of these homogenous societies, the conditions that occurred, and the reasons these societies lost the will to struggle through the crises need to be understood. Hopefully, through study and understanding, the West will prevent a similar demise, and the future will remain bright and prosperous for generations to come.

Writing and literature are important elements in the development of civilizations and the advancement of culture and sophisticated societies. The development of the Greeks' Classical period was greatly advanced through their refined written script, which was derived from a more ancient Phoenician alphabet. The Greeks incorporated distinct letters for vowels and consonants into the older alphabet and formed the basic Greek writing. Their text then formed the basis for other written languages that followed. During the Classical period of Greek culture in the fourth and fifth centuries BC, Greek writing flourished. Their original classical prose included lyrical poems, rhetoric, eulogies, plays of drama, comedies, tragedies, and historical narratives by Greek historians such as Thucydides (460-400 BC) and his history of the Peloponnesian War, and Herodotus (484-425 BC), known as the "father of history." Herodotus organized and categorized the materials he compiled prior to the creation of his historical narrative, which set the template for future historians to follow in building historical-based treatises.

Democracy developed in the Greek city-state of Athens in the late sixth century BC. A city-state was known as a *polis*. Politics, metropolitan, and police are common words that derive from *polis*. From the very early time of the development of Greek culture before the ninth century BC, the Greeks experienced several different types of ruling authorities, including monarchy, oligarchy, and tyranny by aristocrats. The Athenians in the fifth century were again ruled by a group of aristocrats who, as unchecked rulers have often done throughout history, enacted laws and policies that advanced their own best interests and not the interests of the people. This is an old tale of history. The Athenian population revolted against the ruling elites, and what the Athenians did next is the real story.

Securing the support of the middle class, Cleisthenes, who was a lauded and enlightened Athenian statesman, a member of the aristocracy, and a lawgiver, worked to reform the Athenian constitution. With great popular support, he dramatically increased the power of the citizens and started Athenian society on the path to democracy for the first time. That event, almost by accident, was one of the most important in the history of the world. It created an early model for Western societies, including the American Founders in the eighth century, to follow over the centuries, and it has increased the wellbeing of countless hundreds of millions of people. That important historical event brought a higher morality and justice to governance for the citizens of Athens. Under the new political arrangement, Athenian citizens were granted the right to vote, given that they passed a high bar of eligibility. This excluded women, slaves, and migrant workers. Athens had a population of between 250,000 and 300,000 residents, and only about 30,000 were considered citizens and eligible to vote. It was a direct democracy in that voter approval was required for laws, and every citizen who was approved to vote was expected to vote and participate in the political process. It was very different from modern Western representative democracies, including the United States where representatives are elected to vote for laws in a legislature on behalf of the citizens. The exclusion of the majority of Athens' inhabitants might be looked at with a jaundiced eye in the twenty-first century, but it is hard to underestimate the positive impact the development of democracy has had on the human experience in the advancement of justice, equality, and the rule of law.

As the Athenians worked through the details of operating a democracy over the next few decades, they struggled with political forces from within and the external pressures from the military superpower of the day, Persia. The Athenians joined with other Greek city-states, including Sparta, in a protracted war with the Persian Empire that lasted almost fifty years (492-449 BC). The Greeks were eventually successful. The victory by the Greeks over the Eastern Empire of Persia cemented Greece as the cultural center of the ancient world and secured democracy's survival as a model for the future. One of the most legendary battles of that war, and one of Western civilization's most lauded and courageous last stands, was the battle of Thermopylae in 480 BC. Under Spartan King Leonidas, a group of 300 Spartan Hoplites (ancient Greek warriors) intercepted the Persian invasion force at the mountain pass of Thermopylae and held off the Persian Army for seven days. The Persians, under King Xerxes, eventually won the battle, killing King

Leonidas and his storied group of Spartan Hoplites. That rallied the Greeks, and after a subsequent series of successful battles on land and sea by the combined Greek city-states, they prevailed against the Persians. It is difficult to imagine that the great achievements in science, medicine, art, architecture, philosophy, and the beginnings of democracy would have continued to develop in Greece had the Persians won.

The Greeks' victory over the Persians was one of the decisive events of history. The narrative of the Greek triumph over Persia was written by the Greek historian Herodotus. In his work *The History of the Persian Wars*, Herodotus incorporated the Greek method of inquiry into his historical writings, which also included politics. In fifth-century Greek tradition, burgeoning democratic ideas were reviewed in his narratives. He compared democracy, oligarchy, and monarchy, and he concluded that democracy was an exemplary form of government. Herodotus also wrote on equality and freedom of speech, noting that they are things "worthy not in one way alone but in many respects."[1] It is interesting to note that as democracy developed in fifth century Greece, the concepts of freedom of speech, rights of the individual, and consent of the governed developed alongside it.

The Golden Age of Athens or the Age of Pericles was the time when Greek culture reached its peak (448 to 429 BC). The period lasted roughly between the Persian and Peloponnesian Wars. Athens became the intellectual center of the ancient world, advancing concepts in philosophy, education, art, literature, theater, science, and architecture. It was also the time when Athens' direct democracy reached its height due to reforms to the city-state's constitution initiated through the leadership and persuasive oratory talents of Pericles. Pericles also advanced greater participation of the lower classes in the legislative process. Alongside the expansion of democratic ideas, art and architecture set new achievements in aesthetics and grandeur. In an effort to establish Athens as the Imperial City of the Greek world, Pericles was the inspirational force in rebuilding the Acropolis after its destruction in the Persian War. It was during that time that the Parthenon and other great Athenian civil works were built, which made the *polis* the standard of the known world.

The historian Thucydides called Pericles "the first citizen of democratic Athens," more than just a convincing orator statesman and successful politician. Pericles was from an aristocratic family and was a victorious *strategos* (army leader or General) who led several military campaigns against Athens' enemies. In a campaign of note, Pericles led an offensive by the Athenian Army in the expulsion of barbarian invaders from the Thracian Peninsula in 447 BC. For decades, Athens experienced growing wealth from local silver mines in Laurium and financed much of the new construction that was championed by Pericles and others. Athens also received tributes from Greek allies around the Aegean Sea to maintain the Athenian Navy. The Greek trireme (a three-oared slender war vessel used to ram enemy ships) was a very effective naval implement that was used to defeat the Persians at the battle of Salamis in 480 BC. The Athenian Navy stood by to provide protection for the Greek allied states against the potential dangers posed by the Persian Empire in the Delian League. The Delian League was a group of Greek city-states led by Athens.

Athens entered into a destructive war with the city-state of Sparta and its allies in the Peloponnesian War in 431 BC. The war lasted until 404 BC, and the Spartans emerged victorious. The initial strategy of Pericles was to have all of the surrounding population of Athens hold up behind the city's walls. In the first year of the war, Pericles offered a funeral oration for the lost war dead, as was customary. The oration departed from the normal tribute in that he used the occasion to rally the citizens for the coming struggle against the Spartans and to emphasize that the current struggle was a validation of the sacrifices of those who lost their lives for the city. An excerpt from his oration: "I shall begin with our ancestors: it is both just and proper that they should have the honour of the first mention on an occasion like the present. They dwelt in the country without break in the succession from generation to generation, and handed it down free to the present time by their valour."[2] In those words from Pericles, we can find the eternal connections of Western civilization and democratic ideals that transcend generations, time, and space. Lincoln, in his Gettysburg address, clearly drew some inspiration from Pericles:

Four score and seven years ago our fathers brought forth on
this continent a new nation, conceived in liberty, and
dedicated to the proposition that all men are created equal.
Now we are engaged in a great civil war, testing whether that
nation, or any nation so conceived and so dedicated, can long
endure. We are met on a great battlefield of that war. We
have come to dedicate a portion of that field, as a final resting
place for those who here gave their lives that that nation
might live. It is altogether fitting and proper that we should
do this.[3]

Athens' and Pericles' struggles in the Peloponnesian War
did not end well for Athens or Pericles. A plague broke out in the
polis and took many lives, including that of Pericles himself in 429
BC. Democracy lasted for approximately 180 years in Athens with
periodic interruptions and the imposition of oligarchic leadership
after the defeat by the Spartans in 404 BC. The final demise of
Athenian democracy came with the ascendancy of the Macedonian
Greeks under King Phillip II during the fourth century BC.

The Macedonian Greeks dominated the Hellenistic world
after the fall of Athens to the Spartans. Phillip II emerged as a
powerful king, imposed his rule over most of the Greek city-states,
formed the League of Corinth, which he controlled, and cemented
Macedonian rule over Greece. His son Alexander the Great
ascended to the throne upon Phillip's assassination. In 331 BC,
Alexander achieved one of his greatest accomplishments, the
founding of Alexandria, a new city in Egypt on the eastern edge of
the Mediterranean Sea. Alexander did not live long enough to see
his city rise to become one of the great cities of the ancient world.

He died at the age of 33 in 323 BC. The city of Alexandria became the center of the Greek Hellenistic world and a place at the crossroads of the important civilizations of the ancient world, including Greece, Egypt, Rome, and later Byzantium. The city is important to the history of Western civilization and modernity because it developed into a great learning center and repository of the classical writings on science, philosophy, mathematics, and history. A great library was established in 288 BC, and it housed much of the writings in books and scrolls of ancient scholars on all elements of knowledge. The library existed for hundreds of years. One of the great tragedies of history was the burning of the library in 48 BC, attributed to Romans under Julius Caesar during a civil war with the Egyptians.

America's Founders were influenced by the thinking of the ancient Greek philosophers, including Socrates (469-399 BC), Plato (428-348 BC), and Aristotle (385-323 BC), and the methodology they used to formulate their ideas on man, politics, nature, and God(s). The Greeks were instrumental in the development of democracy, natural science, medicine, and philosophy. Socrates was the teacher of Plato. Plato wrote about Socrates and the advancement of the concept of the critical method of analysis, known as the Socratic Method. The concept is based in a regiment of pursuing knowledge by inquiry. Socrates believed that by this method of questioning and inquiry one would attain knowledge and arrive at the truth. The Socratic Method is still a much-used tool in education, and it leads to a more focused regiment of study. Plato, in his dialogues and book # 6 of his *Republic*, noted that Socrates promoted the idea that intellectual curiosity is important for the attainment of knowledge. Socrates believed that wonder is the beginning of wisdom.

The Greek tradition of deep intellectual reflection and analysis of esoteric issues and the natural world also gave rise to the scientific method. In this process of systematic observation, measurement and testing produce answers to questions on a given subject. It is easy to trace the roots of logical analyses and methods of solving problems that were applied to the political issues of the eighteenth century. The Founders and the great minds of Western civilization that came after the Greeks were given a blueprint. In that blueprint were the keys to open up pathways to the attainment of knowledge and understanding.

Socrates never wrote down any of his ideas on philosophy and his analyses of man, nature, or concepts of the quest for knowledge; that was left to Plato and other students of the great teacher. Through Socrates' critical analyses and inward reflections on man's nature, he proposed that the attainment of individual knowledge would advance human virtue and in turn produce happiness. With that, all that we know about the life of Socrates and his teachings we've learned from his students and other secondhand sources. Plato became the leading sophist (teacher of philosophy and rhetoric in ancient Greece) after Socrates' death in 399 BC. Socrates had focused his intellectual energies in an inward reflection of the nature of man, including politics, but Plato's interests were much broader and involved the natural sciences and mathematics as well as philosophy and politics.

Plato was a prolific writer. He wrote upwards of thirty-six books and started a learning center called the Academy, which existed for more than three hundred years. The Academy was a center for the advancement of learning and sharing knowledge. At the Academy, students would study subjects such as philosophy, mathematics, politics, and natural science. Aristotle was one of Plato's important students and studied at the Academy with Plato for twenty years before moving on and forming his own center for learning called the Lyceum. Demosthenes (384-322 BC) was another celebrated student of Plato. He was considered one of the great statesmen and orators of fourth century BC Athens and spoke against the rise and power of Macedon's King Philip II, the father of Alexander the Great. The volumes of writings by Plato spread Greek culture throughout the known world. The aspirational ideal of "knowing thyself" is about man developing an understanding of himself and living according to his nature. The Greek sophists also proffered the concept of "eudemonia," the idea that the pursuit of knowledge, truth, and virtue produces a sense of satisfaction in the understanding.

Aristotle continued the tradition of study, learning, analysis of the natural world, and philosophy as originally established by

Socrates and Plato. Interestingly, Aristotle left his twenty-year study under Plato shortly before Plato's death. He left Athens at the request of King Phillip II of Macedon to teach the king's son Alexander in 343 BC. Aristotle's work had a great influence on Western ideas and concepts up to and including the current day.

The Athenian Greeks experimented with the implementation and operations associated with democracy. That included the revolutionary idea of average citizens having a say in the direction of society through their individual votes. They were able to maintain democracy for hundreds of years; however, the subversive forces of dictatorial rule were and always are present and threatening the continuation of democracy. This fact is true even in contemporary times. America and the West need to remember this important lesson from the ancient Greeks. It is easy to fall back into authoritarian rule by either one or the few. The assuagement by the events of the moment and corruption from the masked forms of oppression can lead to the impulse to surrender out of exhaustion and to cave into the coercion of the hidden forces of authoritarianism and mob-rule. These forces are designed to upend social norms, order, and democracy. To succumb to this element can bring the death of a civil society and in the end drown individualism and inalienable human rights. In American contemporary society, it is easy to see how subversive elements can shame people into surrendering their ideals and principles. Establishing a democratic republic is hard, and it is even harder to keep. The really important principles of the American democratic republic - individualism, human rights, and justice under the law - need to be continuously reinforced and revalidated. These principles are worth fighting for to maintain a vibrant civilization.

In reflection on the stories from the Greeks, America needs to hold onto its values and be strong and reject the coercive elements of subversion, lies, and deceptions of the Progressive Left. In America's darkest moments, when we see riots and buildings burning in American cities, we need to hold onto our core beliefs in freedom, liberty, and justice for all. America is not a systemically racist nation, and we should always push back vehemently against this untrue and perverse characterization of the country. A focused campaign by fair-minded and thoughtful Americans should be mounted in our schools, public spaces, and institutions to fight against this grotesque lie.

As outlined in Plato's works, both he and Socrates were pessimistic-about the idea of direct democracy (rule by the people) in its purest form as practiced in Athens. They believed that selecting leaders in a society was too important to be left to individuals who could be corrupted by the process. They believed that ordinary citizens had not attained a higher level of knowledge or eudemonia; that they lacked wisdom in the selection of rulers; and that the outcome of the process would be the installation of demagogues. Plato believed that democracy was the second worst political system, surpassed only by tyranny. Instead, he proffered the idea of aristocratic rulers who would be educated and trained in philosophy and would attain a high level of knowledge. Based on their higher levels of knowledge, they would be more enlightened in governance. Plato also had concerns about how aristocratic rule could be corrupted. He speculated that aristocratic rule could be undermined over time and devolve into an oligarchy (a small group of people in control) and that the rulers could grow to be motivated by self-interest and no longer by the thoughtful pursuit of knowledge and truth.

Keeping the idea of Plato's aristocratic rulers in mind, most contemporary Western democracies would reject the idea of only a select privileged class of educated and knowledgeable aristocratic rulers having the right to vote. They would find it anti-democratic for a chosen group to have exclusive power in determining the direction of a society. It would appear, however, that there is another idea to be understood from Plato and his concerns of pure democracy. The idea is that he desired to see the political process end with philosopher rulers or kings. The learned philosopher rulers would be endowed with wisdom and virtue, and those characteristics would most effectively manage society.

As America struggles through highly contentious elections, consideration should be given to Socrates' and Plato's pessimism concerning the corruptibility of the democratic process. As civilizations develop with the rapid evolution brought about by advances in technology and science, it is important for every citizen to recognize that their votes are the pillar that democracy stands on. It is incumbent upon the educational systems to establish a curriculum that facilitates the intellectual curiosity of students to examine multiple sides of all issues. In order to preserve democracy and a civil society, an individual citizen's vote should be the product of a critical analysis of the facts and not an emotional response that is fed by abhorrent political ideologies like socialism and communism, which will ultimately subvert the interest of the individual and society. Educating citizens to think critically about the value of individualism, human rights, liberty, freedom, and the richness of the American experience will facilitate the continued maintenance of an orderly society. Tyranny by the machinations of the intellectual elitists and venality of dubious politicians are always lurking in the background. These elements are always trying to undermine and divide society and to create disharmony and chaos. In the end, it is the way the elitists see the world and their best avenue to gaining control. These elements of the Progressive Left are committed; we need to be just as committed to fight against these subversions. Conservatives need to develop countermeasures and provide alternative narratives of hope and reassurance in the values we believe in. In this way, the civil society can be affirmed and the individual can be confident that the election process and the results can be validated. As a result of this more enlightened process, the great original teachers of Western philosophical thinking wittingly or unwittingly extended a cautionary warning to the future. America needs to provide safeguards for the maintenance of democracy and the continued pursuit of a higher level of knowledge and virtue.

The Romans

Rome's founding (753 BC) and mythology are full of colorful stories and tales. One story from Roman mythology is of twin orphan boys reared by a she-wolf and discovered and raised by a shepherd. Over time, the two boys, Romulus and Remus, grew into rivals. Romulus eventually killed Remus and became the first king of Rome. Rome got its name from Romulus. Another story is that Rome was founded by Trojan settlers after the city was sacked by the Greeks. The Roman Kingdom was established on seven hills adjacent to the Tiber River. The Latinas, or Latins, a regional Italic tribe that inhabited the region around Rome, was absorbed into Rome in 338 BC along with many other tribal groups in the region, including the Etruscans to the north and the Sarbanes to the east. The Romans adopted many political, cultural, and linguistic components of the groups they absorbed. The absorption of conquered peoples into their sphere of control, and the adoption of many of the most positive features of those societies into Roman culture, proved to be very successful in the development of the Roman world. That continued over the centuries as Rome grew into the most important civilization of the ancient world.

There was a historical momentum and inevitability to the rise and preeminence of the Roman Empire. Rome grew to eclipse

Greece in terms of power, population, and great construction projects in the second century AD. The Greek decline had been continuing for several hundred years until the Romans defeated part of the Macedonian Empire in 188 AD. Rome's ascendency was gradual and continued over many centuries. The rise of the Roman state was marked first by conquest of new territories and peoples and then by inclusion of those territories' best traditions, customs, and technology into the greater Roman culture. That was particularly true with regards to the Greeks. The Romans emulated and adopted many cultural elements from Greece, including architecture, art, religion, philosophy, education, science, and medicine.

Though Rome would be challenged by many empires, they eventually became the center of the ancient Mediterranean world. There are many similarities in the early development of the Roman and Greek civilizations. They both started with monarchy and gradually moved to the first rudimentary forms of divided government in which the citizens voted on laws, officials, and, in Rome's case, representatives. The Greeks in Athens had a direct democracy, and all of the citizens voted on a wide cross-section of governmental issues and laws. This was somewhat different in the early Roman model, which was symbolized by a senate and divided rule by two consuls with limited terms of one year.

Similar to other civilizations of the ancient world (Egyptians, Persians, and others), Greek and Roman societies were brutal in conquest and rule. Also similar to other ancient societies, they allowed slavery as a part of their social structure. Slavery has been a scourge and moral corruption of mankind since the dawn of civilization. As brilliant and enlightened as the ancient Greeks and Romans were in the inception and development of ideas on governance, laws, philosophy, democracy, architecture, construction, and centers of learning, they were still capable of committing the most unthinkable atrocities toward their fellow human beings. The lesson of history from these great past civilizations reveals a fatal flaw. A society cannot sustain itself with only advances in the physical and intellectual realms of achievement. Without an equal imperative of moral values and, thereby, a true understanding of equal justice, the successes and sustainability of the Greek and Roman societies were, in the end, fleeting.

The Romans established a republic (meaning: public thing) in 510 BC, and it lasted for nearly 500 years. In the period before the Roman Republic, Rome was ruled by its last king, Lucius Tarquinius. The legendary story of the end of the Tarquinius reign conveys that his son Sextus Tarquinius raped a noble woman named Lucretia. The Romans were outraged and overthrew the king and his family. The Romans, concerned about the absolute power of a king, advanced the concept of divided government between two consuls in the establishment of the Roman Republic.

Rome established one of the ancient world's first deliberative bodies, a senate, in 753 BC. Later, in the Roman Republic, two senior leaders called consuls were elected by the senate to rule the republic for a one-year period. When their term was up, new consuls were elected. The senate and the wider citizenry of Rome were concerned about too much power residing with one leader, so they divided authority between two consuls, an early form of checks and balances and division of power. Two ruling consuls with divided leadership was an institutional precaution against the return of monarchy or authoritarian rule over the state by one all-powerful leader. The senate consisted of between 300 and 600 members. In the early stages of the senate, a group of aristocrats called patricians, originally noblemen and members of one of the founding families, ruled the legislative body. Senators were selected for lifelong terms. In the beginning of the republic, lower-class citizens made up of working-class people, tradesmen, farmers, military members, and non-nobility were called plebeians. They had little input in the decision-making of the government. This inequity, in around 495 BC, led to a more-than-200-year struggle in which the plebeians fought against the power of the patricians. That struggle is known as the "Conflict of the Orders," and it resulted in the plebeian class gaining great input in the governmental decision-making.

During the revolution of the Roman Republic, and as a result of the continuing struggle between the aristocracy and the citizens, foundational laws were established. In 451 BC, the first codified laws were established and written down for all citizens to follow. Those original laws, known as the "12 Tablets," were put down on twelve bronze tablets or plates. The laws were described in detail so that all citizens had knowledge of them and could be guided by them. The laws dealt with property, crime, family, theft, marriage, and inheritance, and they also facilitated the roles and responsibilities of the state in the governance of the citizens of Rome. They also established equal treatment under the law for all. Three universal principles of legal jurisprudence were established during the development of the Roman Republic. Those three principles were: (1) the accused person is assumed innocent until proven guilty; (2) the accused person has the right to offer a defense and face his accuser; (3) in order for the accused person to be found guilty, there needs to be clear evidence of that guilt. These Roman Republic ideas of clearly defined and widely known laws were incorporated into the US Constitution and were adopted as bedrock principles of other Western democracies as well. The Romans took a page from the Greeks' application of logic and reason to establish the most effective implementation of the laws for their citizenry. The establishment of given laws that were based in equality and fairness and recognized by all is one of the great contributions the ancient Roman Republic made toward the progress of Western civilization.

The Roman Republic had its share of lauded leaders despite the cruelty and despotism that marked the age. One such leader was Lucius Quintus Cincinnatus, an aristocrat and statesman born in 519 BC who was elected to the senate and served one year as a council. Cincinnatus was known as a strong leader and a patriotic Roman citizen of moral character and "simple virtue." When his time was completed as council, he and his family retired to his small farm across the Tiber River. According to Roman law, the senate could select a dictator for a period of six months in times of crisis. In 458 BC, Rome was threatened by an invasion from two tribes to the south, the Aequians and the Sabines. To repel the threat, Rome and its army were in need of a decisive leader to assume emergency dictatorial powers and shepherd Rome through the crisis. Cincinnatus, known for his high moral standing, was asked by the senate to become dictator and to lead Rome in its struggle against the enemies. Under Cincinnatus' leadership, the Roman Army was victorious against the Aequians and the Sabines in just two weeks. Cincinnatus was celebrated and was asked to stay on as ruler, but in dramatic and storied fashion he rejected the offer and returned power back to the senate. This has been recorded as "laying down of the scroll." Cincinnatus desired to return to his humble farm and family. Many years later, Cincinnatus was once again asked to lead Rome through a crisis, and once again he stepped down after the crisis was over. History has recorded Cincinnatus as a man of great civic virtue and selfless patriotism to Rome.

The story of Cincinnatus "laying down of the scroll" was not lost on George Washington centuries later. As America's war of independence was drawing to a close and the last British soldiers departed New York City on November 25, 1783, Washington made a decision that shaped the future of America. In December of 1783, Washington ventured to Annapolis, Maryland, where congress was in session. In the spirit of Cincinnatus, Washington, too, would "lay down the scroll" and resign his commission as the Commander and Chief of the Continental Army. His desire, as was Cincinnatus' all those centuries ago, was to return to his farm at Mount Vernon in Virginia. Washington would again "lay down the scroll" after two terms as president in 1796 when he decided not to run for a third term. He set a presidential tradition that lasted for 144 years until Franklin Roosevelt chose to run for a third term in 1940.

In reflecting on the parallels between Washington and Cincinnatus, it is important to understand the most compelling leadership qualities that history records. These qualities are defined by a sense of purpose and the willingness to do what is right for the people, no matter what the personal cost is. They are also marked by an abiding affection for one's country, unvarnished humility, and simple virtues. These leadership attributes are very difficult for contemporary leaders on the national scene to live up to. Unfortunately, it is apparent that few even try.

Washington and the American Founders of the late eighteenth Century studied the examples of the great figures from the Greek and Roman Classical period. Another important figure and man of integrity from the late Roman Republic was Cato the Younger (Marcus Proclus Cato (95 BC to 46 BC)). Cato the Younger was a conservative leader and great orator and statesman in the Roman senate. Much to the consternation of his opponents, he fought against corruption and could not be bribed into adopting policies or positions he thought were wrong for Rome and the people. Cato was a vehement opponent of Julius Caesar's rise to power as council of Rome, and he fought against him for years in the senate. In a final act of defiance, Cato committed suicide in 46 BC rather than recognizing Caesar's authority to grant him a pardon. Philosophically, Cato was a follower of stoicism, which was a Greek philosophical belief system adopted by many Romans. Stoicism stressed restraint and reason and the idea that virtue was the highest good. It also stressed the belief in living in harmony with nature and in concert with divine reason that governs events, dismisses pleasure, and encourages a greater tolerance for pain. Stoicism incorporated much of the teachings of Socrates.

During the last half of the first century BC, the Roman Republic-struggled with external pressures and political intrigues. That culminated with the rise of Julius Caesar as he gained great power over the senate and Rome. Caesar, a successful and natural military leader, expanded Roman control and hegemony over territories in Gaul (current day France). He broke with Rome's military tradition by not disbanding his army before crossing the

Rubicon (a river north of the city) while approaching the city. The phrase "crossing the Rubicon" has come to symbolize the making of an irrevocable commitment to a course of action, a fateful and final decision.

Caesar became a dictator, and the senate gave him the title "The Divine Julius." He was given permanent authoritarian powers that allowed him to veto rulings by the senate. As previously noted, Cato was Caesar's most eloquent opponent in the senate. He advocated strongly for the ideas of Republicanism and opposed Caesar's quest for power. The struggle between the two men has often been referred to as a struggle between good and evil. As noted, the culmination of their differences eventually ended with Cato's suicide.

An interesting note of history... George Washington was an admirer of Cato as well an admirer of Cincinnatus. In an effort to convey the attributes of a virtuous individual to his troops, Washington had a theatrical production preformed. The play was Joseph Addison's 1717 production of *Cato,* and it was performed at Valley Forge during the spring of 1778. The production was contrary to congressional prerogatives against theatrical events, but Washington did it anyway.

Caesar's control lasted only four years as he was assassinated in the Roman senate in 44 BC due to growing hatred for him and concerns that he wanted to crown himself king of Rome. The Roman Republic, which had lasted nearly 500 years, came to an end in 27 BC. Caesar's adopted son became Emperor Augustus, and the period of the Roman Empire began. The Roman Empire became very large and was divided into four separate jurisdictions and regions over the next few centuries. During that period, Rome had many Emperors, seventy in total from the beginning of the Roman Empire in 27 BC until the collapse in 476 AD. Some of those Emperors were benevolent and successful; others were despotic, destructive, and brutal toward the people of the regions and the conquered lands of the Empire. Roman legions were often at war with tribes and groups of people on the periphery of the Roman world. At times they were at war with other legions and power centers within the Empire. Roman culture and ideas and the root traditions of Western civilization, originally started by the Greeks, were continually being spread and implanted throughout those new lands.

Emperor Constantine I (280 to 337 AD), known as "Constantine the Great," reigned for more than thirty years. He became emperor in 306 and was a successful military general in the territories of Persia and the west in Britain before and after becoming emperor. According to his biographer Eusebius, while on a military campaign as emperor in 312, Constantine and his legions had a religious revelation when they saw a cross of light in the sky. This Christian revelation was reinforced that night when Constantine had a dream about Christ. Constantine allowed the Christian faith to be practiced throughout the Empire, and in 313 he proclaimed the edict of Milan, which officially endorsed the faith. Constantine himself later converted to Christianity. His conversion enabled monotheistic Christianity and the belief in only one God to spread across the Roman Empire and become the dominant religion replacing Paganism.

The Western Roman Empire continued for another 140 years after the death of Constantine until it collapsed in 476 AD. The demise was due to corruption from within and invasion from the Germanic Barbarian tribes. That ended the nearly 1,000-year-long rule and order that Rome brought to the Mediterranean and to areas of occupation and conquest. Rome (the "eternal city") and its perpetual legacy to civilization would remain an important building block of Western cultural heritage for centuries to come.

It's an interesting footnote of history that during the 3,500-year-long period covering the Bronze Age to the fall of the Western Roman Empire in 476 AD, mankind's struggle with the primal instinct for cruelty and dominance contrasted with the pursuit of morality and justice. Both the Greek and Roman civilizations, as well as others of the time, struggled with this duality of human nature. While mankind was creating great works of art, architecture, and construction, and developing science, medicine, poetry, philosophy, and democracy, civilizations were slaughtering each other in wars of conquest and committing genocide. Let us also not overlook the unknown millions held in bondage and slavery during the high points of those civilizations. Humans in general, and not just those in ancient civilizations, are both enlightened and duplicitous beings full of contradictions. On one hand, mankind is cognizant of intellectual reasoning, analysis, great works, and an abiding appreciation for beauty, compassion, and love. On the other hand, mankind is capable of heinous acts of butchery against his fellow humans. Modern science attributes this duality of man's nature to different parts of the brain. The more primitive part or the primal brain (the hindbrain and medulla) is where drive and survival instincts come from. The frontal cortex or cerebrum is the part of the brain where problem-solving, memory, judgement, and reasoning resides. Humankind's walk through history has been a continuous struggle between these divergent aspects of man's inner nature. The great discoveries and achievements of ancient civilizations, notably the Greeks and Romans, have been studied and analyzed by historians for more than two millennia. The great question is: why did these great civilizations that rose to great heights and achievements eventually fall? Did they collapse under their own weight or did they succumb to the next civilization's positioning to push them over? Do the demises of civilizations and, in a larger sense, man himself, rest with circumstances outside their control? Is it that man is just a casualty of these eternal dynamic forces and that the elements of destruction are imbedded within human nature itself? The answers to and consequences of these questions are not simply to satisfy interested historians studying ancient civilizations; they also have profound implications for modern society and how we deal with the issues of man's permanence. We know that the seeds of destruction lie with man's technological abilities, and how man handles that responsibility will determine his future.

Chapter Three

Age of Reason/Enlightenment

Middle Ages

After the fall of the Western Roman Empire in 476 AD, the European cultural descendants of the Greco/Roman world entered a period of social, economic, and philosophical dislocation and stagnation. That period, the first half known as the Dark Ages and later as the Middle Ages, lasted for approximately 1,000 years from roughly 500 AD to 1500 AD. Consequently, many important events that shaped Western civilization and the American founding occurred during that period.

In England in 1215, one of the most important documents in history was established when the English king's royal seal was placed on the Magna Carta ("Great Charter"). The English nobility had revolted against the unbridled tyrannical rule of King John and demanded restrictions on the king's absolute powers. The Magna Carta, a form of a binding truce between the rebel barons and the king, put limits on the heretical authority of the monarch. The Great Charter established the principle that everyone, including the king, is subject to the law, and it guaranteed the rights of individuals, the right to justice, and the right to a fair trial. The Magna Carta is a foundational document that established basic principles of English Common Law. The Common Law established basic principles of jurisprudence across the English-speaking world, including within American law, as can be found in the Declaration of Independence, the Constitution, the Bill of Rights, and other documents of democratic principles and human rights.

The Middle Ages were also marked by great thinkers and Christian Theologians. Distinct among them was the Catholic saint and follower of the Dominican Order, Thomas Aquinas (1225 to 1274). Aquinas had a preeminent mind and demonstrated it through his writings on a system of intellectual analysis referred to as Thomism. His teachings and writings evolved into the official philosophy of the Roman Catholic Church. Born in Italy and educated in France, Aquinas was not just a Catholic theologian but was also a philosopher who prescribed to the ideas of Aristotle, a new and revolutionary position for a Catholic theologian to advance at that time. *Stanford Encyclopedia of Philosophy* states that Thomas Aquinas "lived at a critical juncture of western culture when the arrival of the Aristotelian *corpus* in Latin translation reopened the question of the relation between faith and reason, calling into question the *modus vivendi* that had obtained for centuries."[1]

It was during the earlier centuries of the post-Roman decline, after the fifth century, that the scholarly teachings of Classical Greece and Rome had largely been deemphasized and displaced by feudalism and adherence to strict religious orthodoxy. Reopening the ideas and teachings from the past, Aquinas wrote about the melding of the two great driving principles of man: faith and reason.

He noted that the greatest gift of God to man was reason. Aquinas merged the secular ideas of Natural Law (a body of unchanging moral principles regarded as a basis for all human conduct) and the religious perspective of Eternal Law (law that God created and infused into man for his direction and preservation). Aquinas proffered that through reason and reflection there is only one truth and that there is no conflict between the truth of God and science. The melding of Christian theological doctrine and the emergence of new attitudes toward the scientific method had important consequences for Euro/Western societies, which developed rapidly over the next several centuries.

This development in science and the advancement of technology gave the West an edge over its contemporary rival civilizations moving forward. In contrast, the Islamic world which had made great strides in culture and the advancement of science and technology in what is known as the Islamic Golden Age, beginning around the eighth and lasting to the fourteenth century. It was during the last part of this period that the European/West societies would revive from their intellectual stagnation and enter a new era of creativity.

Prior to the Wests' renewed interest in the classical ideas and concepts of Greece and Rome, other historic events were taking shape across Asia, Africa and the Mediterranean world. The seventh century witnessed the rise of Islam, the youngest of the Abrahamic religions, which includes Judaism and Christianity. Islam would appear first on the Arabian Peninsula through the revelations of the Prophet Mohammad, of the Angel Gabriel, who they believe conveyed the verses of the Koran (Islamic holy book) to him. Islam would then expand over the next several centuries, through zeal and fervor of it followers and would spread across large portions of the civilized world. The Islamic conquest and conversion brought on structural social changes to these regions and marked hostility and conflict with the Christian European societies. Older cultures once part of Christendom including Egypt, Byzantium, North Africa and parts of Spain, the Balkans and Asia, would fall to Islamic invasion and conversion, often by the sword, including the city of Constantinople in 1453. The Great city of Constantinople (current day Istanbul) which lies at the juncture of the European and Asian continents and was named after the Roman Emperor Constantine. The city had emerged as an important economic and cultural center in the post Roman world. During the Middle Ages, it would also become the capital of the Byzantine Empire, which was the eastern part of the older Roman Empire, and had lasted for nearly 1,000 years after the fall of Rome. As the Islamic caliphate (rule of law by Islam) would sweep across the middle east, Constantinople like Cairo and Baghdad would emerge as important cities in the Islamic world.

As the Christian European societies were confronting new challenges from Islam, the Christian West would experience a different type of revelation and awareness in the centuries to follow. This revelation was one of thought and rediscovery.

As the Euro/Western societies emerged from the Middle Ages, a great intellectual awakening began to occur. The Renaissance (French for "rebirth"), beginning in the fourteenth century, brought in a rediscovery of the Classical periods of Greece and Rome and emphasized European cultural awareness of science, art, politics, and economics. This neo-classical period was also marked by Humanist philosophy (the advancement of individualism, freedom, and progress) and a move away from strict religious orthodoxy.

The Renaissance was born in Italy and gave rise to new ways that individuals could relate to and interact with each other. In a departure from Feudalism, towns began developing into cities and becoming centers for science, art, language, and culture. The renewal of art and expression flourished in Italy and other parts of Europe. Great painters and sculptors such as Michelangelo, Raphael, and Donatello brought creativity, beauty, and perspective to art for the ages to revere and appreciate. Leonardo da Vinci, truly the Renaissance man, was not only a masterful painter and artist but was also a brilliant scientist with a creative and curious mind.

The Renaissance also gave rise to the expanded study of natural philosophy, which later became modern science. The "father of astronomy," Polish-born Nicolas Copernicus (1473-1543), discovered that the planets revolve around the sun and that the earth rotates on its axis. Galileo Galilei (1564-1642) was an Italian physicist whose studies in astronomy and observations through his telescope are credited with the discovery of the moons of Jupiter and other planetary phenomena. Sir Isaac Newton (1642-1727), an English physicist and mathematician, was one of the most important figures in the scientific revolution of the seventeenth century, and his discoveries and teachings were comparable to those of Einstein's in the twentieth century. Of Newton, *Encyclopedia Britannica* states:

> In optics, his discovery of the composition of white light integrated the phenomena of colours into the science of light and laid the foundation for modern physical optics. In mechanics, his three laws of motion, the basic principles of modern physics, resulted in the formulation of the law of universal gravitation. In mathematics, he was the original discoverer of the infinitesimal calculus. Newton's *Philosophiae Naturalis Principia Mathematica* (*Mathematical Principles of Natural Philosophy*, 1687) was one of the most important single works in the history of modern science.[2]

The fifteenth century was also the beginning of the Age of Discovery, first led by the Portuguese and later including the Spanish, English, French, and Dutch. The Age of Discovery was marked by the European nations venturing out past local coast lines, westward into the Atlantic, and southward around Africa and beyond the straits of Gibraltar and the confines of the Mediterranean Sea. Many American school children have been taught that the great explorers of that age were the ones who proved the earth was round, but the theory of the earth as a sphere goes far back to the ancient Greeks of the sixth and fifth centuries BC. Pythagoras, a philosopher and mathematician at that time, taking into consideration the circular shadows on the moon, conjectured that the moon was a sphere and that the earth must therefore be spherical too.

A pre-existing idea of the earth being round did not lessen the risks faced by the men who ventured across the oceans of the world in brave quests of discovery. Christopher Columbus was an Italian explorer who sailed for Spain and rediscovered the New World. He made four trips across the Atlantic and opened up the western hemisphere for future colonization. Portuguese adventurer and navigator Ferdinand Magellan discovered the Pacific Ocean and was the first to circumnavigate the world. Vasco da Gama connected Europe and Asia by an ocean route, and his fellow countryman Pedro Alvares Cabral landed in what is now Brazil and claimed it for the Portuguese Crown. John Cabot, an Italian navigator, explored the coastline of North America for the British king, and his party was the first group of Europeans to visit the continent since the Vikings of the tenth century.

It is presumptuous to note discovery of these areas because human societies had already been established in all of them for hundreds or even thousands of years before the arrival of the European explorers and colonists. Some of the indigenous people, such as the Mayans and the Aztecs and the Inca Empire of Central and South America, lived in structured and organized societies, but all of them were eventually overtaken by the superior military equipment and organization of the European colonial empires, most notably the Spanish.

The destruction of many native cultures and the expansion of the slave trade to the Americas from Africa and the Caribbean by the colonial European nations are not high moral points in the story and evolution of Western civilization.

Contemporary historians condemn the treatment of indigenous people by the European colonial powers and by the later nation states of both North and South America. It is just another example of man's ability to rationalize aberrant behavior toward his fellow man. Indeed, many of the indigenous people had already been committing warfare and genocide against each other for many of the same reasons as the colonists. Those reasons included rivalry, conquest, land and resource acquisition, slavery, and others. The European colonists and later nations did not do anything to the native people of North and South America that the native people were not already doing to each other; the colonists were just more successful at it. This is not to offer a rationalization or justification for such morally abhorrent behavior. The true reason for man's destructive behavior towards people of different tribes and cultures can likely be found in an inward reflection of man's basic nature. Man in his "natural state" is still subject to nightmarish deeds against humanity, even after centuries of assuagement and the mollifying effects of belief in a divine power, morality, and civilization. It is an unfortunate fact of history that, despite the advancements of Western culture in the New World, many atrocities were committed by the European colonial powers in the struggle for dominance of North and South America.

Over time, the nations of the New World broke away from their traditional European monarchies. The new societies adopted various concepts of democratic principles. That was especially true in America where the original ideas of Western political and ideological concepts about the limitations of government and the rights of the individual, including property rights, were incorporated. The foundational ideas of man and the universe were not the exclusive property of the early Greek sophists and eclectic Roman philosophers. In reality, Western societies that came after those early civilizations contributed greatly to the contemporary ideas of Western cultural inheritance.

The Enlightenment

As noted, the American founders were influenced by many of the great thinkers and philosophers of antiquity. They were also greatly influenced by the Renaissance and, most importantly, by the Age of Enlightenment. Many of the philosophers of that age shaped the construction and elements of America's founding documents and governmental system as well as the inspirational direction of the American civil society. When it came to the organization of the

American government in the period leading up to the Revolution and during the Constitutional Convention and ratification process, no Enlightenment thinker was quoted more than Montesquieu. The list included George Mason, Thomas Jefferson, and James Madison among others. Montesquieu's influence on the American Constitution was of such magnitude that Madison was quoted as calling him an "oracle."

Barron Charles de Montesquieu (1689-1755), a French aristocrat, social philosopher, and judge, authored one of the period's preeminent works on government, laws, and jurisprudence titled *The Spirit of Laws* in 1748. Montesquieu was interested in how a government could work most effectively while preserving the rights of the people. He was also interested in providing safeguards to ensure that the executive and legislature did not become too powerful. In Montesquieu's study of laws from ancient societies up to and including his time, he was not simply interested in the function of laws. He examined the effects of laws from a social context with regards to elements of religion, economics, and politics, and he was cognizant of the ever-present danger of tyrannical rule encroaching into government. He noted from his study that there are three forms of government: monarchism, republicanism, and despotism. In *The Spirit of Laws*, he outlined a type of limited government that would provide protections for the preservation of the rights of the people. This could be accomplished by placing limitations on the powers of individuals as well as on elements within the different branches of government (checks and balances). Montesquieu was in opposition to the French monarchy of his time. He examined despotic regimes of the past wherein all elements of government were controlled by a king through his ministers or authoritarian rule by decree. Those types of governments, in Montesquieu's view, would only perpetuate tyranny.

In his theories of government and the relationship of man and society, Montesquieu was building on the inspirational ideas of John Locke and man's escape from the "state of nature." "When the legislative and executive powers are united in the same person, or in the same body of magistrates, there can be no liberty…Again, there is no liberty, if the judiciary power be not separated from the legislative and executive."[3] Montesquieu coined the term *"trias politica"* (Latin for, "separation of powers") and suggested a system of checks and balances that would be provided by three separate but equal and counter-balancing branches of government: the legislative branch, the executive branch, and the judicial branch. He concluded that separating the government in this way would keep the branches of authority in harmony and secure the liberty of the people.

Another important Frenchman, social philosopher, and prolific writer of the period was Francois-Marie Arouet, more commonly known by his simple adopted name of Voltaire (1699-1778). Voltaire was a dynamic champion of human progress in mind and spirit, which was a hallmark of Enlightenment philosophy. His spirited satirical writings and direct criticism of the monarchy and the church led to his imprisonment, and he had to leave France and take refuge in England and later in Holland. He was an idealist, and he played an important role in advocating for civil rights in French society. He challenged the French monarchy and social order, and his most important work, *Candide,* was eventually banned in France for blasphemy and sedition. *Candide* is a satirical novel that explores the travels of a fictional character through whom Voltaire expresses criticism of religion and the ruling authority. He was also a champion of individual expression and a strong advocate for freedom of speech. In a 1906 biography titled *The Friends of Voltaire*, the author, Evelyn Beatrice Hall, paraphrases Voltaire: "I disapprove of what you say, but I will defend to the death your right to say it."[4] She is also credited with another book on Voltaire that was published in 1903, *The Life of Voltaire.*

Voltaire, like Locke and Montesquieu, believed that the purpose of government was to protect the rights of the people. He believed that organized religion could be useful to an orderly society, but he did not accept religious orthodoxy as dictated by the Catholic Church. Voltaire believed in the separation of church and state and in the harmonious interaction of all people working together regardless of their religious affiliations or beliefs. He thought prejudice against different religious beliefs might lead to persecution and cause communities to break into different religious camps, which would hinder commerce and other normal activities within society. He pointed to Britain as an example of a more successful social organization because of its practice of freedom of religion and the positive effect it had on the overall society.

Voltaire was a follower of Deism, an Enlightenment belief based on reasoning and imbedded with a sophisticated view of continuity between God and universal scientific principles. It is a natural religion, and it professes the existence of a supreme being or "Nature's God" who created the universe and all things. In theory, it rejects supernatural interaction between man and God. In fact, pure Deists believe that God does not intercede in human affairs at all. It was a belief system held mostly by the intellectual elites of the Enlightenment period. Since Deism was based in reason and grounded in the laws of nature, most followers could loosely accept some or most of its tenets and still hold many core Christian beliefs. That appears to have been the case for many Deist followers. This group can be referred to as Christian Deist. Along with Voltaire and Montesquieu and possibly John Locke, other Deists included Isaac Newton, Leonardo da Vinci, James Hutton, and Adam Smith. The American founders also had a contingent of malleable Deist followers, including Benjamin Franklin, George Washington, Thomas Jefferson, James Madison, Thomas Paine, John Adams, and Abraham Lincoln. Though Lincoln was not a founder, he was by any measure an important figure in the nation's development and was referred to as a Christian Deist.

It is arguable, however, that no single philosopher had more influence on American original political thought than English Physician and political sophist, John Locke (1632-1704). Locke is often referred to as the "father of classical liberalism" (classical liberalism being the concept of economic individualism, civil rights, and rule of law). Locke proffered ideas on many subjects that were under consideration by many seventeenth century theorists in England and other European countries. His reflections and writings included several treatises on religion. In his work *A Letter Concerning Toleration,* his view was that the suppression of various religious beliefs within the English society was counterproductive to civil harmony. He believed in the separation of church and state and that religious freedom was part of man's natural inalienable rights, rights given to individuals directly by God. According to his concept of the "liberty of conscience," individuals should have the right to practice any faith they choose without dictates from the government.

Locke was also influential in the education of children. He had a practical view of teaching and thought that morality was a very important element of learning and that the teaching of subjects that advance the orderly function of individuals within a society was most important.

In his work *An Essay Concerning Human Understanding* (1689), Locke proffered the idea of the *"tabula rasa"* (Latin for "blank slate"), the concept that individuals are born without built-in mental context and that all knowledge therefore comes from experience and perception. Within the context of epistemological analysis (the study of knowledge), he believed that knowledge is learned and not innate to humans at birth. Locke's views on human nature were somewhat different than his contemporary Thomas Hobbes. Hobbes believed that man, in a "state of nature," is a brutish unregulated being and that humans are inherently and egocentrically focused on their individual wants and needs. Unlike Hobbes, Locke believed that humans have instinctive inclinations toward reason and tolerance and that these traits are building blocks that people can use to develop and survive in nature and thrive in communal environments.

Locke made his greatest intellectual contribution to Western societies in the field of political theory. It is not too much of a stretch to say that the original theory of America and its governmental system was conceived by John Locke nearly ninety years before the Declaration of Independence. In his *Two Treatise of Government*, he advanced ideas that were in direct contradiction to the contemporary ruling status quo of absolutism in late seventeenth-century England. In his treatise he proffered that all people, no matter the station they are born into, are given basic rights directly from God and that these rights cannot be taken away. These rights include "life, liberty, and property." This morality-driven position gives all humans equal standing in their humanity under God, and it eventually shook the foundation on which kings and sovereigns justified their powers of "divine right." Under the idea of "divine right," kings and nobility received their authority from God, but if all people, kings and paupers alike, have equal rights granted to them directly from God, it would restrict and even nullify the prerogative of absolute authority that kings had over their subjects. In Locke's ideas we see the root concept that was advanced by Jefferson in the Declaration of Independence. Locke was the inspiration and Jefferson was the architect and writer. This collaboration culminated in the great America experiment in limited government and the acceptance of inalienable rights of the individual.

Another area in which Locke and Hobbes differed was the social contract theory. The social contract was the supposition that man was originally born in a state of nature. Hobbes contended that this state of nature is a very dangerous and precarious environment for individuals because in it they are void of any controlling authority. As he wrote in his work *Leviathan*, in a state of nature, man's existence would be "all against all," and in order to escape this environment, man should establish authoritarian rule to protect individuals within society from destroying each other. He contended that once authoritarian rule (a king or sovereign) was established over society, the people surrendered all individual rights to protect themselves from one another and that the arrangement was permanent and irrevocable. His perspective is referenced by the title of his book, *Leviathan,* which is an Old Testament biblical reference

(Psalms 74:14) to a powerful sea monster. This somewhat colorful elucidation was Hobbes' vision of an all-powerful ruling sovereign.

John Locke disagreed with Hobbes' assertions on the absolute power of the sovereign and rejected the idea of divine right of kings. He believed that individuals always retained their natural rights and that a government's authority should come from the consent of the governed. It was his belief that governments are erected to protect the rights of the people and that when governments no longer act in the people's interest, the people have the right to change or replace that government. He believed that revolution in some circumstances is not only a right but an obligation. Locke was also concerned about government power becoming overbearing and controlled by a single element of authority. He believed in separating the powers between the executive and legislative functions of government. The concept was similar to the old Roman Republic's appointment of two councils to defuse power of any one individual or institution, and it was similar to Montesquieu's view of the separation of powers.

It is important that America continues to hold reverence for John Locke and his ideas and teachings on the relationships of God to man and man to government. All men are created equal with rights that existed before any government and that are paramount over government. Government was established to protect the rights of the people it serves, and when government stops serving the interest of the people, the people have the right and the duty to change or replace that government as they see fit. These ideas from Locke are so fundamental and embedded in the American consciousness that they are inseparable. Inexplicably, though, in recent years there has been a disturbing and somewhat incoherent revisionist movement and rise of socialism and even communist influences among some elitist young people in America. These ideas have proven to be false prophecies and delusions of utopia that have failed wherever they have been tried. These ideologies are completely antithetical to the intellectual genius of John Locke. One of America's preeminent young intellectuals and social and political commentators, Ben Shapiro, has recently stated his agreement that "if we lose John Locke, we lose America."[5]

Scotland experienced its own notable period of intellectual inspiration similar to the larger European Enlightenment. The Scottish Enlightenment had several important thinkers and teachers, including James Hutton (1726-1797), who was a geologist and naturalist. Hutton, through observation and reason, offered that the earth has always changed in uniform ways and that the present is the key to the past. This theory is known as Uniformitarianism, and it is important for understanding the earth's past. Hutton's ideas went on to influence Charles Darwin. Another influential thinker of the Scottish Enlightenment was David Hume (1711-1776), a philosopher and historian who is known for his writings on skepticism and empiricism (the theory that knowledge is acquired via the senses). He believed in the somewhat intellectually unflattering notion that humans are more influenced by their feelings than by reason.

The most noted member of the Scottish Enlightenment and one of the truly influential figures of the period was Adam Smith (1723-1790), an economist and moral philosopher. Smith is known as the "father of modern economics and capitalism," but that, in and of itself, does not fully describe him. Along with being an economist and a social philosopher, he was very interested in the human condition. The state and value of the human condition was a driving force of the intellectual energies that fueled much of the discourse of the period. Smith was a willing participant in those interactions aimed at developing models to improve how man can prosper and find a sense of value in his work and efforts. Smith's first work, *The Theory of Moral Sentiments* (1759), lays out his views on ethics and virtue including individual rights and liberty. Smith was a realist and recognized that, within the context of human nature, individuals are driven by self-interest. This is not necessarily a bad thing but a reality of the human condition. Smith's most noted work, *An Inquiry into the Nature and Causes of the Wealth of Nations* (1776), outlines the principles and elements of a new economy. He contended that an economy centered on individuals acting in their own self-interests in the exchange of goods and services in a "free market" would have benefits for the whole society. He referred to the idea metaphorically as the "invisible hand."

> Every individual necessarily labours to render the annual
> revenue of the society as great as he can…he intends only
> his own security…and he is in this, as in many other cases,
> led by an invisible hand to promote an end which was no part
> of his intention…By pursuing his own interest he frequently
> promotes that of the society more effectually than when he
> really intends to promote it. I have never known much good
> done by those who affected to trade for the public good.[6]

Smith was writing against the backdrop of the early stages of the industrial revolution, and new modes of economic development motivated him to propose a system that would free individuals from the drudgery of mundane work tasks. Smith was against the existing economic system of mercantilism that was in vogue in the seventeenth and eighteenth centuries. Mercantilism was a system based on national trade policies that would increase a nation's power and wealth through exports and protectionism. This would, in the end, amount to a zero-sum game. Smith noted that greater efficiencies in production could be achieved by breaking work tasks through a "division of labor" into smaller specialized elements. The concept of work specialization would equal greater productivity and efficiency within society, facilitate an increase in labor rates, and improve the people's standard of living. Another benefit of increased productivity would be the overall lowering of product costs. Smith was a strong advocate of the free market and a laissez-faire economic policy. He believed these policies were the best way to improve the conditions of the workers and society as a whole and increase the wealth of a nation.

There were many important voices that spoke out on the issues of the day, including human rights and the role that governments have in supporting a civil society. One of those voices was Irishman Edmond Burke (1729-1797), born in Dublin to a Catholic mother and Protestant father. Burke was a great orator, writer, and social and moral commentator who served in the English Parliament for nearly thirty years. He is credited with laying down the basic principles of conservatism in theory and is considered the "father of modern conservatism." Burke valued the virtuous message that religion conveyed in a society. He believed in the value of traditional social order and that long-established institutions needed to be preserved and protected. He believed that "good order is the foundation of all good things."[7]

Burke was a supporter of the American Revolution. In theory, he would not have supported the colonies detaching from the order and traditions of Britain, but he justified his support because he saw that the British were the aggressors and that they had denied the colonists their rights as Englishmen with the impositions of the Stamp and Tea Acts. In the end, the colonists were just meeting force with force and defending themselves against abusive treatment by the Crown. Burke knew that liberty does not exist in the absence of morality, and he understood that "the greater the power, the more dangerous the abuse."[8]

Burke was strongly opposed to the French Revolution. In his work *Reflections on the Revolution in France* (1790), he outlined his position and the reasons he was against the movement. His view was that the Revolution was retrogressive in its effect, and he felt it would be destructive to the society. Burke was thought of as a moderate reformer, and he knew that making appropriate changes within a society was at times necessary so long as the society held onto its ancestral customs in social order and rule of law. The French Revolution was a complete departure from this traditional concept of inheritance. As the Revolution progressed, it not only ended the monarchy and reign of King Louis XVI, it completely fractured the framework of the French societal estates (tiered classes in French society). It also brought about the persecution of the French nobility and the Catholic Church. Burke would not argue that French society did not need social reform and greater equality, but he believed the result of the French Revolution would be calamity. He thought some of the elements of the movement were naive and that they did not take the very complicated nature of man into account. He also denounced the oppression of the Catholic Church and the lasting negative consequences it could have on a society. Burke understood that those who don't know history are destined to repeat it.

In the 1790s, there was great concern all across Europe and beyond about the French Revolution and the lasting effects the dislocating movement could have on the existing social order. The Revolution was seen as a direct challenge to the long-established rule of sovereigns, the church, and the nobility. Burke was concerned about the atheistic tenor of the revolutionary Jacobins. He believed that the combination of atheism and the destruction of social norms and legal traditions would invariably lead to tyranny of the masses. Society would, in the end, lose its stabilizing inheritance of accepted jurisprudence and moral grounding. In summing up his views of legal predicate and moral responsibility, Burke stated "it is not what a lawyer tells me I may do, but what humanity, reason, and justice tell me I ought to do."[9] Burke did not live long enough to see the result of the French Revolution. He died in 1797 at the age of sixty-eight, but much of his trepidations came to be realized. Generations of Conservatives and Liberals alike have drawn wisdom from Burke and his perspectives on the relationship and continuity of inherited traditional social standards and the sometimes-unappreciated value those qualities impart to an organized community.

The French Revolution

During the last half the eighteenth century, two pivotal events that came to define the Enlightenment period developed in both America and France. Those two events were the American Revolution and the French Revolution, and they brought together the intellectual awareness that was developed during the Renaissance and Enlightenment. During the Enlightenment period, man developed a greater understanding of his place in the universe and his position among his fellow creatures. Ideas of basic human rights and freedom of speech, religion, and the press were all part of the dialogue. In France, "liberty, equality, and fraternity" were part of the cries of the masses. Unrest and injustices surrounding the plight of the people were fermenting in the taverns and meeting places among the less privileged. Concern was growing in the halls of the affluent and dilatant circles throughout the country. Sedition and revolt against the king, nobility, and the strata of social estates were at the heart of the conflict.

The French Revolution started in 1789 and lasted for ten years, during which the entire French social order and governing system were disrupted and overturned. The French King Louis XVI supported the American Revolution against his rival, the British King George III. King Louis' material and financial support for the American cause along with decades of extravagance, misallocations of national resources, and institutional corruption depleted the French treasury and created a crisis. There are many reasons the French Revolution began, including decades of crop failures that caused widespread food shortages and famine. There also growing anger over the disparity in wealth between the rich and poor within the ancient class system, which was a holdover from the Middle Ages. The bourgeoisie (middle class merchants) were excluded from political power and suffered the imposition of high taxes and an inability to enact fiscal reforms.

Pre-revolutionary France was divided into three classes or estates. The first estate was the Catholic Church and the clergy. The second estate was the nobility and the aristocracy with links to the monarchy. The third estate represented the remaining 98% of the population and was made up of merchants and businessmen along with farmers and peasants. The first two estates were excluded from the tax burden of the nation, and the less well-off and the poor were obligated to pay increasing amounts of their dwindling resources. For years prior to the Revolution, there had been a growing desire for societal reform and to move away from the country's traditional feudal system. The recent success of the American Revolution in throwing off the British Crown gave many in the third estate a model for a similar type of revolt against King Louis XVI's rule.

The financial situation grew worse in France, and it prompted the king to summon the Estates General in May 1789. The Estates General was an assembly comprised of all three estates of the French population. It was the first time the Estates General was called since 1614. The Estates General had the power to invoke new taxes and establish reform in French society, and it represented a potential threat to the king's absolute authority, but desperate times required desperate measures. As the Estates General proceeded, the three estates were not able to come to an agreement on measures to close the budgetary deficit. In defiance, the third estate broke away and formed a revolutionary movement called the National Assembly. This convention led to the French National Constituent Assembly, which constructed and adopted the Declaration of the Rights of Man and of the Citizen drafted by Abbe Sieyes and the

Marquis de Lafayette. Thomas Jefferson was the US Ambassador to France during that eventful summer of 1789. In the closing months before he left France to go back to the United States, Jefferson consulted with Lafayette on the development of the Declaration of the Rights of Man. This gives Jefferson a singularly unique role in history in that he participated in the creation of two of the most important documents in the development of individual rights and human progress. Not only did Jefferson author the American Declaration of Independence, but he consulted on the Declaration of the Rights of Man in France. The Declaration of the Rights of Man drew inspiration from the concepts developed during the American Revolutionary period. It also drew inspiration from Enlightenment philosophy of natural laws and individualism and from Rousseau's ideas on the Social Contract.

The writings of Swiss philosopher Jean-Jacques Rousseau (1712-1778) were widely read and followed among many pre-revolutionary French intellectuals. Opposite to Thomas Hobbes, Rousseau believed that man's nature was naturally good but corrupted by society. In his book *The Social Contract* (1768), he wrote that "Man is born free; and everywhere he is in chains."[10] Rousseau did not believe that a "civil society" based on individual needs could provide the mechanism for securing man's natural inherited rights; instead, he thought that man would best find himself and liberation in the total acquiescence of will to a community of all the people. He proffered that man should give up "all his rights, to the whole community; for, in the first place, as each gives himself absolutely, the conditions are the same for all; and, this being so, no one has any interest in making them burdensome to others."[11] The people he described as being sovereign in this state would make laws for enforcement over the community. Rousseau's ideas challenged the idea of the divine right of monarchs and helped advance the French Revolution. Though popular in French intellectual circles, Rousseau's concept of surrendering your individual rights to a "community" of earthly authority was in direct contradiction to the views of John Locke and are completely antithetical to American political theory and practice in which the individual's God-given rights of life, liberty, and the pursuit of happiness are paramount.

The ideas of Rousseau had a great impact on the late eighteenth-century French Revolutionary period, particularly on elements of the radical clubs including the Jacobins and Maximillian Robespierre. The Jacobins were left-wing revolutionaries committed to overthrowing the king and establishing a republic. In 1793 and 94, during a period known as the "Reign of Terror," the country was ruled by a group called the Committee of Public Safety. The committee was comprised of Jacobins and other revolutionaries led by Robespierre who was known as "the incorruptible" because of his strong stance in defense of democratic values. The group implemented violent judgements and terror against those they viewed as being counter-revolutionary. In the end, the Jacobins commenced with their own destruction by executing the elements of the movement who were not radical enough. Those individuals were labeled as interfering with the goals of the Revolution and included many original members, even Robespierre himself.

The Revolution ignited in July of 1789 when a group of Parisian rioters stormed the Bastille, a prison thought to hold political prisoners. The Bastille was an armed fortress, and it came to symbolize the authority of the king and his oppression over the people. Over time, the armed revolutionary mob grew larger, and the Commander of the garrison, Bernard-Rene de Launay, and his soldiers inside the prison were forced to surrender. The mob dragged de Launay through the streets of Paris and eventually killed him. It was a portent of violence to come and sparked the beginning of the ten-year-long ordeal of the Revolution. The revolutionary fever spread throughout the countryside and cities of France. The mob burned the houses of tax collectors and assaulted the monarchy's symbols of authority. In September of 1792, the National Assembly abolished the Monarchy, and King Louis XVI and Queen Marie Antoinette were both imprisoned. In that same year, the National Assembly drafted a constitution, and the first French Republic was established, giving rise to the French motto of "liberty, equality, and fraternity." In the following years, a period of social unrest and "societal cleansing" erupted throughout all of French society. The Reign of Terror saw many clergy, aristocrats, and counter-revolutionaries become familiar with the guillotine, and between 16,000 and 20,000 French citizens lost their lives. A movement was unleashed all over the country to erase the old ways of feudalism, class structure, and the privileges granted to the nobility, Catholic Church, and the clergy. France emerged from the Revolutionary period when, in November of 1799, Napoleon Bonaparte seized power through a military coup. Napoleon, like the Romans, established rule through consuls. Rome had two consuls and Napoleon had three, with himself being counted as one of them. In 1804 he returned France to a hereditary monarchy and reinstated many of the old traditions of French society including reversing the effort of de-Christianizing the country.

It is important when reviewing the French Revolution that we remember Thomas Jefferson and the Declaration of Independence:

> Prudence, indeed, will dictate that Governments long established should not be changed for light and transient causes; and accordingly all experience hath shewn, that mankind are more disposed to suffer, while evils are sufferable, than to right themselves by abolishing the forms to which they are accustomed.[12]

Jefferson was noting that to upend a governmental system and all the accompanying social infrastructure is an extreme measure that should not be undertaken but for the most egregious circumstances. The Declaration goes on to state:

> But when a long train of abuses and usurpations, pursuing invariably the same Object evinces a design to reduce them under absolute Despotism, it is their right, it is their duty, to throw off such Government, and to provide new Guards for their future security.[13]

The compelling cautionary note here is: "if you break it, you own it" and "once the genie is out of the lantern, it is very difficult to put him back in."

The French Revolution was a messy and protracted affair that manifested in the disarray of the entire society. The overthrow of the anachronistic monarchy and the eventual establishment of a Republic and a Constitution for the French nation was a worthy endeavor. That is despite the disruption and trauma of the ordeal to French social order. In the end, the events advanced the cause of human progress. The Declaration of Independence, similarly, was the justification for the American Revolution and eventually for American independence. The positive aspects and consequences of both revolutions for human dignity and progress cannot be underestimated. They are both landmark developments and lasting legacies of the Enlightenment. The last two-plus centuries have validated the forms of government that both nations advanced, and those governments have been replicated by countries all over the world, but it must be stated that not every insurrection or revolutionary movement is a worthy or a noble cause. This is exemplified by the distortions and corruptions of socialist and communist revolutions, notably in their shallow and baseless promises of utopia that only result in the denial of basic human rights and ascendency into authoritarian rule by the new elite. The reality is and history has taught us that these insurrections are extremely dangerous. They can take on lives of their own and lead to societies being unmoored from their ancestral legal and cultural roots. The French Revolution, with all of it chaos and complexities, is an example. The French struggled through social and political instability and the return of a monarchy under Napoleon. They saw several more decades of political dislocation, but eventually France culminated into a constitutionally based democratic republic.

The period of the late seventeenth and eighteenth centuries was a time of revolutionary thinking on the relationship of man in society and with God. A large part of the discussion was about the best governmental arrangement for securing individual liberty and for the individual to develop and thrive within society. How could older systems of government and civil organization be reshaped into new and better systems to promote equality, civil rights, freedom of religion, and the prerogatives of the individual? The development was not merely evolutionary, but revolutionary. Possibly for the first time in human history, ideas of morality were at the center of philosophical imaginations. That was followed by implementing practical applications for new systems of governance. In the Hobbesian view of man's original condition in the "state of nature" and of the metaphorical Leviathan, the outlook was bleak, but in the new Enlightenment thinking offered by Locke and his views on the inalienable rights of the individual, man had standing with the sovereign. Locke, Montesquieu, and others contended that the purpose of government is to protect the rights of the people and that if government fails in that function, the people have the right and responsibility to change that government. Montesquieu provided a new governmental structure based in separation of powers and checks and balances to protect the rights of the individual. As the Enlightenment progressed, those new concepts received greater acceptance, and the intellectual governing emphasis moved away from the interest of the affluent and powerful and focused on the interest of the people. Those thoughts and concepts had a profound effect on the American system of government that emerged.

Part Two

The World Turned Upside Down

Chapter Four

By the Rude Bridge

The American story began as a consequence of the Age of Exploration of the sixteenth and seventeenth centuries. In that new world, the European powers jockeyed for position and dominance in the territories of the Western Hemisphere. The English competed with the Dutch, French, and Spanish for control of North America and what would become the eastern part of the United States. The English development of the new land was different than their European competitors. The English focused on establishing colonies and encouraged new settlers to immigrate to the land for economic and political reasons. The first English settlement was on Roanoke Island off the coast of North Carolina in 1585. It was established by Sir Walter Raleigh. The settlement was neglected by the British and interrupted by the Anglo-Spanish War (1585-1604). The English later returned to the site to find that the settlement was abandoned and that the inhabitants had vanished. The first lasting and permanent settlement by the British was established in 1607 at Jamestown, Virginia (named after King James I), which then developed into the Virginia colony. That was followed by the Plymouth colony, which was established in 1620 by the English Puritans or Pilgrims, a religious separatist group. Over the next several decades, other British colonies were established along the east coast of North America.

England in the late sixteenth and early seventeenth centuries was struggling through difficult social and economic times, as was much of Europe. Populations were growing, and shortages of many of the necessities of life were common occurrences. That was particularly true with food. Profit motives of the wealthy were at the center of much of the shortfall of life-supporting goods. The then-current economic system of mercantilism turned over large tracts of land that had been used for food production and began to use them for profit-oriented commerce in the raising of sheep for wool and other commercial products. The vast wilderness of North America was considered a great opportunity to expand commerce and relieve the issues associated with shortages and the expanding population problems. In 1606, English King James I, with support from wealthy merchants and Parliament, issued two charters for the commercial expansion and development of the land on the east coast of the North American continent. The southern section was given to the London Company (later the Virginia Company), and the northern section was given to the Plymouth Company. That was the beginning of the great migration to America and the establishment of commercial ties and connections between the growing American colonies and the mother country of England.

Over the next 150 years, America developed into thirteen colonies: Virginia, Massachusetts, Rhode Island, Connecticut, New

Hampshire, New York, Pennsylvania, New Jersey, Maryland, Delaware, North Carolina, South Carolina, and Georgia. The colonies grew and prospered, and a vigorous commercial relationship grew with England. Most of the colonists were farmers, fishermen, and merchants, and by the middle of the 1700s the standard of living in America was higher than in England. The Americans relied on trade with the English for manufactured goods and specialty items from the Caribbean and other regions.

The colonies also relied on England for protection from the other colonial powers such as Spain and France. The relationship between the American colonies and England during that period was marked by common interest and amicable formality. The American colonies had firm roots and shared social and political traditions with the mother country. The colonies also represented the English-speaking contingent of the British Empire in North America. Economically, during the colonial period, the American colonists enjoyed a degree of autonomy in trading among themselves and had a free hand in trade with England. There were, however, restrictions placed on the colonies in trade with other European countries. Politically, the colonies had their own legislatures and enacted laws for the orderly operation of their society. Moreover, the American colonists viewed themselves as subjects of the English king with the rights of Englishmen. The American colonists also generally recognized the English king as their absolute paternal authority.

The era of benign neglect by the mother country started to come to an end in 1754 with the onset of the French and Indian War. The French and Indian War was the local North American conflict of a larger engagement of arms between England and France known as the Seven Years' War. In North America the conflict began over disputed dividing lines between the English and French territories of the Upper Ohio River Valley and other diverging claims. In the 1750s, the American colonists wanted to expand west of the Appalachian Mountains toward disputed lands and further encroach into Native American territories.

By the 1750s, the French settlements in North America were organized mostly with trade in mind and for the exportation of the bountiful riches of the wilderness. Beaver and fox pelts along with other furs were important cash crops in demand throughout Europe. French trappers, traders, and hunters took full advantage of the vast and sparsely populated territories to secure a hold on the continent. The French claims in North America ran from the area of current day Ontario and Quebec down through the Great Lakes and the Mississippi River to the Gulf of Mexico. The French also occupied land of the Ohio River region west of the Appalachian Mountains. It was that region of French settlements, west of the Appalachian Mountains, that brought them into direct conflict with the expanding Anglo-American colonies. The French had established trading outposts and settlements at various key points along their axes of occupation. Those settlements and fortifications included Quebec,

Montreal, Fort Richelieu, Fort Duquesne (later Pittsburg), Fort Detroit, Fort Saint Louis, Baton Rouge, Mobile, La Nouvelle-Orleans (New Orleans), and others.

By the middle of the eighteenth century, the French territories of North America were vast, many times the size of France itself and larger than the Anglo-American colonies, but there was also a great disparity between the size of the French and British colonial populations. The French had a population in North America of between 60,000 and 80,000 inhabitants while the British had approximately 2,000,000, a disparity mostly due to the different emphases the two powers placed on colonization. The French focused on commercial use of the vast territory's resources and sought to use mercantilism to advance the French state. In contrast, the British were interested in permanent settlements and encouraged and attracted migration to their colonies for various reasons including land and religious freedom.

The middle part of the 1700s crescendoed with England and France struggling against each other in several hyphenated wars. The long-term struggle between the two European powers had roots that went back to William the Conqueror and the Norman invasion of England and the Battle of Hastings in 1066. The latest struggle, beginning in 1757, and climax of those conflicts was the Seven Years' War. The revised conflict between France and England would take on global dimensions and come to include the continents of Europe, Asia, Africa, and the Americas. In North America the

French became concerned as Anglo settlers moved into new lands west of the Appalachian Mountains in the Upper Ohio River Valley. Both the English and the French had conflicting claims to those lands. Of great concern to the new French governing authority under the last Governor General of New France, Pierre de Rigaud, Marquis de Vaudreuil-Cavagnialas, was that the Anglo settlers far outnumbered the French in the region. The conflict heated up when the regional French authorities of New France ordered the settlers to be removed from the region in 1749. The hostility between the two countries would come to involve Native American tribes that occupied the region of conflict. The tribes would also war against each other as they chose sides in the struggle.

The war in North America started in 1754, two years before the larger conflict of the Seven Years' War. Both England and France desired to build a new empire in North America. In both cases the other power was in the way along with the native people. The centuries-old antagonism between the two countries was a standing match always ready to ignite into a new conflict. The restrictions on new Anglo colonial expansion into regions claimed as New France territory was the spark that ignited the fire of war. The French, in an effort to strengthen their position along the line of conflict, built several fortified positions at strategic locations. The French and Indian War, which was the North American theater of conflict between the two countries, involved much of the contested area along the dividing line and covered Upper Ohio and Western

Pennsylvania, including the confluence of the Monongahela and Allegany Rivers that join to form the Ohio River at Fort Duquesne (current day Pittsburg). The conflict also involved the Great Lakes region, parts of eastern Canada, New York, and the St. Lawrence River and gulf, including Nova Scotia.

In May of 1754, Governor Robert Dinwiddie of the Virginia colony became concerned about the growing fort system the French were building along the frontier line of the two territorial claims. A Virginia militia under orders of Governor Dinwiddie requisitioned a contingency of militiamen and supporting Indians under the command of a young Lt. Colonel. The mission of the group was to finish construction of fortifications and a road in the wilderness along the way to the juncture of the Ohio River. The Lt. Colonel was twenty-one-year-old Virginia surveyor and planter George Washington. During the course of the expedition, the militia ambushed a French scouting patrol in the Pennsylvania wilderness. The leader of the French patrol, Ensign Joseph Coulon Jumonville, was killed in the engagement under dubious circumstances. Washington and his militia, along with Indian support, erected Fort Necessity in anticipation of a counter attack from the French and their Indian allies, who greatly outnumbered the Virginians. Later, the French did attack Washington and his men and forced Washington to surrender and sign a confession as to the questionable circumstances surrounding the death of Ensign Jumonville. Washington's confession would later be an embarrassment to him.

In the statement, possibly a mistranslation, he took responsibility for the death of the French officer. That was Washington's first experience in combat, and in it he found a place of purpose for his future. He later noted, "I heard bullets whistle and believe me, there was something charming in the sound."[1]

The British and the French engaged in combat all across the frontier. In 1755, the British sent two regiments of foot (approximately 2,000 men) under the command of Major General Edward Braddock to the colonies. Braddock's mission was to expel the French from the Ohio River Valley and eliminate the French fortifications at various points, including the strategic juncture at the confluence of the Monongahela and Allegany Rivers at Fort Duquesne. Washington and his militia joined Braddock on the campaign, absent of the inclusion of local Indian support. The excursion into the Virginia and Pennsylvania wilderness turned out to be a disaster for Braddock and the British. On the campaign, Braddock was killed, and his forces were routed by the French and their Indian allies. Washington demonstrated important leadership qualities and personal courage during the fighting, but the result of the effort was the French securing a temporary hold on the region under dispute.

In the summer of 1757, the French defeated the British again in Upstate New York at the obscure dividing lines of French Canada and English New York. A British garrison of regulars and local militias under the command of Lt. Colonel George Monro was holding out against a superior force of the French at Fort William Henry, located at the southern tip of Lake George, but the French force of more than 10,000, including French Regular Infantry and 2,000 Indian allies from various tribes including the Hurons, ultimately laid siege to the British. The French contingent embarked on a campaign south from Fort Carillon at the southern end of Lake Chaplain. As the siege advanced and supplies ran low, and with no hope of reinforcements, the British were forced to surrender the fort to the French General Louis-Joseph de Montcalm. The terms of the surrender allowed the British to leave the fort and proceed in good order to British territory at Fort Edward further south. Along the way, the British force was attacked by Montcalm's Indian allies in an apparent breach of the surrender agreement, and dozens of British soldiers and dependents were killed and scalped. Subsequently, many prisoners were taken back to Canada and were ransomed. The British viewed the incident and subsequent massacre as a betrayal of eighteenth-century military protocols, and it became a motivating factor to fully prosecute the war against the French and their presence in Canada.

The war entered a period of stalemate with the French holding the upper hand for the first few years of the conflict in North America. As the larger conflict with the English and French raged across the globe in the Seven Years' War, the British, in 1757, under their new Prime Minister, William Pitt, raised the ante in North America. The British intention was no longer just to remove the

French from the contested boundary regions but to remove the French completely from New France, including the regions of the Upper Ohio River Valley and Canada. To that end, Pitt committed large sums of resources and more than 20,000 British troops.

In 1758, the British, under General James Abercrombie, advanced from the south and launched a frontal assault against the French Fort Carillon in Upstate New York. The assault proved to be a costly error, and the British suffered a major defeat against the French forces there under General Louis-Joseph de Montcalm. The Battle of Carillon was the largest engagement of arms in the war. More than 1,000 British were killed and many more were wounded. The French losses were much smaller in comparison. Despite their victory at Carillon, the French recognized the precariousness of their overall position in the region and abandoned the fort to the British and their Iroquois Indian allies the following year in June 1759. The fort would from that point forward be known as Fort Ticonderoga.

The British, under Prime Minister William Pitt, decided to spend large amounts of resources on the campaign in North America to expel the French from Canada. To advance that effort, the British Navy, which was considerably larger than the French fleet, allowed Britain to easily supply and support their forces and to provide the British Army with the initiative to advance the campaign for the next two years.

The British invaded Canada through the St. Lawrence River and defeated the French Army and the inhabitants of New France.

The conflict, or, as the French would call it, *La Conquest*, started in 1758 when the British, under General Jeffery Amherst, successfully sieged Fort Louisbourg in Nova Scotia. From Louisbourg, the British, under Major General James Wolfe, continued the advance through the St. Lawrence and landed near Quebec. In September of 1759, the British and French forces engaged in a fierce struggle. The French were under the command of the resourceful and capable General Marquis de Montcalm, the victor of the Battle of Fort William Henry at Lake George in New York the previous year. The battle joined on the Plains of Abraham outside of the city, providing the British with a more advantageous and conventional venue of battle in open fields and with fixed formations of engagement. The British were victorious, but the actions claimed the lives of both commanders, the Marquis de Montcalm and General Wolfe. In 1760, the British completed the final campaign of the war when they advanced on the French city of Montreal in a three-pronged attack that resulted in the French surrender of the city and the end of any flames in the hearts of Frenchmen for a new French empire in North America.

As a result of France's defeat to the British in the French and Indian War, the French were forced to cede their territories east of the Mississippi River as well as the vast territories of Northeast and Central Canada to England. To add insult to injury, the French were also compelled to cede Louisiana west of the Mississippi to their ally Spain in an effort to stop the British from gaining control of the territory. The move also compensated the Spanish for their loss of Florida, which Spain ceded to the British to maintain control of their colonial possessions in Cuba and the Philippines. The British had captured those two Spanish possessions in the larger struggles between the conflicting allied nations.

The British and their allies soundly defeated the French and their Spanish allies who had joined with France in 1761 against Britain in the Seven Years' War. The war raged all across the world in dramatic fashion and became the first true global conflict. It involved most of the European powers, including Prussia and Fredrick the Great who were aligned with the British. Joining the French side were the Spanish, Austrians, Swedes, and Russians. The British won victories in Europe, India, the Philippines, and the Caribbean as well as North America. Britain's empire grew exponentially by the end of the conflict and the signing of the Treaty of Paris in February 1763, which ended the Seven Years' War. As a result of England's victories over France and Spain across the globe and the addition of new territories in North America, the English Empire eclipsed the old Roman Empire in size.

England won impressive victories all across the globe, and the successes were codified in the Treaty of Paris in February 1763. In order to achieve those victories, Britain had to commit large sums of financial resources to support its army and navy and to maintain the new lands and territories of their empire. The British treasury had accumulated a massive debt, doubling from the period before the war in 1756 to 122 million pounds by the war's end. Britain had to find ways to offset the debt, and that took the form of increased taxation, some of which fell to the American colonies. From the outset of the British colonial establishment in America, the colonies had enjoyed a degree of self-governance, and England showed a level of tolerance and patience that fostered a sense of entitlement in America. England's attitude toward its prized colonies in America began to change as the war debt mounted, and it had a new need to more closely control the operations of the colonies in order to secure the revenue from the new taxes. The amicable relationship between England and the American colonies began to change.

From an American perspective, the elimination of the French from the bordering regions gave the American colonists the liberty to breach the confines of the Appalachian Mountains and establish new settlements in the fruitful lands to the west. American enthusiasm was short lived, however. England soon realized that American expansion westward would present adverse consequences for cohesion and peace. The Native Americans of the region, led by the Pontiac and Ottawa tribes, would revolt against the new settlements. After the long and costly Seven Years' War and the corresponding campaign in North America, England looked to appease the native tribes of the region at the expense of the colonists and settlers. In October of 1763, King George III through a royal proclamation closed further expansion of settlements west of the Appalachian Mountains.

In 1764, the British Parliament enacted the Sugar Act or Revenue Act to raise capital for the Crown. The Sugar Act aimed to reduce smuggling of sugar and molasses and to provide enhanced administration to collect duties. In 1765, Parliament established the Quartering Acts, which mandated the colonies pay for the quartering and feeding of British troops. In the same year, Parliament also imposed the Stamp Act on the American colonies. The Stamp Act placed a duty on paper goods and printed materials, including all legal documents, such as wills, bills of sale, licenses, newspapers, pamphlets, and almanacs. The act even covered playing cards and dice. The Stamp Act was an additional burden on the lower- and middle-class merchants and farmers, much of whose businesses relied on credit. The act imposed a costly tax on legal documents, court proceedings, and other materials. The result was a swell of resistance and animosity toward the British that, for the most part, did not exist prior to the act. Resistance to the Stamp Act was one of the early embers that eventually ignited the bonfire of revolution.

The resistance included a direct in-person appeal to Parliament by none other than Benjamin Franklin, and the Stamp Act was repealed in 1766 after extensive American boycotts and protests from state legislatures. Even with the successful repeal of the Stamp Act, for the Americans it was not the end. In 1767, the Stamp Act was followed by the Townshend Act, which imposed a tax on all imported tea and other goods including china, lead, glass, and paint. The new tax elicited a focused and determined response from the American colonies, and many of the goods were boycotted. During that period, the British enacted other impositions in the form of acts aimed at achieving greater control over the colonies and producing revenue for the Crown. The acts combined with earlier laws such as the Hat Acts, which placed restrictions on the manufacturing, sale, and export of American-made hats, and were viewed by the Americans as being overbearing and even punitive. The provisions exerted British power and dominance over the lives of the growingly beleaguered Americans. The relationship between the mother country and her American colonies was becoming strained, and the voices of resistance were becoming louder.

In the early days of the founding of the British colonies in North America, the state legislatures enjoyed a degree of self-governance and autonomy from the British Crown. The first of those state legislatures was formed in 1619 in a General Assembly in Jamestown, Virginia. Later it elected representatives to the Virginia House of Burgesses in Williamsburg. The House of Burgesses was modeled after the British House of Commons and enacted state laws that could be revised or vetoed by the governor, who was appointed by the Crown. It was in the House of Burgesses and other similar legislatures across the colonies that issues of the day were discussed and debated, and it was there that America first experimented with and then establish a legacy of democracy that matured for more than 150 years.

Patrick Henry, a prominent planter as well as a self-taught and educated lawyer, was elected to the Virginia House of Burgesses in 1765. He was a powerful orator and a passionate opponent of the overbearing power of British authorities over the colonies. He first gained notoriety because of his speeches against the perceived injustices of the Stamp Act and the subsequent Stamp Act Resolution, which questioned Parliament's authority to tax the colonies. Henry's passionate opposition to the Stamp Act, which bordered on treason, branded him as a radical among the privileged gentry class that occupied the assembly. His revolutionary tendencies were further reinforced by his early advocacy for secession from England. Other respected representatives in the House of Burgesses, such as Edmond Pendleton, disagreed with Henry's fiery and inflammatory rhetoric, but in the end they agreed with the resistance to the Stamp Act and subsequent constraints to American liberty by the British Crown.

George Washington was elected to the House of Burgesses in 1758 and served for more than fifteen years. It was there that he learned the art of political nuance and statesmanship. He was not a great orator like Henry or a skilled legislator in the traditional sense of authoring or advocating for specific legislation, but when you add political acumen to the military experience he gained in the French and Indian War, he was developing a unique resume. The House of Burgesses provided him with connections to many of the best minds that were reviewing and debating the important issues of the time.

They included Thomas Jefferson, Payton Randolph, John Robinson, Edmond Pendleton, and others. Through those experiences, coupled with a rock-solid disposition and moral compass, Washington was building a formidable skill set for his future interactions with William Howe, Henry Clinton, Charles Cornwallis, and providential destiny.

At the other end of the colonies in Massachusetts at that time, other loud voices were disparaging the heavy taxes and regulations placed on the colonies by the British. Samuel Adams, the son of an affluent brewer, became the leader and vocal officer of the Massachusetts House of Representatives. He was more interested in the growing resistance movement and prospects of revolution than he was in his family's commercial interest. Adams, like Patrick Henry in Virginia, strongly advocated for boycotts of British goods and led the resistance to England's heavy-handed policies toward the colonies. Resistance movements grew into loose bands of separatists and revolutionaries across the thirteen colonies. The Sons of Liberty, born from the resistance to the Stamp Act in 1765, took proactive measures against the king's representatives. The measures were not limited to boycotts and protests; they included threats and intimidation of officials and sometimes physical retribution by tarring and feathering. The underground movement struggled against the Crown for the next decade, at first promoting the rights of Americans as Englishmen. The Americans' original grievance against Parliament and its taxing policies was the lack of American representation in the body. As James Otis, Massachusetts representative in the legislature and later radical, lamented, "taxation without representation is tyranny."[2] The Americans believed that if they were going to be taxed by the king's administrative minions, they, as Englishmen, should by natural rights have representation in Parliament. The Sons of Liberty grew to have members in all the colonies and became more radical over time as they advanced the idea of independence. They helped promote cohesion among the colonies and the notion that they were all in the struggle together. Their speeches and pronouncements became more and more radical, and they organized the vandalism and destruction of British goods, further driving a wedge between those individuals who wanted a radical break with the Crown and the local Tories who still supported the king.

As animosity grew between the American colonies and the Crown, Massachusetts emerged as a particular hotbed of discontent, and the city of Boston became the focal point of the resistance to British authorities. The residents of Boston became so increasingly angry and hostile over the continued imposition of the Townshend Act that the British decided to take action. Local British officials and Tories requested support against, as they saw it, the radical elements of resistance. On October 2, 1768, a British fleet arrived in Boston Harbor. Part of the cargo onboard the ships was the 14th and 29th regiments of British foot, to whom the Americans disparagingly referred as "redcoats" and "lobsterbacks." The British also had a nickname for the American patriots; they called them yankees, a name possibly derived from the Dutch word *janke*, or little John). At first there were small-scale run-ins between the British troops occupying Boston Commons and the inhabitants of the city. The run-ins began to take on larger dimensions as open hostility and physical altercations were becoming destabilizing to local British control. Another point of conflict was the redcoats' pursuits of the local female inhabitants. During the occupation, British soldiers became discouraged and frustrated due to low pay and boredom in a growingly hostile town. Over the next year and a half, the mutual irritations continued and manifested in an altercation on King Street outside the Customs House where the British authorities kept the revenue from the duties and taxes they collected.

On the night of March 5th, 1770, which was an unusually cold night, a single British soldier, Private Hugh White, was manning a post outside the Customs House. He was accosted by several locals who had apparently just left a local tavern. The altercation became more vehement, and Private White, after being poked in the chest, struck one of the protesters with the butt of his Brown Bess musket, knocking him to the ground. An alarm was shouted, and soon the street was filled with hundreds of angry Bostonian rioters looking for a fight. The night of the Boston Massacre was underway. Additional British troops were marshaled from the nearby barracks and joined in the fray of the unwieldly and volatile encounter. The British contingent was eight soldiers including an officer, Captain Thomas Preston, who stood in front of his men forming a semi-circle with their backs up against the Customs House. He ordered the crowd to disperse, but the angry mob continued to throw snowballs and other objects at the outnumbered redcoats. One of the British soldiers, Hugh Montgomery, was struck by a club and fell to the ground. Montgomery rose and fired his musket, and several other soldiers also sporadically discharged their muskets into the crowd, killing five, including Crispus Attucks, possibly the first patriot to fall in the American Revolution. It was noted that Attucks was a vocal member of the crowd, along with Samuel Gray who was also killed by a musket ball to the head. Attucks was part Black and part Native American. Considering the march of American history, it is ironic that one of the first patriots to lay down his life for the cause of America's freedom was a man of part Black and Native American roots.

Captain Preston ordered his men to stop firing, and the crowd dispersed, leaving Boston on the verge of open rebellion. The Sons of Liberty began meeting and preparing to confront the force of 600 redcoats that were occupying the city. Among the patriots were Paul Revere and Samuel Adams, both strong advocates for independence and the American cause. It was around that time that Revere, a silversmith and sometimes artist, made his famous engraving *The Bloody Massacre Perpetrated in King Street*, which provocatively depicts the actions of the British soldiers as blatant barbarism toward unarmed civilians. Revere successfully used the image as propaganda to rouse public animosity toward the British and to garner support for the American cause throughout the colonies.

Tensions in Boston subsided when, under pressure, British Lt. Governor of Massachusetts, Thomas Hutchinson, agreed to put Captain Preston and his men on trial for murder. The British troops were arrested and imprisoned for upward of six months as the trial progressed. In another example of the ironies of American history, while Samuel Adams promoted the punishment of the British soldiers who were on trial for their lives, his cousin John Adams became their defense attorney. Recognizing the bitter feelings his local Bostonian neighbors held toward the soldiers, he knew he was taking a great personal risk by agreeing to be their counsel, but John Adams was a man of integrity and believed in fairness and justice. Even if he personally disagreed with British actions and policies in America, he believed the soldiers were entitled to a fair trial. Adams was a bright and talented attorney and provided the men with a skillful defense. His advocacy for the soldiers was successful, and the men were mostly acquitted of the charges against them. Two soldiers were found guilty of manslaughter and were branded on their thumbs with an M for murder and received reduced sentences for their actions that night. Captain Preston and the other five soldiers were found not guilty. Later in April of 1770, Parliament, as it had done with the Stamp Act, repealed the Townshend Act to appease the Americans. In addition, British troops were temporarily removed from Boston.

With the repeal of the Townshend Act, emotions in Boston and all the colonies were temporarily quelled, but deep resentment still persisted toward the British in general and toward their taxation policies in particular. American boycotts of British goods were having a negative effect on the British economy, and the English treasury was still deep in debt after the commitments made during the French and Indian War. Even after the repeal of the Townshend Act, the boycotts continued, especially on tea. An unintended positive consequence of the boycotts was that the Americans were becoming more self-sufficient in getting many of the items that they previously purchased from British merchants. Tea was the main item that Parliament reserved the right to continue levying a tax on. American tea consumption had grown to 1.2 million pounds yearly and was a potentially lucrative revenue source. To satisfy American desire for tea, entrepreneurial merchants such as Samuel Adams and John Hancock smuggled tea into the colonies from Dutch and other sources. By keeping a tax on English tea, Parliament lessened the risk of appearing to capitulate and show weakness under American pressure and reaffirmed its prerogative to tax the colonies as England and England alone saw fit.

In November of 1772, Samuel Adams became the driving force behind a letter-writing campaign among the thirteen colonies.

The Committee of Correspondence established an extensive network of like-minded leaders among the intellectual cadre of the separate colonies. They provided an important mechanism for conveying news, venting mutual grievances, and sharing ideas on a unified response including security issues. The initial focus was on how best to deal with Britain's harsh and supercilious conduct toward its American brethren. The correspondences also provided consolation that all members and colonies could take solace that they were not in the struggle alone and that they could rely on each other. Additionally, the Committee of Correspondence provided the basis for the formation of a future convention of the states, the purpose of which was to discuss and debate among the selected leaders the future relationship between Great Britain and the American colonies.

The English East India Company, the largest multinational entity of the period, was bordering on financial instability due in part to the American boycott of English tea. Parliament, in interest of the company (of which several members of Parliament were stockholders), passed the Tea Act of 1773. The intention was to provide a lifeline to the East India Company in its financial struggles and reduce its inventory of stored tea. The Act permitted the company to ship the tea directly to American ports, bypassing the merchants (middlemen) and duties and undercutting the price of smuggled tea in the colonies. It was a calamitous miscalculation on the British part. The Americans resented any new taxation, even if the sum price of the product was cheaper, and in many ports like New York and Philadelphia the British cargo ships from the East India Company were not allowed to dock. In Boston three merchant ships were able to dock with 342 chests of tea. Resistance organized by Samuel Adams and the Sons of Liberty stopped the shipment from being offloaded. The ships sat at dockside with their cargo intact until the night of December 16, 1773.

The Sons of Liberty, under the cover of darkness and direction from Samuel Adams, prepared for action. Upwards of sixty of their contingents painted their faces, donned Indian clothing as a disguise, and marched along with hundreds of supporters to the long wharf where the ships were docked. The group easily pushed aside the customs agents who were guarding the ships, broke open the cases of tea, and dumped all 92,000 lbs. of contents into Boston Harbor. The Boston Tea Party was the final straw of measured tolerance between the king's authorities and the rebellious Massachusetts colony. After the Boston Massacre in March of 1770, British troops were stationed outside of Boston to reduce the prospects for violent altercations between the soldiers and the locals. All of that was about to change. The British saw the Boston Tea Party as a wanton act of destruction of private property and a direct challenge to British authority and the king's rule.

The king clamped down hard on the Massachusetts colony. The port of Boston was closed, suspending all commercial activity in and out of the harbor. The British reacted quickly to the Tea Party by enacting the Coercive Acts in March of 1774. The Coercive Acts, which came to be known as the Intolerable Acts by the Americans, placed several new punitive measures on the Massachusetts colony. As indicated, Boston Harbor was closed until the tea debt was paid. The Massachusetts Government Act of 1774 placed restrictions on meetings, suspended the Massachusetts Legislature, and appointed leaders to replace those that were previously locally elected. Additionally, British officials were no longer subject to local prosecution, and the Quartering Act required local residents to house British soldiers at will. The last of the acts was the Quebec Act. Along with other provisions, the Quebec Act gave French-speaking Catholics of Quebec domain over the region of the Upper Ohio Valley and west of the Appalachian Mountains, regions previously off limits to American settlement by the king's proclamation to appease the Native American tribes after the French and Indian War. The Quebec Act added insult to injury for all the American colonies. It also nullified American deed claims in the region and put in place new administrative controls by Parliament. It also had the potential to limit self-determination, to which the Americans had been accustomed for more than 150 years in the colonies.

The English believed that imposing harsh measures and closing Boston Harbor could isolate Massachusetts from the rest of the American colonies. The Intolerable Acts had the opposite effect. The other colonies rallied to the defense of Massachusetts. That was in no small part due to the extensive two-year-long campaign of letter writing and conceptualizing about their mutual predicament of British rule over the American colonies. The Committee of Correspondence had given the colonies a sense of cohesion and a head start in building the intellectual argument for a new world order in which man should govern himself. They envisioned a place where free people would be allowed to think for themselves and thrive and prosper based on their providential inheritances as sons and daughters of humanity. The infrastructure was in place along with immutable dynamic forces working towards an intractable conclusion.

British policies were constricting all the American colonies, not just Massachusetts. The rest of the colonies could take note that if they didn't acquiesce to new British rule, the same fate that was imposed on Massachusetts would be imposed on them. Building on the communication network they had established, the principal members of the Committee of Correspondence met to discuss the effects of British policies toward the colonies and to formulate a response in defense of their rights. In a secret session, fifty-six representative delegates from all the states except Georgia formed the First Continental Congress, which met in Carpenters Hall in Philadelphia from September 5th to October 26, 1774.

Some of the noted attendees of the Congress included Samuel Adams, John Adams, and John Hancock from Massachusetts; Patrick Henry and George Washington from Virginia; John Jay and William Floyd from New York; Roger

Sherman from Connecticut; Samuel Chase from Maryland; William Livingston from New Jersey; John Dickenson from Pennsylvania; and many others. Payton Randolph of Virginia was unharmoniously elected to be the first president of the Congress. Randolph was a friend of Washington and a cousin of Thomas Jefferson. Later, during the Second Continental Congress in 1775, the connection between Randolph and Jefferson had a considerable significance to the American cause for independence. Randolph was highly regarded by the delegates and had previously served as the president of the Virginia House of Burgesses. His official duties called, and he returned to Virginia after the first month of the congressional session in part to add his efforts to Virginia's struggles when their Colonel Governor, John Murray the 4th Earl of Dunmore, dissolved the House of Burgesses because of Virginia's solidarity with Massachusetts and because of taxing issues.

There were several critical issues that brought about the First Continental Congress. Among them was the need to show strong support for Massachusetts and unity between the colonies against British strong-arm rule. The delegates agreed that the Intolerable Acts needed to be repealed by Parliament. To that end, the delegates in Congress established a Resolution on October 20 that the people possessed the rights of life, liberty, and property and that no authority could take those rights away. They also put forth that their forefathers were Englishmen, and they, as their descendants, did not surrender their rights as Englishmen because of their migration to

America. They also formed the Continental Association and petitioned the various colonies to begin organizing and training their militias for whatever was coming their way. Absent of a repeal of the Intolerable Acts, the colonies would expand the boycott of British goods to take effect on December 1, 1774. The delegates sent an appeal directly to the king to address the myriad complaints and usurpations that Parliament and his agents had imposed on his colonies in America. They also established that if Parliament had not met their demand to rescind the Intolerable Acts, they would meet again in a Second Continental Congress starting on May 10 of the following year in 1775.

The First Continental Congress resulted in the development of a new state of mind, and some of the delegates might not have recognized that a transformation was underway. That transformation was a departure from the old way of thinking that the state from which one hailed was the touchstone of one's identity. A new identity was developing from a place of infinitely more potential and significance, and that identity was as an American. Patrick Henry rose at the Congress to dispel the old identity and affirm the new, leading the way for others to follow: "The distinctions between Virginians, Pennsylvanians, New Yorkers and New Englanders are no more. I am not a Virginian, but an American."[3]

Parliament did not repeal the Intolerable Acts, and over the next several months the relationship between the king and the Americans developed in a more combative direction. Colonial militias were working in the fields, sharpening their skills and preparing for the inevitable interaction of emotions and arms. A new militia calling itself the Minutemen was forming. The first group was formed in Worcester, Massachusetts, in September of 1774, and in the following months other groups formed across all the colonies. Their first task was to weed out any Tories in their midst and require them to resign.

As the winter of 1775 led into the spring, tensions were running high in and around the city of Boston. The British appointed a new Royal Governor of the Province of Massachusetts Bay, General Thomas Gage, who arrived in Boston in May of 1774 with several regiments of occupation troops. His orders were to restore law and order to the province. He continued to enforce the punitive measures put in place by the Intolerable Acts, and those measures continued to provoke angry reactions from the local inhabitants of Boston and its surroundings. The match head only needed to be struck for the flame of conflict and open rebellion to be ignited.

Revolution ignited on April 19, 1775, when close to 700 British Army regulars, Welch Fusiliers, and Royal Marines under the command of Lt. Colonel Francis Smith set out on a surprise midnight march. The contingent of troops left the confines of Boston the night before and ventured out to seize arms and military stores and to arrest Samuel Adams and John Hancock. The British believed that a large weapons cache was stored in the town of Concord approximately twenty miles from the city. Paul Revere and others received information about the coming raid and arrests from Dr. Joseph Warren, a respected leading patriot and member of the Sons of Liberty. Dr. Warren might have received the tip about the British incursion from an unlikely source: General Thomas Gage's wife, Margaret Kemble Gage. Margaret was an American and was thought to have sympathy for the American cause. On learning the information, Revere along with William Dawes and Samuel Prescott rode out to alert the countryside of the intended British maneuver. Revere left word for his associates inside the city to hang either one or two lanterns to indicate from which direction the British would be coming: "One if by land, and two if by sea," as noted in Henry Wadsworth Longfellow's poem titled *Paul Revere's Ride*. Two lanterns were placed in the belfry of Boston's Christ Church (Old North Church), indicating that the British were coming by the sea route and the Charles River through Charlestown.

On the way, the British encountered a local militia on the Green at Lexington led by Captain John Parker. After some of the militiamen refused to yield, shots rang out from an unknown source. The British then fired volleys into the militia, killing eight and wounding another ten. The war of the American Revolution had begun. The British then moved on to Concord in an effort to seize as much of the stored arsenal as they could. Lt. Colonel Smith divided his forces into separate columns to facilitate the search. Two companies of approximately 100 British regulars guarded the Old North Bridge, which crossed over the Concord River at the approach to the town. There the British were met by approximately 400 Minutemen. The Americans advanced on the British at the bridge and exchanged fire with the regulars. Major John Buttrick of the local American militia gave the fateful order to *"Fire...For God's sake fire!"*[4] Half of the British officers present at the bridge were hit by musket fire and ordered to withdraw, giving the Americans a tactical victory. Ralph Waldo Emerson referred to the event in his 1837 poem titled *Concord Hymn*: "By the rude bridge that arched the flood, / Their flag to April's breeze unfurled, / Here once the embattled farmers stood, / And fired the shot heard round the world." Another American writer, Nathanial Hawthorne, noted that the meaning of concord is "peace and harmony." History has deemed that, at least for the morning of April 19th, 1775, Concord be remembered in posterity for something other than a peaceful and harmonious interaction.

The Minutemen engaged in unconventional warfare by harassing the British soldiers and firing on them from behind trees and stone walls and securing defilade from concealed positions. The British suffered 73 killed, 174 wounded, and another 26 missing in the assault on Lexington and Concord. It was a costly exercise for British General Thomas Gage and his men who secured only a small amount of the arms that they intended to seize. They did, however, receive a certain amount of the desired munitions from the fired smoothbore muskets of angry Minutemen.

As the British garrison inside Boston hunkered down for a siege, thousands of American militiamen from surrounding areas in Massachusetts and several other colonies joined the newly forming American Army encampments that encircled the city. That was despite the arrival by sea of British General Sir William Howe, 5th Viscount, on May 25th, 1775. Howe was joined by two other British generals who played roles in the revolutionary struggles over the next several years. They were General Sir Henry Clinton and General John Burgoyne, and they were accompanied by 4,200 additional British troops to reinforce the current garrison. The additional British soldiers raised the total in the city to upwards of 10,000 under the command of General Thomas Gage.

General William Howe came from a distinguished military family. His older brother, Brigadier General George Howe, was a highly regarded officer in the British Army. He served with the British Army during the French and Indian War and was killed during an engagement with the French near Fort Carillon in 1758 (Fort Carillon later became Fort Ticonderoga). The American colonists who fought alongside the British during the French and Indian War honored the older brother for his service. Admiral Lord Richard Howe, a third military brother, served with the Royal Navy and also participated with William in attempting to quell the rebellion in North America. Both brothers (particularly William) remembered the recognition the Americans gave to their fallen brother. While still in London, William Howe along with Edmond

Burke and others voiced sympathy for American grievances against the Crown. In the end, however, he was a solider and would do his duty for king and country.

Howe, it seems, was anticipating a somewhat less contentious arrival when he returned to America, likely due to his own service during the French and Indian War when he fought alongside local militias and the memory of his lost brother. It must have been somewhat discouraging to learn upon his arrival that open hostility had already commenced. Howe, along with Gage and the other British commanders, set out to develop a strategy to secure their position and put down the rebellion. The Americans held an advantage in numbers and were able to choke off land routes for supplies to the British inside the city. Boston was the third largest city in America during the colonial period and had about 15,000 residents. That summer, the number of local inhabitants in the city decreased to roughly 7,000, due primarily to the British occupation and the state of the siege. With the British occupation, the number of the city's inhabitants again grew to almost 20,000 including British dependents and all personnel. The numbers caused shortages and degraded the quality of life for all of the inhabitants. British supplies of all materials and food mostly came from their naval support ships via routes from other parts of North America and England.

As the spring of 1775 was coming to a close, the British garrison inside Boston looked to improve its military position on the high ground around the city. Across Boston Harbor, in Charlestown, the rebel militia had control of Bunker and Breed's Hills, which overlooked the British inside Boston. The British plan, under the command of General Howe, was to occupy those two positions. The Americans learned of the British plan the night before, and early in the morning of June 17th, 1,200 militiamen set to work fortifying the hills with earthen redoubts. The efforts were principally focused on Breed's Hill. The militias were commanded by Colonel William Prescott, General Israel Putnam with the Connecticut militia, and local Bostonian physician and Militia General Dr. Joseph Warren. Warren had also been serving as president of the Revolutionary Massachusetts Provincial Congress. That morning, the British learned that the Americans had occupied the strategic positions, and British ships of the line were ordered to cannonade the militias on the hills in an effort to force them off.

The Revolutionary War was marked by various spy rings, and both the Americans and the British had their spies in and out of the city. One not so successful spy was the traitor and one-time Revolutionary military hero Benedict Arnold, known for his ill-fated plot to take West Point with British Spy Master Major John Andre. Others, however, especially on the American side in and around Boston, were more successful. Those American spies, especially later in the war as part of the Culper Spy Ring on Long Island and in New York City, monitored British troop activities and provided Washington and his army with continuous valuable intelligence on British troop strength, movements, and intentions.

Intelligence was obtained that the British were going to make a move to secure both Bunker and Breed's Hills. Colonel John Prescott, Israel Putnam, and Dr. Joseph Warren planned the resistance and organized the fortifications to repel the British. Entrenched in their positions atop the hill, the patriots, though ready for the fight, had insufficient supplies of ammunition. Conservation of their vital supply needed to be part of the militia's strategy. The idea was to draw the British close in on their fortified positions so as to make every shot count. History recognizes John Prescott with the phrase, "Do not fire until you see the whites of their eyes." In the afternoon of June 17th, British forces numbering around 2,200 landed on the Charlestown peninsula and mounted an assault on Breed's Hill. The British attack was a direct frontal engagement up the slopes of the hill. The Americans lacked the military discipline and organization that was characterized by British troops and military philosophy of the period. What the Americans lacked in classical military practices, however, was more than compensated for by their expert marksmanship as the unfortunate British regulars were about to find out. As the British were preparing to launch their first assault up the hill, they received sniper fire from Charlestown. The British forces then set fires to suspected structures in the town, which caused significant damage. The first two British assaults on the hill were repelled by the Americans, and the British suffered major casualties, especially among the officers. As the Americans ran low on ammunition, the British eventually succeeded in the third assault. In that final advance, the British used their bayonets on the remaining Americans that stood their ground on the crest of Breed's Hill.

The British were able to claim victory after they secured positions on top of both Bunker and Breed's Hills. But at what cost? American musket fire had inflicted more the 1,000 British casualties and killed more than 200, and the price was particularly high among British officers. The Americans suffered more than 100 killed and 400 wounded. Among the American losses was the renowned Bostonian leader and American patriot Dr. Joseph Warren. Upon being recognized by a British officer, Warren was shot in the head, and his body was repeatedly bayonetted by enraged British soldiers. His family searched the battlefield for his body for many months so that they could provide him with a proper burial. In the aftermath of the battle, the British recognized that the Americans could and would fight and, under the right set of circumstances, could inflict grievous casualties on any opposing force. British General Thomas Gage remarked that "The loss we have sustained is greater than we can bear."[5] Arriving in Boston after the battle, General Nathaniel Greene, leader of the Rhode Island militia and later recognized by Washington as his number two, noted, "I wish we could sell them another hill at the same price."[6] The Americans gained confidence as a result of the battle. They learned that they could stand man-to-man and musket-to-musket with the best army in the world and make it pay a heavy price.

At the close of the First Continental Congress in October 1774, delegates returned home to their respective state legislatures to report on the events of the Congress. At the Second Virginia Convention on March 23, 1775, Patrick Henry made a rousing and compelling case as to why Virginia should send troops to fight for the cause of American liberty and self-determination:

> It is in vain, sir, to extenuate the matter. Gentleman may cry, peace, peace—but there is no peace. The war has actually begun! The next gale that sweeps from the north will bring to our ears the clash of resounding arms! Our brethren are already in the field! Why stand we here idle? What is it that gentlemen wish? What would they have? Is life so dear, or peace so sweet, as to be purchased at the price of chains and slavery? Forbid it, Almighty God! I know not what course others may take; but as for me, give me liberty or give me death![7]

Virginia and the other colonies did, in fact, commit to the American war effort. Virginia dedicated not only troops to the struggle but also its most lauded son, George Washington, to lead the fight for American liberty and freedom.

The Second Continental Congress convened on May 10th, 1775, at the Pennsylvania State House in Philadelphia as previously planned. The Congress established the American Army on June 14th, 1775, and Washington took command of the Continental Army as General and Commander-in-Chief on June 19th, again by an Act of Congress. He then ventured from Philadelphia to join his troops outside of Boston. Upon arrival in Boston, Washington was eager to launch a direct assault against the British positions inside the city. His second in command, Major General Artemas Ward, and others successfully prevailed on Washington to wait out the British and not commit to a direct attack. A stalemate ensued through the rest of 1775 and the winter of 1776. Though contrary to Washington's inclinations, waiting out the British proved to be the right decision. The British had completed very formidable defensive positions inside the city, and Washington's army would have suffered heavy and unnecessary casualties.

In January of 1776, Washington received a gift from one of his most trusted aides, General Henry Knox. The gift was fifty-eight pieces of artillery, mostly 12-pounder and 18-pounder cannons that Knox had secured from Fort Ticonderoga. Ethan Allen and the Green Mountain Boys, along with a force under Benedict Arnold, successfully assaulted and captured the British-held fort the previous summer. Knox, under orders from Washington, pulled off one of the most daring and resourceful campaigns of the war by transporting the cannons across frozen wilderness to Boston. The militia went to work cutting down trees and reinforcing placements for the cannons in makeshift fortifications on Dorchester Heights overlooking Boston. Once the British officers inside the city saw the cannon placements on the heights overlooking their positions, they knew their hold on Boston was untenable. The British evacuated the city by sea on March 17th, 1776, and Washington and his army moved in without risk of an assault.

Throughout the early stages of the war, Washington was an aggressive military leader, and often his subordinates had to assuage him from directly assaulting enemy positions. It is clear that he was not the equal of British generals when it came to tactics and deployment strategies. Washington's real strength as a leader was that he was a quick learner and unconventionally resourceful. Time and time again, he also demonstrated personal courage on the battlefield and leadership while under duress. Those personal characteristics were a profound inspiration to the officers and men who served under him. Washington often put himself in direct line of fire along with his soldiers. Not only was he recognized by personal attributes of integrity, courage, determination, and conviction; he was also noted for poise, character, and grace under pressure. During the long eight-year struggle for American independence, Washington called on those personal attributes to see his army and the fledgling nation through the darkest times. One of Providence's great gifts to America at its inception was the personification of all those lauded human characteristics in one extraordinary, yet fallible, human being.

As Washington and his staff contemplated the next move by the British, consequential events were happening in Philadelphia. Payton Randolph was once more elected president of the Second Continental Congress. He again returned to Virginia and later died in October of 1775. John Hancock then assumed the duties as president. Virginia replaced Randolph as part of their delegation with a tall, slender, red-haired, young planter and attorney from the mountain region of Western Virginia. That young Virginian was Thomas Jefferson. Throughout the spring and early summer of 1776, the Second Continental Congress, which had been in continuous session since the year before, was moving closer to a complete break with British King George III.

Chapter Five

When in the Course of Human Events

As Congress met and the grievances against the British Crown were debated, it was decided that a committee should be appointed to draft a position statement. War was already underway, and the committee began contemplating the future relationship between the American colonies and the British king. On June 11, 1776, Congress chose John Adams and Benjamin Franklin along with Roger Sherman and Robert Livingston to work on the draft with Thomas Jefferson, the principal architect of the document. Jefferson was never considered to be a great orator in the presence of Patrick Henry, but he was a truly talented writer.

The Declaration of Independence overviewed the shared ancestral legacy between the English and their American brethren. It also provided justification for severing the connections the colonies had with England and proclaimed that the decision was difficult and had been concluded only after a long deliberation. It listed the grievances the people of the colonies had suffered at the hands of the English king and how their natural rights as men were being usurped by his authority. The Declaration emphasized contemporary Enlightenment ideas of the government's role and responsibilities to its citizens, and it proposed the revolutionary concept of the rights of the individual. The individual and his/her wellbeing is, in fact, the reason for government. It declared that all men, due simply to their humanity, possess natural God-given rights that cannot be taken away by earthly authorities and that "all men are created equal, that they are endowed by their Creator with certain unalienable Rights, that among these are Life, Liberty and the pursuit of Happiness."[1]

The Declaration proclaimed that government is subservient to the people and is required to act in the interest of the people. When government does not act in the interest of the people, the people are empowered to abolish that government and institute new government as they see fit. The Declaration of Independence was the defining document of the war period, and in the end it dissolved the relationship between Britain and America and established a new nation.

America's founding is a landmark event of singular importance along the road to human progress and dignity, and it has provided inspiration to people and nations around the world. The Declaration advanced the principles of freedom and how man interacts and flourishes in a civil society that is based on the rights of the individual and justice under the law. It advocated for liberty and for individuals to enjoy the fruits of their labors. The system in which the American colonists found themselves was antithetical to the concepts of individual liberty and freedom. Individuals could be imprisoned without due process, and justice was obstructed by royal decrees and overbearing administrative dictates. The royal authorities would unjustly usurp people's financial resources and labor through arbitrary and unjustified taxation. When governmental authority acts in that manner, it is a theft of liberty, and resistance is the only legitimate recourse. Those were the fundamental concepts the founders advanced to justify the Revolution.

The fifty-six signers of the Declaration took great personal risk; if the rebellion failed or they were captured by the British, dire consequences would lie ahead for them, including potential rendezvous with the gallows. The Revolution tested their will and courage in standing up to England, the most powerful nation of the time. The signers were a mixed group of individuals. They were farmers, plantation owners, merchants, landowners, and physicians, and some were even ministers, like John Witherspoon of New Jersey. Several had multiple occupations, including Abraham Clark of New Jersey who was a lawyer and surveyor; Benjamin Franklin from Pennsylvania who was a printer and scientist; Lyman Hall of Georgia who was a minister and a physician; and the 33-year-old Thomas Jefferson of Virginia who was a lawyer, plantation owner, and, like Franklin, a scientist. Nearly half of them were lawyers, and many of the signers were very well-educated scholars and intellectuals who had read much of the classics, including Greco Roman history and English literature including Shakespeare.

Washington didn't receive the formal and traditional education that many of the other founders did, but he was very well read and learned in classical literature and history. Franklin also was not formally educated, but he was possibly the most renowned scientist of his time. His occupation as a printer and writer gave him a lifelong quest for knowledge, study, and the nuances of the written word. Many of the attorneys attended the best universities in eighteenth-century America and England. They included Jefferson who attended William and Mary in Virginia; Adams and Hancock who attended Harvard in Boston; John Jay who attended Columbia in New York; and Dr. Benjamin Rush who attended The University of Edinburgh and Princeton University. At that time, a classical education was part of the curriculum, and study emphasized learning languages such as French, Latin, and Greek and included history, mathematics, and literature.

Most of the founders were wealthy and had attained status in their communities and states. Their wealth and positions were, for the most part, not obtained in the old European sense by which nobility and family wealth was inherited. The long-established example of European prestige of class and generational privilege was generally absent in colonial America, providing one of the benefits of building a new society. In fact, the founding generation and generations of Americans that came after scoffed at the idea of hereditary nobility and a privileged class. In America the idea of the "new man" was rooted in self-reliance. That was the beginning of the American "meritocracy," and wealth was created based on personal accomplishments and making the most of opportunities that arose from carving a new civilization out of the virgin wilderness.

Most historians over the last 250 years have viewed the founding generation with high regard. Some historians, however, have unfairly cast a jaundiced eye at the founders. One such example is the writings of Charles Beard. In 1912 he authored a cynical book titled *An Economic Interpretation of the US Constitution*. Beard contended that the founders were mostly interested in their own economic gains and only casually interested in the development of a new social order in America. That view is patently wrong. The founders were well aware of the consequences of their actions and the risks they were taking, and they were mindful of the importance of their efforts for the future of America.

To understand the motivations of the American founders, we need to examine the thinking of their time and how they constructed the principles by which a new system would operate. To organize and build a new approach to governance and societal reform, it was important for the founders to incorporate processes for testing new ideas. The Age of Reasoning and Age of Enlightenment ushered in renewed appreciation for a host of topics, including the natural sciences, medicine, architecture, art, philosophy, and democracy. The founders relied on conventional historical precedent and generations of political and philosophical thinking that went back to the Greeks, Romans, and English Common Law. Ancient Greek philosophical ideas had become widespread throughout the West.

Methods of evaluating concepts and testing ideas, which were the foundation of eighteenth-century thinking, created the supporting structure of American political thinking.

Many accept the false idea that America's founding was a natural outcome of events and not something exceptional within the general parameters of historical development, but nothing could be further from the truth. Britain was the superior military power of the day, and America was an underdeveloped agrarian society. To take on the world's superpower was a very presumptuous affair for the American colonies. The Revolutionary War could have gone in a very different direction without the support of France and Washington's will and presence. Things could have ended in a disaster for the colonists.

In the Declaration of Independence, Jefferson refers to Nature's God and divine Providence, which, contrary to Deist philosophy of the time, play a role in the course of human events. God also established basic principles of human conduct that are embodied in Natural Law. Divine Natural Law is rooted in the basic order of the universe and morality. Though many of the founding generation were Deists who accepted a belief in a creator, they did not believe that the creator intervened in human affairs. Deism was consistent with eighteenth-century Age-of-Reason ideas that humans were, by way of reason and logical analysis, able to decide between right and wrong. God was a decisive factor in the separation between the colonies and the British Crown, and the moral principles of Natural Law were a guiding force in the formation of the new country.

The Declaration of Independence was much more than a notice of the thirteen colonies' intention to separate from the British king and dissolve his authority over them; it was an assertion of the inalienable rights given to every individual by God. The Declaration declares:

> Governments are instituted among Men, deriving their just powers from the consent of the governed. That whenever any form of government becomes destructive of these ends, it is the Right of the people to alter or abolish it, and to institute new government, laying its foundation on such principles and organization on such form, as to them shall most likely to affect their Safety and Happiness.[2]

The Declaration contends that the primary purpose of government is to serve the people and that the people, as the legitimate sovereign over government, can change or abolish the government if they determine it no longer best serves their interest. That was the first time in history that such an important proclamation about the relationship between the individual and government was proposed. Jefferson used the theoretical concepts first advanced by the Greeks and Romans and then by the Enlightenment philosophers Locke, Montesquieu, and Hobbes when he drafted the Declaration.

To understand the American founding and the ideas that were developed in the Declaration and the Constitution, it is important to understand that their intellectual origins and progression were first conceived in the traditions of Western civilization.

1776…Bagging the Old Fox

In the summer of 1776, the world's greatest invasion fleet of more than 300 British ships arrived in New York Harbor over a period of several weeks and disembarked on Staten Island. It was said at the time that those who witnessed the arrival of the tall ships thought all of London was at sail. The force of warships and transports was the greatest armada of ships ever to enter New York Harbor until the middle of the twentieth century. The armada brought the British back to the American colonies after the evacuation of Boston several months earlier. The newly arrived British forces were completely under the command of General Sir William Howe. After the assault on Bunker Hill and Breed's Hill in Boston, British General and Royal Governor Thomas Gage appointed Howe as Commander–in–Chief of British land forces in America. The British under Howe redeployed a vast army from Britain and Halifax, Nova Scotia, to New York City on June 29th 1776. General Howe was supported by his older brother, Lord Admiral Richard Howe, who commanded the vast naval armada that brought the invasion forces. Washington anticipated the move and marched his army south to Manhattan from Dorchester Heights and the surroundings of Boston shortly after the British evacuation.

General Howe established a base camp on Staten Island where he could train his men for the upcoming campaign against the Americans. To counter Howe, Washington moved a large section of his army (approximately 10,000 men) across the East River and continued to construct entrenchments on high ground in Brooklyn across from Manhattan. Despite the odds, the Americans were optimistic about their prospects against the British. They had shown great resolve the year before in the fight for Bunker Hill and Breed's Hill in Boston. Though the Americans eventually conceded the hills to the British, the rebel militia under Dr. Warren and Colonel Prescott had inflicted hundreds of British casualties in the process. The siege of Boston reinforced the confidence of the militias — the soon-to-be American Army.

The American Army under Washington was mostly made up of militias from the various states. They were composed of farmers, tradesmen, shopkeepers, laborers, and fisherman. They clearly lacked in training, equipment, supplies, and discipline as a coherent military unit and were no match for the British regulars and Hessians they would be coming up against. The Hessians were mercenaries or more accurately auxiliaries from principally two German states: Hesse-Kossel and Hess-Hanau. The Hessians fought for the British and comprised approximately 25% of all British forces engaged in the Revolutionary War. The tactical importance of New York, with its deep harbor and the Hudson River's connection to the North as well as the friendly British colony of Canada, was not lost on Washington and his staff. Strategically for the British, New York was also near the center of the colonies and had the potential of isolating New England, where the hostilities began.

Defending the city and stopping the British from securing the harbor that they needed to supply their vast army was the objective of Washington and his defensive strategy. Defending New York City was a daunting task for Washington as it would be for any military force that was void of a navy. The city and its surroundings are an archipelago providing many places where an army coming from the sea could easily secure unobstructed landings. To counter the coming British force, Washington and his staff built defensive positions and fortifications on Manhattan Island and Long Island in Brooklyn. The locations were strategically chosen and believed to be the most likely places the returning British forces would land.

During the summer of 1776, Washington had at his command approximately 17,000 troops preparing to join battle against upwards of 33,000 British regulars and Hessians. Washington and his army arrived in Manhattan in April and started to build defenses in preparation for the anticipated British assault on the city. In the year of the Declaration, New York was the second largest city in the American colonies. Philadelphia was the first with around 25,000 inhabitants. During the Revolutionary War, Washington could only rely on the support of, at best, fifty percent of the population. The rest were Tories who still supported the king or were ordinary people who were ambivalent to the Revolution and just wanted to avoid the negative consequences of taking sides. As

Washington prepared to engage the British in New York, he had to avoid alienating the locals and turning them against the cause of the rebellion, which would complicate his already-difficult situation.

The most important year in American history was 1776. It was a time of infinite possibilities and potential for the newly declared nation. The text of the Declaration was printed in pamphlets, and papers were read allowed to thousands of Americans in meeting halls, town squares, churches, and private residences across the thirteen states. There was a thrilling anticipation for the future new nation among hundreds of thousands of its citizens. The euphoria of the moment, however, was muted by the cruel reality that the pathway to that bright and independent future was blocked by the world's preeminent military, which had just landed in the middle of New York and was on the move.

On August 22, British General Howe and his officers, from their base on Staten Island, orchestrated a brilliant amphibious assault on the relatively small American defending force in Brooklyn. Howe landed his force of approximately 20,000 soldiers (both British regulars and Hessians) at the Narrows at Gravesend, not far from where the Verrazano Narrows Bridge is today, and established a basecamp in Flatbush. His plan was to meet the Americans in what General Howe and his staff hoped would be the decisive battle that would end the rebellion. The British strategy at the time was to lure their opponent into a decisive battle that played to the strength of the British regulars in fixed lines and formations.

The British trained in tactics of tightly held formations and disciplined musket volleys that would break the enemy's line and then charge with bayonets. That was the strategy used in the Battle of Quebec in 1759 on the Plaines of Abraham outside Quebec City in Canada. There, the British under General James Wolfe were able to defeat the French under General Marquis de Montcalm in the French and Indian War, which removed the French from Canada and ceded the region to the British.

As the British Army arrived in Brooklyn and were preparing for battle, Washington held back a portion of his army in Manhattan in case the British movement in Brooklyn was a trick and the real attack was coming by sea. Washington appointed General Israel Putnam as Commander of the Brooklyn operation. The Americans deployed their forces to protect the approaches through and around the Heights of Guan, which is a group of hills with road passes between the higher ground. The Americans had also set up several fortifications and a base camp with a reinforced perimeter on the Brooklyn Heights peninsula adjacent to the East River. The Battle of Long Island would turn out to be the largest engagement of forces in the entire Revolutionary War with upwards of 50,000 troops on both sides.

The battle began on the morning of August 27th when approximately 6,000 British regulars, led by General James Grant, attacked the American force, led by General Lord Stirling (William Alexander), that was protecting the Gowanus Pass. The Americans fought well at first, as they occupied the high ground of that part of the battlefield. The British reinforced their numbers and continued putting heavy pressure on Stirling's American defenders. As the morning progressed, Washington realized that the major British assault was in Brooklyn, so he crossed the East River with an additional 1,000 troops, bringing the American deployment in Brooklyn to 11,000. At that point, the Americans were under increasingly heavy attack, and Washington, Putnam, and their staff soon found out that they were outnumbered two to one.

In the center of the fight, the Americans under General John Sullivan were defending the Flatbush Pass (Battle Pass). Opposite them were Hessians under the command of General von Heister. The Hessians fought a delaying action of minimal intensity, holding in place more than 2,000 Americans. Also in the center was the Bedford Pass, which the Americans were guarding. As the fighting on the American right intensified, Sullivan sent 400 of his men to support Lord Stirling and his struggle with British General Grant. Grant eventually overwhelmed Stirling and pushed the Americans back, forcing them to redeploy.

In a brilliant flanking maneuver, Howe and a contingent of nearly 10,000 British regulars under a joint command marched to the east. The command included the big three: Howe himself, General Henry Clinton, and General Lord Cornwallis. Their march to the east took them to the American left and to a 4th pass, the Jamaica Pass, which was inexplicably guarded by only a very small contingent of Americans. The British were led to the Jamaica Pass by three local loyalist farmers. The large British force pushed past the Americans and came in behind Sullivan's men guarding the Flatbush Pass. The British force signaled to the Hessians who were fighting in the middle of the engagement, and they stepped up their assault against Sullivan's center. The American position was in jeopardy of a full collapse. British General Grant on the right and the Hessians in the middle pushed back the Americans, who were under attack from three points. Sullivan attempted to redeploy some of his soldiers to meet the new challenge from Howe's flanking force, but he had little success. His men took heavy casualties, and many, including Sullivan, surrendered. The situation was no better on the right as Stirling's forces were pushed back. The American forces broke to find sanctuary at the basecamp position of Brooklyn Heights.

There were brave moments for the Americans. A group of approximately 400 men from the 1st Maryland Regiment under the command of Lord Stirling put up stiff resistance to the advancing British. The Marylanders heroically charged the British six times so others could escape back to the basecamp. Washington was quoted as saying in deference to the sacrifice of the Marylanders, "Good God! What brave fellows I must this day lose!"[3] The Marylanders were slaughtered in their valiant counterattacks against the British. In the end, 265 brave soldiers from the 1st Maryland Regiment were killed. Many others were wounded or captured, and Lord Stirling was forced to surrender. He later returned to the American side in a prisoner exchange and was highly regarded by Washington. The Battle of Long Island was a disaster for the American cause. The British suffered relatively light casualties while the Americans suffered more than 300 killed, 800 wounded, and 1,000 captured, including several senior officers.

To complete the destruction of the American Army, Howe moved on the American basecamp at Brooklyn Heights. Washington and the battered American Army were in a seemingly untenable position with their backs against the East River and no apparent outlet for withdrawal. Howe and the British Army had the most advantageous position for a complete victory and were primed to destroy the American Army and end the rebellion. It was then that something almost inexplicable happened. Howe hesitated and decided to hunker down and delay his siege on the American position. Additional British troops arrived from Staten Island. If the British had continued the initiative and took full advantage of their three-to-one superiority, the outcome would have been a complete victory for the king and his Army. They most likely would have hanged Washington and re-established British rule.

As the British siege on the American position was to commence in the late afternoon of August 29, Washington decided to make a daring and dangerous move. He directed Colonel John Glover and his regiment of skilled fishermen/soldiers from Marblehead, Massachusetts, to initiate, under the cover of darkness, an extensive ferrying mission. The plan was to secretly move the entire American Army — men, cannons, wagons, horses, and equipment — across the one-mile stretch of the churning East River from Brooklyn Heights to Manhattan. There were many obstacles in their way, including British frigates and Royal Navy man-of-war ships patrolling the waters off Brooklyn. Stealth and silence had to be a priority. No one was permitted to talk, and precautions needed to be in place to soften the sounds of their wagons and cannon wheels and oars and the movement of men and stores. Colonel Glover and his group of men rounded up every available boat, ferry, and raft they could. On that night, a heavy rain began to fall, further helping the Americans hide the noise of their more-than 9,000 soldiers and all of their equipment. As midnight of the 29th approached, the river-crossing operation began. To further disguise their plan, a contingent of Americans under the command of Major Benjamin Tallmadge of Setauket, Long Island, stayed in their trenches and continued to keep campfires burning through the night so the British would think the American Army was still in place. Along with the good fortune of the rain, the wind also worked in the Americans' favor as it shifted and prevented British warships from venturing up the East River and detecting the crossing. Glover and his men worked hard all through the night and made as many as ten to twelve crossings. Only experienced seamen familiar with tides and currents could have pulled off such a bold plan. As daylight broke on the morning of the 30th, many of Washington's men still had not made it across the river to temporary sanctuary in Manhattan. Then a thick fog rolled in and covered the East River and Brooklyn Heights, further masking the movement of men and equipment. Tallmadge and his men became anxious as they anticipated British patrols and the possible detection of the Americans' intentions. Tallmadge gave a testimony of the events.

> As the dawn of the next day approached, those of us who remained in the trenches became very anxious for our own safety, and when dawn appeared there were several regiments still on duty. At this time a very dense fog began to rise, and it seemed to settle in a peculiar manor over both encampments. I recollect this peculiar providential occurrence perfectly well; and so very dense was the atmosphere that I could scarcely discern a man at six yards' distance...we tarried until the sun had risen, but the fog remained as dense as ever.[4]

As the last of the American boats left Brooklyn for Manhattan, the American hope was that Providence would grant a better day and more favorable grounds for a future rendezvous with the British. Tallmadge and his men accomplished their mission and escaped at the last minute to catch their boat ride across the East River. Washington was on the last boat to leave Brooklyn that morning as patrols of redcoats approached the evacuation site and began firing at the fleeing Americans. Washington and the men from Marblehead had pulled it off. The entire American Army and all of its equipment was saved to fight another day, and the American cause was still alive.

Nearly 150 years later, a similar nation-saving evacuation occurred. Recognized as one of Western civilization's greatest orators and one of the most important figures of the twentieth century, Winston Churchill noted in a 1940 speech to Parliament that "wars are not won by evacuations."[5] He was referring to the British evacuation from Dunkirk and the saving of the British Army to fight Adolph Hitler and his Third Reich another day. Washington had to be aware, like Churchill was, of that cogent fact. Wars are not won by evacuations. Both cases provided two important reflective considerations. Churchill and Washington were both provided with second chances for success, and each was taught that he had to be better prepared for the next battle and never to underestimate his enemy. The Brooklyn affair afforded Washington a costly lesson in generalship, and it was one he would not forget.

Providential Design

People of faith and those who believe in the goodness of America see the hand of God interceding to save the new nation on the night of August 29th and the morning of the 30th, 1776. It is a spiritual affirmation of the country's salvation, and it has always implied an obligation for the country to live up to the tenets of its founding document. In the centuries that followed, America has assumed the role of mankind's guarantor of security and guardian of freedom, justice, and dignity. It is hard to deny that something extraordinary was at play that night. Rarely in history have the stakes been so high and a move been so daring and bold that the future of a nation hinged on a single decisive act. Three simultaneous meteorological elements played a hand in the survival of the American Army. The absence of any one of those events could have meant doom for the American cause. One — the rain that muffled the noise of the departing men and equipment. Two — the wind that shifted and prevented the British fleet from coming up the East River. Three — the morning fog that obscured the movement of the last remaining troops, including Washington himself.

Washington and the American Army were temporarily secure in Manhattan as Howe and the British Army stood atop Brooklyn Heights with a view across the East River. Sanctuary in Manhattan did not last very long for the Americans. It was clear that New York was strategically important, but the British Navy had the ability to strike any point of its choosing, and after the disastrous Battle of Long Island, Congress gave Washington permission to leave New York at his discretion. The next step for the British was an amphibious attack against the island of Manhattan, once again in an effort to trap Washington and refuse him an escape route. On September 15th a large-scale British naval bombardment commenced on the east side of Manhattan, north of the city at Kips Bay (current day 34th Street near where the Midtown Tunnel enters Manhattan). The bombardment smashed the American positions guarding the shoreline as 4,000 British redcoats landed under the command of Henry Clinton. The American defenders fled the British assault, and the landing was mostly unopposed.

Many of the American troops in the vicinity of the landing at Kips Bay were militiamen who were mostly ill trained and ill equipped in the art of eighteenth century warfare. The assaulting British regulars made quick work of those who had the tenacity to stand and fight. The American defenders under the command of Israel Putnam and Nathanael Green were thinly positioned across the island. A large contingent of approximately 9,000 Americans under General William Heath and Joseph Spencer were north of the British landing area of Kips Bay. Heath's men were tasked with guarding an American withdrawal off the island at the Kingsbridge Crossing at the northern end of Manhattan. Spencer's men were building fortifications along the high ground in Harlem. Nathanael Green, possibly Washington's most trusted and able subordinate, in a meeting and war council on September 12th, urged Washington to abandon the city and move his army off the island of Manhattan. That effort by the Americans was already underway when the British landed at Kips Bay.

Washington and Putnam were both to the north of the British landings in Harlem Heights as the British assault began. Washington then rode along the Boston Post Road south toward the action. The Boston Post Road ran in a north/south direction along the east side of the narrow island of Manhattan. Similarly, on the west side of the island was another road that ran north/south — the Bloomingdale

Road. As Washington arrived in the area of the battle, he witnessed, to his extreme distress, Connecticut militiamen in full retreat. He was quoted as saying with disgust, "Are these the men with whom I am to defend America?"[6] Washington temporarily lost his temper and good judgement, and he severely shouted admonishments at his men for abandoning their posts. He hit many of them with his riding crop and drew his sword and pistol. At that point, Washington was exposed to direct enemy fire from approaching British and Hessian troops. All his attempts to rally his men had failed. Washington, along with his horse, Blueskin, and one of his aides, moved in a direction away from the battle and back toward Harlem Heights.

Fortunately for the Americans, much of the army was already north of the British landing at Kips Bay, but thousands remained in or near the city in fortifications built to repel a direct assault from the sea. When the British showed their hand as to the location of their assault, the key for the Americans and General Putnam was to move the rest of the army north to join Washington at Harlem Heights. British and Hessian troops would move to both the north and south along the Boston Post Road to corner the Americans and capture as many of them as they could. They could then force the Americans into an unfavorable position with their backs once more up against the waters surrounding New York.

The British hesitated again and did not take full advantage of the strategic position they had secured at Kips Bay. Manhattan Island is only 2.3 miles across at its widest section. The British failed to push across to the west, which would have sealed off the island and blocked any movement north by the Americans. General Putnam raced to gather his force and as much of the equipment as possible and attempted to join Washington at Harlem. A key for the Americans was Lieutenant Arron Burr, a resident of New York who knew the routes in and around the city. Burr helped guide the American forces north up the west side of Manhattan along the Bloomingdale Road (renamed to Broadway in the nineteenth century). At the same time, the British were advancing to the south down the east side of Manhattan along the Boston Post Road. The two opposing Armies passed within several hundred yards of each other undetected, and the Americans arrived in Harlem and joined Washington and the rest of the Army.

Kips Bay was another disaster for Washington and the Americans. They suffered the loss of more the 400 soldiers killed or captured, and the British losses were minor in comparison. The Americans also lost large quantities of valuable supplies and equipment including cannons that had to be left behind. The loss of New York was, on top of everything else, a serious psychological blow to the American cause. New York provided the British with a great harbor to supply their army and a connection to the North via the Hudson River to Canada. Nearby Long Island became bountiful with livestock and crops for the British as they hunkered down for a protracted occupation that would only end with the Treaty of Paris and a distant Evacuation Day.

The British, newly in possession of New York City, moved north in pursuit of the elusive American Army. One of Washington's highly regarded and bright young officers from West Boxford, Massachusetts, was Thomas Knowlton. Knowlton was with the American cause and the army from the beginning of the struggle, including the siege of Boston and the Battles of Bunker and Breed's Hills. During the Battle of Breed's Hill, he fought with fellow Patriot Dr. Joseph Warren who was killed during the final British assault. Knowlton had recently been promoted by Washington to Lieutenant Colonel and was given responsibility for selecting a group of men to form an elite group. The group came to be known as "Knowlton's Rangers" and was the first of its kind in the American Army. Its mission was to carry out reconnaissance and spying operations. On the morning of September 16th, Knowlton's Rangers engaged a patrol of British Light Infantry under British General Alexander Leslie as it advanced north toward Harlem. The fighting became very intense, and the Battle of Harlem Heights progressed through the afternoon. Knowlton's Rangers, after falling back through the surrounding woods, counter-attacked with support from other joining American units from Virginia under Major Andrew Leitch. Knowlton and his rangers continued the fight and exchanged fire with advancing British Infantry. The British augmented their thrust with cannons to drive the Americans back. Washington then ordered more units into battle and put heavy pressure on the over-extended British Infantry. The British pulled back, and a protracted exchange commenced as more British entered the struggle and joined with Leslie. As the day wore on, the British withdrew as ammunition ran low, ceding the field to the Americans.

In the dark days of the early part of the war, Washington and his army won their first battle against the British. The victory, though greatly needed for morale, came at a cost. The American losses at Harlem Heights were light in comparison to other recent battles, but one of the losses was the venerable leader of the Rangers, Thomas Knowlton. In a general order on September 17th, Washington paid homage to his young comrade when he described him as "The gallant and brave Colonel Knowlton, who would have been an honor to any country, having fallen yesterday while gloriously fighting" for his country.[7] Knowlton was one of America's first examples of a brave and talented young soldier who gave his life so his country could live. It is one of history's sad truths that for the validation of human freedom, liberty, and justice too many of the best among us have sacrificed their lives for the greater good of the nation. It is an unfortunate reality that has played out again and again on numerous battlefields and in numerous campaigns over the two and a half centuries since then. America should never forget Thomas Knowlton and the countless others who were willing to pay the ultimate price.

In the following days, Washington and his army moved to King's Bridge, which crossed over Spuyten Duyvil Creek. *Spuyten duyvil* is Dutch and translates to "spitting devil" or "devil's whirlpool" due to the turbulence of the waters of the creek. In Dutch New Amsterdam folklore, prior to the British renaming the city New York, it was also referred to as "spite the devil." Spuyten Duyvil Creek separated Manhattan Island from the mainland and the Bronx. Metaphorically, the Americans, by crossing the bridge and continuing the struggle, were "spiting the devil" by advancing the cause of human dignity and standing up for the ideals of freedom, liberty, and justice. On the 20th of September, the retreating Americans witnessed columns of smoke rising from New York City south of their position. A great fire had started on the west side of city during the night of the 20th and burned until the morning of the 21st. More than 20% of the structures in the city were destroyed. The British claimed that the fire was started by American sympathizers, but no direct evidence of causation was ever attributed to either side.

In late October, Howe and the British Army again followed the Americans. The British Naval force landed at Throggs Neck in the Bronx on October 18th and then at Pell's Point in Westchester. The British landed upwards of 10,000 British and Hessian soldiers including four British regiments of foot, a Hessian grenadier battalion, and cavalry of light dragoons. The British strategy was to once again attempt to trap the American Army in Manhattan by getting in behind it and closing off its escape routes. The British moved northwest through Westchester and the villages of New Rochelle and Scarsdale. American resistance along the roads and musket fire from hidden positions thwarted British progress and slowed the British advance, allowing the bulk of Washington's army to arrive at its supply stores in White Plains on October 22nd. Again, Washington was able to slip through the noose that Howe and his friends were preparing for him. Upon arriving in the village of White Plains, Washington had his army of approximately 13,000 build defensive lines and fortifications on the hills in and around the village. The American command and distribution of units was becoming more integrated as the frequency of battles engulfed all aspects of Washington's army. State and regional parochialism continued to exist in the makeup of the American Army, but over time the units began to acquire confidence and rely on each other. The strains of battle drew soldiers together in a common cause as no other endeavor has the capacity to achieve. The new American Army was a cross-section of the colonies. By the war's end, the army would be the glue that held thirteen different states together in one cohesive country.

The Americans left a large contingent of men in two forts to their rear: Fort Washington in Manhattan and Fort Lee on the other side of the Hudson River in New Jersey. The Battle of White Plains lasted for several days and was hyphenated by bad weather from October 28th until November 1st. The engagement began when an American advance party under General Spencer assaulted the British and Hessians as they were forming for attack. The British and Hessians organized in eight columns on the Americans' defensive right and advanced on Chatterton Hill. The Americans fought well in the beginning of the battle and were successful in pushing back two assaults and inflicting many casualties on the British and Hessian forces. A final assault by the Hessians was able to push the Americans off, and the Hessians initiated a flanking move against the adjoining American defensive positions. The British and Hessians continued to advance on the right of the American positions. The field that day was under the command of General Henry Clinton, and he, as well as his superior General Howe, had found a tactic on the battlefield for which the American Army didn't have an effective counter measure. That tactic was to attack the Americans' flank in force and turn it and come in behind their defensive lines to envelop them. Washington and his staff once again realized what Clinton was attempting to do and ordered a withdrawal, ceding the field and another tactical victory to the British.

Once again, the Americans were able to avoid a disaster as they withdrew toward Peekskill and an eventual crossing of the Hudson River to New Jersey. Howe did not pursue Washington and his army. Instead, he focused his army's attention on the American forts left behind. Fort Washington was the last remaining stronghold the Americans held in Manhattan, and after the Battle of White Plains, Washington gave a discretionary order to abandon the fort. The American General in charge at the fort, Colonel Robert Magaw, believed that his force could hold against a British attack. He was wrong. On November 16th, Howe ordered an attack led by a combined British/Hessian force of nearly 8,000 men under General Hugh Percy. The fort surrendered, resulting in another disaster for the American Army. The Americans suffered more than 150 casualties, and nearly 3,000 soldiers joined the thousands of American patriots who were already occupying prison ships in New York Harbor. On the other side of the Hudson River, in New Jersey, Fort Lee was abandoned to avoid a fate similar to Fort Washington. The two forts were constructed to prevent British warships from having free access up and down the lower Hudson River. Howe ordered General Lord Cornwallis to cross the Hudson River to New Jersey and defeat any points of resistance from the severely battered and dwindling American Army. Cornwallis and his contingent of combined forces of British/Hessian soldiers invaded New Jersey on the night of November 19th. The combined British forces of approximately 5,000 landed at the Palisades and pursued the retreating Americans.

The remnants of the American Army retreated across New Jersey. The Americans had been battered by the British in a series of punishing battles during the summer and fall of 1776 as the New York campaign ended. As Washington moved his men across northern New Jersey, hope for the army and the American cause seemed bleak. With colder weather setting in, the Americans faced new challenges. Smallpox, a virulent virus that plagued the army through a good part of the war, broke out, and Washington ordered his men to be inoculated, which most likely saved many from the ravages of the disease. Disease (smallpox in particular) was responsible for an estimated 15,000 or more deaths among the Americans, which was more than all the causalities suffered by the army in battle throughout the entire war. Disease was also a major cause of death on British prison ships. The British took upwards of 20,000 Americans as prisoners during the war, and at least half of them died under deplorable conditions.

During the closing months of 1776, the army was additionally depleted due to desertions and expiring terms of service among the militiamen. Washington and the American cause received vital assistance from the pen of Thomas Paine, a former British subject who had recently emigrated to America through the urging of Benjamin Franklin. Throughout American history, America has been continuously blessed by the actions and inspiration of immigrants. The period of the American struggle for independence was no exception. Individuals who come from places where life's struggles and limitations restrict the human spirit have unique insights into the wondrous possibilities that America offers. Is it that immigrants can see more clearly the value of the American experiment that native-born Americans take for granted or overlook? America has always been a place of great promise where humanity could throw off the bonds of oppression and individuals could have the best chance of living more fulfilling lives.

Thomas Paine was born in England and arrived in America in 1774. He was a political theorist and activist and was mostly unsuccessful in the occupations he tried before coming to America. He was also an unusual figure who provided the inspiration to lift the nation up in its darkest moment and provided shelter from the storm of failure and discouragement. Paine authored two principal works during the Revolutionary period. One of those works was a pamphlet titled *Common Sense*. It was published in January of 1776, and it provided a compelling argument for why the American cause was justified and why a break with England was the only recourse for America. In December of that year, while the prospects for the American cause were at a low point, Paine traveled with the American Army and wrote the first in a series of thirteen pamphlets describing the American crisis. Paine's compelling and emotional writing style provided inspiration that reignited morale, steadied the course of the army, and helped bring new life and purpose to the American cause. The following excerpts are from Thomas Paine's *The American Crisis*.

> THESE are the times that try men's souls. The summer solider and the sunshine patriot will, in this crisis, shrink from the service of their country; but he that stands it now, deserves the love and thanks of man and woman. Tyranny, like hell, is not easily conquered; yet we have this consolation with us, that the harder the conflict, the more glorious the triumph. What we obtain to cheap, we esteem to lightly: it is dearness only that gives every thing its value. Heaven knows how to put a proper price upon its goods; and it would be strange indeed if so celestial an article as freedom

should not be highly rated. Britain, with an army to enforce her tyranny, has declared that she has a right (not only to tax) but "to bind us to in all cases whatsoever," and if being bound in that manner, is not slavery, then is there not such a thing as slavery upon earth. Even the expression is impious; for so unlimited a power can belong only to God.

Whether the independence of the continent was declared too soon, or delayed too long, I will not now enter into as an argument; my own simple option is, that had it been eight months earlier, it would have been much better. We did not make a proper use of last winter, neither could we, while we were in a dependent state. However, the fault, if it were one, was all our own; we have none to blame but ourselves. But no great deal is lost yet. All that Howe has been doing for this month past, is rather a ravage than a conquest, which the spirit of the Jerseys, a year ago, would have quickly repulsed, and which time and a little resolution will soon recover.

I have as little superstition in me as any man living, but my secret opinion has even been, and still is, that God Almighty will not give up a people to military destruction, or leave them unsupported to perish, who have so earnestly and so repeatedly sought to avoid the calamities of war, by every decent method which wisdom could invent. Neither have I so much of the infidel in me, as to suppose that He has relinquished the government of the world, and given us up to the care of devils; and as I do not, I cannot see on what grounds the king of Britain can look up to heaven for help against us: a common murderer, a highwayman, or a house-breaker, has as good pretence as he.

'Tis surprising to see how rapidly a panic will sometimes run through a country. All nations and ages have been subject to them. Britain has trembled like an ague at the report of a French fleet of flat-bottomed boats; and in the fourteenth (fifteenth) century the whole English army, after ravaging the kingdom of France, was driven back like men petrified with fear; and this brave exploit was performed by a few broken forces collected and headed by a woman, Joan of Arc. Would that heaven might inspire some Jersey maid to spirit up her countrymen, and save her fair fellow sufferers from ravage and ravishment! Yet panics, in some case, have their uses; they produce as much good as hurt. Their duration is always short; the mind soon grows through them, and acquires a firmer habit then before. But their peculiar advantage is, that they are the touchstones of sincerity and hypocrisy, and bring things and men to light, which might otherwise have lain forever undiscovered. In fact, they have the same effect on secret traitors, which an imaginary apparition would have upon a private murderer. They sift out the hidden thoughts of man, and hold them up in public to the world. Many a disguised Tory has lately shown his head, that shall penitentially solemnize with curses the day on which Howe arrived upon the Delaware.

As I was with the troops at Fort Lee, and marched with them to the edge of Pennsylvania, I am well acquainted with many circumstances, which those who live at a distance know but little or nothing of. Our situation there was exceedingly cramped, the place being a narrow neck of land between the North River and the Hackensack. Our force was inconsiderable, being not one-fourth so great as Howe could bring against us. We had no army at hand to have relieved the garrison, had we shut ourselves up and stood on our defensive. Our ammunition, light artillery, and the best part of our stores, had been removed, on the apprehension that Howe would endeavor to penetrate the Jerseys, in which case Fort Lee could be of no use to us; for it must occur to every thinking man, whether in the army or not, that these kind of field forts are only for temporary purposes, and last in use no longer than the enemy directs his forces against, the particular object which such forts are raised to defend...

I shall conclude this paper with some miscellaneous remarks on the state of our affairs; and shall begin with asking the following question, Why is it that the enemy have left the New England provinces, and made these middle ones the seat of war? The answer is easy: New England is not infested with Tories, and we are. I have been tender in raising the cry against these men, and used numberless arguments to show them their danger, but it will not do to sacrifice a world either to their folly or their baseness. The period is now arrived, in which either they or we must change our settlements, or one or both must fall. And what is a Tory? Good God! What is he? I should not be afraid to go with a hundred Whigs against a thousand Tories, were they to attempt to get into arms. Every Tory is a coward; for servile, slavish, self-interested fear is the foundation of Toryism; and a man under such influence, though he may be cruel, never can be brave...

I once felt all that kind of anger, which a man ought to feel, against the mean principles that are held by the Tories: a noted one, who kept a tavern at Amboy, was standing at his door, with as pretty a child in his hand, about eight or nine years old, as I ever saw, and after speaking his mind as freely as he thought was prudent, finished with this unfatherly expression, "Well! Give me peace in my day!". Not a man lives on the continent but fully believes that a separation must some time or other finally take place, and a generous parent should have said, "If there must be trouble, let it be in my day, that my child may have peace;" and this single reflection, well applied, is sufficient to awaken every man to duty. Not a place upon earth might be so happy as America...

By perseverance and fortitude we have the prospect of a glorious issue; by cowardice and submission, the sad choice of a variety of evils – a ravaged country – a depopulated city – habitations without safety, and slavery without hope – our homes turned into barracks and bawdy-houses for Hessians, and a future race to provide for, whose farther we shall doubt of. Look on this picture and weep over it! And if there yet remains one thoughtless wretch who believes it not, let him suffer it unlamented.[8]

Despite the emotional boost from Paine's prophetic writings, the situation on the ground for Washington and the American Army in December 1776 was still precarious. The army moved through New Jersey with British General Cornwallis on its heels and crossed the Delaware River to an encampment in Pennsylvania. While the British soldiers marched across northern New Jersey's ravaged farms, they confiscated household belongings and conducted themselves like plundering barbarians from antiquity. They were indifferent to whether their victims were rebels or loyalists.

Washington's army, once a numerous force, had dwindled from attrition, desertion, and disease to between 4,000 and 5,000 men who could be counted on for action. Moreover, expiring terms of enlistment were fast approaching for many in the army. Washington needed to do something dramatic, resourceful, and unexpected to keep the cause alive and to keep his command a viable military instrument. He chose a bold plan. As the winter set in, the British dispersed many forces among exposed outposts in New Jersey, leaving them isolated and potentially vulnerable to attack. From his position in Pennsylvania, Washington's plan was to have his army cross back over the Delaware River, which separated Pennsylvania from New Jersey, and attack an enemy outpost. He hoped that he and his men would be undetected as they braved the perils of the ice-clogged Delaware. The target was Trenton, and the movement would be conducted at night, just like the crossing of the East River several months earlier and the escape from Long Island and the clutches of General Howe and his friends.

The crossing was to occur on December 25, 1776, in the dead of winter, and the plan integrated three separate crossings and directions of attack on Trenton. To complicate matters, it was cold that night, and falling snow and hail made travel on the roads and across the river hazardous. Washington was facing manifest obstacles. The army was in a battered shape. There were many fewer soldiers available, and they were tired and eyeing the prospects of going home. The winter elements were brutal, but the enemy was not suffering the hardships that Washington and his men were. The British and Hessians were enjoying success and thinking the war was nearly over and that the Americans were about to give up. That was in reflection of the successful operations of his Majesty's Army over the prior several months. It would have been irrational to think otherwise, or so it seemed.

Generations of Americans have celebrated nearly 250 Christmases since Washington and his army crossed the Delaware River. The holiday festivities have most often been spent in the warmth and comfort of homes surrounded by family and friends. I wonder how many Americans, as they enjoy the joyful religious holiday, pause to contemplate the sacrifice those brave American soldiers made that night of America's first Christmas. It is hard to consider that in those dark moments of America's first Noel the hand of divine inspiration did not, once again, provide the lamp of direction for Washington and his men to follow. The exertion provided by the patriots during the season of grace and hope kept the American cause alive.

Washington again called on Colonel John Glover and his men from Marblehead to apply their boat-handling skills and acumen to navigate the army across another difficult body of water — the Delaware River. Washington's plan went awry from the beginning. Of the three separate columns and crossings that were involved in the initial plan, only Washington's main contingent was able to cross. Washington determined that despite having a reduced force on hand he would carry on with the attack against the Hessians at Trenton.

The army crossed at McConkey's and Johnson's Ferries and traveled approximately nine miles south on frozen roads on the night of December 25th and morning of the 26th. The destination was Trenton, and the plan was to surprise Hessian Colonel Johann Rall and his garrison of approximately 1,400 men. Washington was supported by Generals Nathanael Green and John Sullivan, and they commanded 2,400 men, including cannons. The Americans were able to secure strategic positions in and around Trenton, and the battle began to provide the attacking American force with a vital advantage. The Americans were on top of the Hessians before they could mount and organize an effective defense. A short but fierce battle ensued, and much of the Hessian force surrendered. The Americans' losses were small. They did not lose any men in the action, and less than one dozen were wounded. They did, however, lose two men to the elements during the march. The Hessians suffered more than one hundred casualties, but most of the force of nearly nine hundred were forced to surrender and were taken as prisoners. One of the Hessians' losses was their commander, Johann Rall, who was killed by musket fire during the engagement.

Washington and his men returned to their basecamp in Pennsylvania. They had pulled off a daring victory when all seemed to be slipping away from them and the American cause for independence. The victory at Trenton invigorated morale among the soldiers and the supporting population, but it still remained that enlistments were coming to an end at the year's close. Something needed to happen to address the enlistment issue and keep the army in place. Congress helped by granting a ten-dollar stipend to the men who re-enlisted. Washington also appealed to their patriotism and the dream of a brighter future for them, their children, and posterity. Washington addressed his men on December 31st.

> My brave fellows, you have done all I ask you to do, and more than can be reasonable expected; but your country is at stake, your wives, your houses and all that you hold dear. You have worn yourselves out with fatigues and hardships, but we know not how to spare you. If you will consent to stay one month longer, you will render that service to the cause of liberty, and to your country, which you probably can never do under any circumstances.[9]

It worked! Most of the men stayed, and new recruits joined the ranks as more of the population began to see a pathway forward for the new nation. Out of desperation and being cornered, Washington and his men sprang into action like a coiled rattlesnake and hit at the vulnerable underbelly of their enemy.

Washington and his army were buoyed by the Trenton victory, and it was not the time to hunker back and sit out the winter. There was more work to be done. They crossed back over to New Jersey on December 30th. The belief among Washington, Nathanael Green, and the other American officers was that Cornwallis was not going to let the Battle of Trenton go unanswered. They were right. Cornwallis was on the move. Near the battle space, the British had around eight thousand men, though many were dispersed at various points throughout northern New Jersey. Cornwallis' command was again a combined force of British regulars and Hessians, and they were going to force an engagement. Washington was going to preempt the British movement. The "old fox" (a nickname for Washington by Cornwallis) was learning! He set up defensive positions three miles long on the south side of Assunpink Creek outside of Trenton. Those defenses were to guard against another flanking movement by the British. Washington and his army had paid a heavy price for being exposed to British flanking movements in previous battles earlier in the year.

The main part of the British Army under Cornwallis made its way south from Princeton on a ten-mile march toward Trenton and another meeting with Washington and the American Army. The first engagement started on January 2, 1777, when an American advance guard of riflemen formed skirmish lines and attacked the British column as it moved south. The American contingent was under the command of Colonel Edward Hand. The idea was to fatigue the British along the march south and slow their advance. It worked. The British did not make the crossing of the Assunpink until the late afternoon, limiting the time for them to launch an attack against the Americans. The Americans were well positioned as the British started to advance across the creek bridge that separated the two opposing forces. The first and second British assaults were thwarted by musket and cannon fire from the Americans. The third assault by the British also failed as the Americans inflicted several hundred casualties on the attacking British. At that point, daylight was running out in the early winter sky and Cornwallis called off the attack. They would renew their assault on the Americans in the morning. Cornwallis and his staff were confident that they had the upper hand on the Americans. Notwithstanding the skirmish around Harlem Heights, the British had thrashed the Americans and soundly outgeneraled Washington in strategy and deployment of forces. Cornwallis was quoted as saying on the evening of January 2nd, "We got the old fox safe now. We'll go over and bag him in the morning."[10]

Washington had other plans. At that point, the Battle of Assunpink Creek was a victory for the Americans. They had nothing more to prove at Assunpink and potentially everything to lose if they stayed and fought out a fixed battle against the main body of the

British forces. The issue for Washington was how to preserve the success of the engagement at Assunpink and not appear to retreat, which could have had an adverse effect on morale. The answer was to redeploy and fight the British at a point where the American Army had an advantage. Cornwallis left in his rear a force of fourteen hundred British regulars under Lt. Colonel Charles Mawhood at the town of Princeton.

As night set in on January 2nd, the Americans left a contingent of rear guards on the ground surrounding the south side of Assunpink Creek. As Benjamin Tallmadge had pulled off at Brooklyn Heights, the Americans once again were planning to fool the British into thinking they were still in place on the opposite side of the creek. Cornwallis held a "council of war" with his officers. His Quartermaster General William Erskine advised him not to delay the attack as they had at Brooklyn and to continue the assault on the American positions that night. He noted, "If Washington is the General I take him to be, his army will not be found there in the morning."[11] Erskine was right! Washington and his army were gone in the morning. With the help of a local militia, they pulled out during the night and headed down a back road toward Princeton.

The action at Princeton began the morning of January 3rd after Cornwallis ordered British units at Princeton to join the main body at Trenton. At that point, two regiments of British regulars under Mawhood engaged in a firefight with a brigade of Americans commanded by General Hugh Mercer. The British were getting the best of the Americans in the initial action and pushed Mercer and the Americans back. Mercer was surrounded by angry British soldiers, and he refused to surrender and was bayonetted.

Washington ordered the militia into the action and took control of the battle for the Americans. Three companies of Marines were with Washington's army at Princeton. They joined in the engagement against the British at Clarke Farm, and several of them were killed, including one of their officers, Captain William Shippin. Those men were among the first Marines to fall in the service of their country. At first the militia and some elements of Mercer's brigade retreated, but the men were inspired by Washington's leadership and the risk to his own personal safety that he accepted. It was like Washington's actions at Kips Bay where he put himself at risk. At Princeton, he also placed himself in the direct line of fire. Unlike Kips Bay, Washington was successful in reversing the direction of his soldiers and motivating them back into the fight at Princeton. The Americans regained the initiative and forced the British redcoats under Mawhood to retreat. The British ran from the pursuing Americans as Washington cajoled his men forward. The bulk of Mawhood's men did, however, eventually make their way back to Trenton in scattered units to join Cornwallis and the main body of the British Army. The Americans also defeated two British regiments and Brigadier General John Sullivan in a fierce fight causing additional British soldiers to surrender at Nassau Hall in Princeton. That final action essentially ended the

Michael Urtnowski

engagement, culminating in a surprising and consequential victory for the Americans.

As the new year began, Washington led his army to winter quarters in Morristown. British General Howe ordered Cornwallis and his army to withdraw back to New York. As Cornwallis withdrew his army, they were harassed by New Jersey militias supported by Continental Army soldiers. The British took additional casualties as the Americans became masters of unconventional warfare. Between December 25 and January 3, 1777, the prospects for the American cause were revived. Washington was given "dictatorial powers" by Congress, and he grew to be known as the Virginia gentleman who stood out among men. Washington and his army had learned how to fight the British and their abundant supplies of resources and capabilities. The Americans could not defeat the British on British terms. To counter British conventional superiority, the Americans created ways to bleed them through protracted and costly engagements. Those ways were elusive and were designed to make sure the British would never have a decisive victory that would end the rebellion. One of the eighteenth century's great military figures, Fredrick the Great, king of Prussia, noted that Washington's movements and engagements with the British in the period from December 25, 1776, to January 3, 1777, were "the most brilliant of any recorded in the annals of military achievements."[12]

A change had taken place. When it seemed the American cause for independence was on the verge of collapse, Washington, through unalterable will and tenacity, infused life back into his army and the nation. British forces were being depleted through attrition and drained of the fighting spirit. Grudgingly, General Sir William Howe, Sir Henry Clinton, and Lord Charles Cornwallis came to realize that they were up against a formidable and unconventional adversary and that defeating the Americans was not going to be an easy task. The Americans were extremely resourceful, and with every success they had, enlistment for the cause of independence increased among the three million inhabitants of the thirteen states. Still many hardships remained ahead for the Americans over the next seven years. Dark clouds appeared on the horizon as the direction of battles and circumstances ebbed and flowed. American will and resolve to stay united and fight on were tested time and time again.

Chapter Six

A New Constellation Appears

On June 14, 1777, the Second Continental Congress passed a flag resolution, a resolution "that the flag of the United States be thirteen stripes, alternate red and white; that the union be thirteen stars, white in a blue field representing a new constellation."[1] Also in that summer of 1777, the British launched a new campaign, once again using the power of their more-than 250 ships. A force of approximately 12,000 British regulars and 5,000 Hessians landed at the northern end of the Chesapeake Bay at Head of Elk, Maryland. The plan was to attack Philadelphia, which was the capital of the new nation.

Another part of the British plan that summer was to launch an army south from Canada and the St. Lawrence River. The force would set out from St. John's, Canada, travel by boats across Lake Champlain, proceed south through dense forest to the northern end of the Hudson River, and advance on Albany. The combined British/Hessian force was under the command of a colorful and boastful aristocrat playwright named General John Burgoyne, often referred to as "Gentleman Johnny" because of his desire for high-class living, ladies, flashy uniforms, and gambling. The British strategic initiative was approved in London by King George in January and was designed to control the Hudson River corridor and isolate New England from the rest of the colonies. The attack plan was a three-pronged assault. The northern contingent, under Burgoyne, would move south. The western contingent, under the command of Brigadier General Barry St. Leger, originated from Lake Ontario and would move east along the Mohawk River. The forces would meet at Albany. A third army, under Howe, would come up the Hudson River from the south and New York City. This all-important southern army would be the vital link of the British plan. To Burgoyne's distress and ultimate demise, neither the force from Lake Ontario nor Howe's southern force ever arrived. The proposed plan never materialized, inexplicably due to a lack of communication between Burgoyne and Howe.

The British contingent under St. Leger that was moving east along the Mohawk River began an engagement with an American force at Fort Stanwix near Rome, New York. The Americans were led by Colonel Peter Gansevoort of the 2nd New York Regiment. St. Leger ordered Gansevoort to surrender the fort, but the American commander refused. A protracted siege resulted on August 2nd and lasted for nearly three weeks.

A peripheral engagement developed as loyalists under Sir John Johnson and his king's regiment of New York, supported by Hessians and a contingent of Iroquois Indian allies, fought a fierce action approximately five miles from the fort. That engagement, known as the Battle of Oriskany, was fought on August 6th and was a tactical victory for the British. The Crown's force was predominately loyalists and Iroquois. At that stage in the war, there was a good deal of animosity between American patriots and loyalists, and bad blood existed between the Americans and many Native Americans, particularly the Iroquois. The pro-Crown forces ambushed an American relief column under General Nicolas Herkimer, which was headed for Fort Stanwix. The engagement was a blood bath as the American force suffered nearly 400 killed, including their commander. In an ensuing action, the Americans did manage a raid on the loyalist camp, which caused a rift between the loyalists and their Indian allies. The rift caused the Iroquois to abandon their loyalist allies and head home. The loss of Native American support had a consequential effect on the overall British plan to advance toward Albany and support Burgoyne.

That same month, another American relief column, under the command of Benedict Arnold, pulled off a crafty deception. Arnold was able to convince St. Leger that he commanded a much larger force, which caused the siege of Fort Stanwix to come to an end on August 22. St. Leger withdrew his forces back to Oswego, New York, abandoning Burgoyne's plan of a thrust from the west along the Mohawk River and a rendezvous at Albany.

Concurrently, Howe moved the bulk of his main British Army in New York not to the north to support Burgoyne, but instead to the west in an attempt to draw Washington into battle. Howe's justification for the move was based on his understanding of the orders from London. He sent his army first to New Jersey and then by sea to attack Philadelphia, leaving Burgoyne on his own to contend with whatever resistance the Americans could mount against his force of approximately 8,000 regulars, Hessians, loyalists, and Indian allies. Howe's plan was to assault the American capital, and it was based on eighteenth-century concepts of conventional warfare whereby if you took your enemy's capital it would force him into concessions or even capitulation. Should his strategy not succeed, Howe hoped that by moving toward Philadelphia he could lure Washington into that all-important and decisive battle that would end the conflict. At a minimum, capturing Philadelphia would have an adverse effect on American morale and would convey to Congress and all Americans the futility of their continued resistance and the inevitability of a British victory.

Washington did not take the bait to fight the British in northern New Jersey. In late August, Howe and the British Army left New Jersey from Sandy Hook and ventured by sea up the Chesapeake to come at the Americans from the west and put Philadelphia in jeopardy. With Howe and the major part of the British Army less than fifty miles from Philadelphia, the situation had changed for the Americans. Washington would choose to engage Howe at the most advantageous location between the advancing British Army and the American capital.

Washington moved his army south to the Brandywine Valley in southeastern Pennsylvania. The region was settled by Quakers, who were pacifists, and the upcoming battle would evolve all around their farms and houses. Washington took up defensive positions on the east side of Brandywine Creek at Chadds Ford. The American defensives were intended to block the crossings of the creek and the main road to Philadelphia. It was similar to the defensive position that had worked well for Washington earlier in the year against Cornwallis at Assunpink Creek. The plan was to funnel the British advance through a narrow crossing and rain fire down on them. The British would move slowly through the Brandywine Valley as they would once again be harassed by militias and Continentals on the main roads in the region. Washington's Continental Army had been rejuvenated with new recruits since the Battles of Trenton and Princeton earlier in the year. By September, the Continental Army, including militias, was approximately 16,000 men, nearly as many as before the Battle of Long Island. The American Army was nearly as large as Howe's British Army that was approaching Brandywine Creek.

On September 11, the Battle of Brandywine began as Hessian and British regulars, joined by a contingent of loyalists called the Queen's Rangers, engaged the Americans on the west side of Chadds Ford. The British center force opposite Washington was comprised of a joint Hessian/British force of approximately 7,000 men commanded by Hessian General Wilhelm von Knyphausen. Once again, Howe, under the cover of fog and aided by local loyalists, sent the main part of his army on a wide flanking move around the American right. Washington and the Americans believed that they had covered the crossing in the battle space, but they were wrong. The British had better intelligence than the Americans did about the local terrain, a major shortcoming for which the Americans paid as the battle progressed. By mid-day, Washington was receiving reports from scouts and militia members that a large British force was moving around his right to flank his army. The British flanking force under Howe and Cornwallis set out on a seventeen-mile looping maneuver that crossed the creek at two locations before heading south to confront the Americans. Washington by nature was aggressive and a gambler, and he believed he had an opportunity to inflict a significant blow to the enemy. He recognized that if the main part of the British force was coming around to his right, then the force in front of him must be an inferior force. Armed with that information, Washington decided to launch a head-on attack against von Knyphausen's force that stood across from the American position. General Nathanael Greene's division began to advance across the creek to assault the Hessian/British force in front of them.

Shortly after Greene's men began their assault, Cornwallis' redcoats and Hessians showed up at the American right and ended any chance of an organized assault against the British center. Greene's men fell back across the creek as von Knyphausen began to apply pressure in an attempt to keep them in place. As the afternoon wore on, the Americans' position became increasingly precarious and they began a withdrawal.

The American effort was greatly advanced by a young French aristocrat from the Auvergne region, the Marquis de Lafayette. Lafayette was sent to Washington by Franklin who at that time was maneuvering his way through the halls of power in Paris attempting to win support for the cause. Lafayette's noble roots and connections to the court of King Louis XVI were not lost on Franklin or Washington, and Lafayette would play a key role in securing vital support from the French. Lafayette at the time was nineteen years old and was a brave leader of men despite his youth. During the American withdrawal at Brandywine, he demonstrated leadership and bravery on the battlefield as he rallied the troops and received a musket ball to his leg. Despite being wounded, he continued to inspire the troops to withdraw in an orderly fashion. Washington ordered three divisions under Sullivan and Sterling to hastily construct defensive positions against the growing threat from Cornwallis on the right flank.

The entire American position was becoming untenable. The defense against Cornwallis' advance from the north was not well organized, and American units were falling back. As the day wore on, Washington realized that the battle was lost and ordered Nathanael Greene's division to cover a general withdrawal to the east to prevent the complete destruction of the army. Washington, while attempting to organize the American defense, was joined by another new European immigrant volunteer.

The new immigrant was also sent to Washington by Benjamin Franklin in Paris. He was Polish-born cavalry officer Casimir Pulaski. Pulaski was born in 1745 and trained in cavalry tactics, which had a long and proud tradition in the Polish military. In his home country, Pulaski had fought in a rebellion against Stanislaus II, the king of Poland, who was controlled by Russia and influenced by other foreign powers including Prussia and Austria. The rebellion was a struggle for freedom and independence for the Polish people against those foreign influences. Unfortunately for the Polish people, the rebellion was unsuccessful and was defeated in 1772. During the rebellion, Pulaski developed a reputation in European circles for being a brilliant cavalry commander. The defeat of the rebellion compelled Pulaski to live in exile outside Poland. While in exile, he eventually met Franklin and was persuaded to go to America and fight for the American cause. He arrived in America in July of 1777 and wrote a letter to Washington seeking an officer's commission in the American Army. Washington was persuaded by the letter, in which Pulaski wrote, "I came here, where freedom is being defended, to serve it, and live or die for it."[2] Pulaski eventually received his commission from Congress and served as a Brigadier General. He formed a cavalry unit called Pulaski's Legion, which was generally recognized as the best of its kind on the American side. Similar to Von Steuben, Pulaski wrote the book on American cavalry tactics.

Washington ordered Pulaski to gather as many retreating Americans as possible and organize a hasty defense. Pulaski's defense was effective in stopping the enemy from enveloping the army and facilitated the American withdrawal. Pulaski is also credited with saving Washington's life as, once again, Washington put himself in the middle of the action. After the battle, Washington made Pulaski a Cavalry Brigadier General. The American withdrawal from Brandywine was orderly, though they received another drubbing from Howe and the British/Hessian forces. The American losses were more than 1,100 men killed, wounded, or captured. Howe and the British did not pursue Washington and the Americans as they retreated to the east. The British also suffered significant casualties of nearly 600 killed and wounded. The door was open for the British to take Philadelphia, which they did unopposed on September 26, 1777. As the British moved toward the city, Congress left Philadelphia for Lancaster and then York, Pennsylvania. Washington moved his army to Valley Forge about twenty miles to the east from occupied Philadelphia. As the British settled into the occupation of Philadelphia, Howe fell under increased criticism in England due to the mounting cost of men and material and the direction of his strategy in overcoming the rebellion and bringing the war to an end.

As the main British Army occupied Philadelphia, an equally significant campaign was underway in the north in Upstate New York along the Lake Champlain/Hudson River waterway.

Burgoyne's army of 8,000 combined British/Hessian soldiers, including a contingent of American/Canadian loyalists, were joined by nearly 400 mostly Iroquois Indian allies as they advanced south along the Hudson River. Many Native American tribes sided with the British during the Revolutionary War. They viewed the Americans as competition for land and resources. The British tried to stop the Americans from encroaching on what previously were native lands after the French and Indian War. The British were willing to supply material goods and sign treaties recognizing boundaries of native occupation and natural resource prerogatives. Though some tribes peacefully interacted and coexisted with the American settlers, many interactions were contentious, and bloody atrocities were committed on both sides. It is understandable how many native tribes, including the Iroquois, concluded that the Americans were a bigger threat to the continuation of their way of life then the British were, and it is easy to see that the British were a better bet for success in the struggle.

As Burgoyne's army made its way south, the fighting force was accompanied by upward of 2,000 dependents, including wives, children, servants, and a supply train of more than 200 wagons. The burdened mass of humanity had to struggle through the virgin wilderness of dense forests. Earlier in the war, in May of 1775, a group of Americans under Ethen Allan and the Green Mountain Boys from Vermont, along with Benedict Arnold and his force, surprised a British garrison and captured Fort Ticonderoga. The fort had been in American hands for more than two years as Burgoyne's army approached in early July of 1777. The Americans had a force of 3,000 men at the fort under the command of Generals Arthur St. Clair and Phillip Skyler and were ordered to hold as long as possible. The British captured a nearby redoubt on high ground at Mount Independence on the Vermont side of Lake Champlain and placed cannons on top, causing the American garrison on July 6th to abandon the position with embarrassingly little resistance.

The British reoccupied Fort Ticonderoga and continued their movement south. The following day, after the Americans evacuated the fort, the British won a rear-guard action at the Battle of Hubbardton against American regiments from Massachusetts and New Hampshire as well as against Colonel Seth Warner's Green Mountain Boys. The Americans believed they had put sufficient distance between themselves and the pursuing British force. They were wrong! The British, under Brigadier General Simon Frasier, who was a highly regarded officer by his peers, were on their heels. The British/Hessian force fell on the Americans, and a fierce battle involving approximately 1,000 soldiers from each side ensued. The Americans put up a determined resistance but eventually fell back and ceded the field to the British. The casualties were high on both sides with the Americans losing more than 300 killed, wounded, or captured and the British losing approximately 200 killed or wounded. The British suffered high losses among the officers, a story that would play out on subsequent battlefields as the war continued.

As the summer wore on, the difficult wilderness terrain slowed the progress of Burgoyne and his army moving south. Burgoyne landed his force by boat at the southernmost point of Lake Champlain. Burgoyne's mile-long caravan had to cut and slash its way through the dense woodland and advanced less than a mile a day. They also had to erect numerous makeshift bridges to cross streams and creeks. The large and unwieldy caravan was further hampered by American militias that placed fallen trees in their path and constructed obstacles at stream crossings. They were also running low on various food items, particularly beef, and required a large quantity of additional horses. Burgoyne was informed that a large cache of supplies could be had at Bennington, so he sent a detachment to secure it.

As he and his army approached more populated areas on their march south, Burgoyne issued ominous warnings and threats to the local population. "I have but to give stretch to the Indian Forces under my direction, and they amount to Thousands, to overtake the harden'd Enemies of Great Britain..."[3] The threat from Burgoyne was evidenced in July when a young woman named Jane McCrea who was engaged to a loyalist officer was brutally murdered, allegedly by Indians who were allied with Burgoyne's army. The strategy of intimidation had the opposite effect of what Burgoyne intended; it galvanized American militias all across New

England. The militias gathered their weapons and left their farms and homes throughout Vermont, New Hampshire, Massachusetts, and Upstate New York to join the effort to stop "Gentleman Johnny" and his army.

Burgoyne sent a detachment of 700 Hessian, Canadian, and American loyalists, including Indian allies led by Hessian Lt. Colonel Friedrich Baum, east toward the town of Bennington to secure the supplies his column needed to continue its advance toward Albany. Ten miles short of their destination, at Walloomsac, New York, Baum and his contingent engaged with an American force. They never made it to Bennington.

The American forces were led by John Stark, an irascible native of New Hampshire who led his state's militia. Stark was joined by other militia forces as they arrived from all parts of New England and New York to stop Burgoyne and his army. Stark served as an officer with the British Army in the French and Indian War, and he was also a veteran of the siege of Boston and of Bunker Hill and the subsequent battles through the spring of 1777. He left the American cause briefly after a dispute over not receiving a promotion. He also refused to take orders from Continental Officers, such as General Benjamin Lincoln whose qualifications, he felt, were inferior to his own. But with Burgoyne on the move and threatening to bring occupation to his region, Stark rejoined the fight.

That August, as the Battle of Bennington developed, Stark had more than 1,500 militiamen at his command. The numbers of American fighters grew daily as more and more New England militiamen arrived to join the fight. As Baum's forces advanced, he received reports that Bennington was defended by a superior American force. On August 14th he decided to build defensive positions and sent word back to Burgoyne to send reinforcements. Stark and his militia arrived at Baum's defensive positions on August 16th. Stark devised a plan to assault the enemy position from three different points. There have been some different versions of what Stark told his men prior to the battle: "There are your enemies, the Red Coats and the Tories. They are ours, or this night, Molly Stark sleeps a widow!"[4] Stark sent a group around to the right and another to the left of Baum's defense positions and kept the main force of 1,200 under his direct command in the front. Other American forces assaulted peripheral positions held by American and Canadian loyalists, many of whom fled the battle only to be hunted down by the Americans. Anger and bitterness prevailed as neighbor reaped vengeance on neighbor.

Stark's American force outnumbered the Brunswick and loyalist force by more than two to one. Stark's militia surrounded Baum's defense, and a bloody engagement took place as the American militia assaulted the Hessian position. As the Americans were rounding up the last elements of Baum's force, Hessian reinforcements arrived from Burgoyne's column. The new Hessian detachment under Lt. Colonel Heinrich von Breymann arrived too late to save Baum. After a stiff encounter with newly arriving American units under Colonel Seth Warren and his Green Mountain Boys, Breymann was forced to leave the field to the Americans and withdraw back to Burgoyne's column. The Americans suffered less than eighty killed or wounded, a small loss in comparison to those of the experienced Hessians. The forces under Baum and Breymann suffered more than two hundred killed and more than seven hundred taken as prisoners. Among the killed was Lt. Colonel Friedrich Baum.

Stark's leadership of the American militia at Bennington was a demonstration on how best to use the unconventional forces. Bennington was a decisive victory for the Americans and an ominous portent for Burgoyne's diminishing hopes for a glorious northern campaign. At the Battle of Bennington, Burgoyne lost 1,000 of his best troops, and his Indian allies were becoming increasingly disaffected with the campaign and began to abandon the English cause.

Washington was also taking note of the important events to the north and began to send additional supplies and troops to aid General Horatio Gates, who was newly appointed to command the American Northern Army. The additions included General Benjamin Lincoln and, more importantly, General Benedict Arnold, possibly the most creative and courageous field commanders of the American war for independence. Washington also sent Colonel

Daniel Morgan and his riflemen. "Morgan's Riflemen Corps" was made up of five hundred skilled woodsmen from Virginia, Pennsylvania, and Maryland and were selected for the unit due to their expert marksmanship. Their weapon of choice was the Kentucky Long Rifle (a rifle is a gun with a barrel of internal spiraled grooves that greatly increase the accuracy of the weapon at longer ranges). The rifle had a 40-inch barrel and was accurate in the hands of a skilled shooter to a range of 250 yards. The spinning .40 to .62 caliber ball from their rifles far exceeded the range of smooth-bore musket fire. The smooth-bore musket had an expected accuracy to only 50 yards. The musket was the weapon of choice during the eighteenth century because it could be loaded more quickly and increased the volume of fire that could be achieved in fixed lines of battle. In the fixed line, the entire line would fire at once in close proximity to the enemy. It was a conventional tactic that sent a volume of lead in the enemy's direction, thus nullifying the advantage of a single rifle's accuracy. Morgan had a different idea about how to use his riflemen on the eighteenth-century battlefield. His men used their rifles to devasting effect on British troops, particularly the officers, in the coming engagements. The American sharpshooters with their rifles earned the title of "widowmakers."

In mid-September and after the losses at Bennington, Burgoyne crossed over the Hudson and continued to move his army toward Albany. He also sent messages to New York imploring assistance from Howe. By that time, Howe's main army was engaged with Washington's army around Philadelphia and out of position to provide any consequential assistance to Burgoyne. British General Henry Clinton, who was Howe's second-in-command and in charge of the remnant garrison still in New York, attempted to draw American forces away from Burgoyne. Later in the campaign, Clinton attempted to support Burgoyne by advancing up the Hudson River to the Highlands with a force of 4,000 redcoats. The British then took two small American forts, Fort Clinton and Fort Montgomery along the river. It was too little and too late to help Burgoyne.

Gentleman Johnny was on his own, though he still held out hope he would get support from New York. As his army moved south, it approached Freeman's Farm in what is now Schuylerville, New York. On September 19th the Battle of Saratoga began. Since the earliest stages of the conflict, the Americans employed the unconventional tactic of targeting enemy officers on the battlefield. As the battle at Freeman's Farm started, Morgan's Riflemen were the perfect instrument to implement that deadly strategy against the advancing British. The main portion of the American defense was entrenched on high ground at Bemis Heights. Horatio Gates' main body of Americans on Bemis Heights blocked any further movement south by Burgoyne's army. Additionally, the Americans had more than 12,000 men deployed for the battle and outnumbered

Burgoyne's army nearly two to one. The American forces continued to grow over the next several weeks as the battle played out.

At Freeman's Farm, Burgoyne divided his command into three probing columns. On the British right was General Simon Frasier commanding 2,000 British Light Infantry supported by Colonel Breymann and his Hessians. The force was, in traditional British fashion, to conduct a flanking move around the American left. The Americans under Arnold on the American left anticipated the move and placed a large force in the path to block British movement. In the center was British General James Hamilton with the largest contingent of British soldiers, including several regiments of foot, advancing directly into Morgan's Riflemen. On the right was General Friedrich von Riedesel's Hessians advancing along the river road with the Hudson on their left.

Morgan's Riflemen perched themselves in trees and other concealed positions in a wooded area in front of the British center column. A fierce exchange ensued between Morgan's men and the British regiments. The fighting went back and forth for hours with both sides giving way. Gates reinforced Morgan's men with several additional regiments from Bemis Heights as the battle progressed. Morgan's men and the other American forces inflicted heavy casualties on the British with particular lethal consequences on the officers. Some on the British units on the field lost almost all their officers. The loss of so many British officers caused disruptions in the command structure and had an adverse effect on unit cohesion.

As the afternoon of the 19th wore on, the American units fighting on the American left under Arnold prevented Frasier's column from flanking the position on Bemis Heights and taking the high ground. Morgan's men and the American units fighting in the center against Hamilton's main force began to fall back as the full weight of the main British force applied pressure. The American center received fire from both flanks. Frasier's column engaged the Americans from the left, and Riedesel's Hessians, whose column was protecting the river road, brought several cannons into play from the right. The Americans were forced to withdraw back toward Bemis Heights. The British suffered more the 600 killed and wounded. The American losses were half that. Those were losses Burgoyne could not afford.

Burgoyne, still hopeful he would receive support from New York, waited for the next eighteen days before taking any additional action against the Americans who blocked his path forward toward Albany. British General Simon Frasier and General Friedrich von Riedesel, who was in command of all German troops during the campaign, advised Burgoyne to withdraw his army back toward Canada. Burgoyne felt it would be a disgrace to go back, and he disregarded his two subordinates' counsel. During the lull in major action, both sides skirmished in the woods, and the Americans continuously harassed the British. They also cut off their line of communications to the north and Ticonderoga and were able to intercept messages Burgoyne was sending to New York. Those intercepted messages made Gates aware of the desperate shape that Burgoyne and his army were in. As September gave way to October, it became clear that reinforcements were not coming from Clinton in New York. Burgoyne knew that time was not on his side and that the Americans would grow stronger for as long as he continued to delay.

Gates' Northern American Army that was blocking Burgoyne was well entrenched on Bemis Heights, an advantageous position overlooking the Hudson River and the surrounding area. The earthen fortifications on Bemis Heights were designed by another recent immigrant and convert to the American cause, Polish-born military engineer Thaddaeus Kosciusko. He and the other American officers present inside the fortifications on Bemis Heights witnessed a major break in the relationship between two senior officers in the American camp — Gates and Arnold. Gates relieved Arnold of his command because of differences in strategy and reports of the circumstance of the opening battle. Gates approved orders for Arnold to return to Washington's main army. Arnold refused to leave the battle area and feuded around the camp during the interlude between the main battles.

On October 7, Burgoyne and his army were in a desperate situation. He decided his best option was to launch an attack against the American position around Bemis Heights. The British launched a reconnaissance force against the American left to find a weakness they could exploit, but the Americans were wise to the move and had forces, including Morgan's Riflemen, in position. The British had also built two redoubts — the Breymann Redoubt on their right and the Balcarres Redoubt on the center left. Those were strong points in the British line that could stop an American counterattack. As fighting became intense on the American left, Benedict Arnold arrived on the scene. He was moving on his own prerogative, as he had been removed from command by Gates. In dramatic fashion, Arnold took command of the battle for the Americans. He demonstrated great leadership and personal courage while willing his men on and exuding confidence and a clear sense of the needs of the battle space. The British began to fall back as the American marksmanship and numerical superiority began to take effect.

Gates ordered units not to obey Arnolds' commands and sent a rider out to recall Arnold. Before the day's fighting was over, Arnold defied Gates and directed other American units into the action. The men on the battlefield looked up to Arnold and recognized him as a dynamic and resourceful field commander. Arnold rode through the lines that separated the Americans and the British and directed the Americans forward. The Americans rallied and pushed the British back and took the Breymann Redoubt, exposing the entire British position. Hessian Colonel Breymann was killed in the engagement, and one of Morgan's Riflemen fired a round into British General Simon Frasier who was removed from the field and died the next day from his wound. The loss of Frasier had consequential effects on British morale as the battle was turning clearly in the Americans' favor. Arnold was also hit. He took a musket ball to his leg. The musket ball also killed his horse, which then crushed his leg, the same leg he had wounded in the Battle of Montreal earlier in the war. As the day and the battle came to an end, Burgoyne and his battered army were forced to withdraw back north to their previous encampment, thus ending all hopes of continuing their original movement south. Burgoyne left his wounded and much of his equipment on the deserted battlefield as his army fell back.

The Americans under Gates, with vital help from Arnold, Morgan's Riflemen, and local militias, had achieved a clear and decisive victory over Burgoyne and his army. Over the next week, the British withdrew back toward the town of Saratoga. Gates' Northern American Army continued to grow to 15,000 and eventually encircled Burgoyne as New Hampshire militiamen arrived and blocked any further movement north. In the two battles, Burgoyne suffered more the 450 men killed and nearly 700 wounded. The Americans suffered less than 100 killed.

Burgoyne was surrounded and outnumbered three to one. He called a council of war with his officers, all of whom agreed to seek terms of surrender. The British began negotiations with Gates, and on October 16th, 1777, the remainder of General John Burgoyne's army surrendered to Gates' Northern American Army ending the British campaign and any hopes of dividing New England from the rest of the colonies. It was the most consequential event of the war to that point. In the long and illustrious history of the British Army and its exploits in combat across Europe and the other continents, it was the first time a British Army surrendered to an enemy force. The event sent shockwaves around the world, particularly in London, Paris, and other capitals in Europe. The American cause for freedom and independence had gained credibility, and victory at Saratoga was the justification French King Louis XVI needed to commit to supporting the Americans.

The American force at Saratoga was made mostly of militiamen. Those nontraditional men-in-arms demonstrated what a well-armed and motivated militia, "citizen soldiers," can accomplish when freedom and liberty are at stake. In the early days of the American struggle for independence and up to and including today, the citizen soldier stood and continues to stand as the vanguard of an ordered and civil society and the defender of the immutable rights of the individual.

Prior to the final engagement at Saratoga and the defeat of Burgoyne's army, Washington's main army attacked the British at Germantown outside Philadelphia on October 4th. Howe had divided his army, having part of it in Philadelphia and another in Germantown outside the city. Washington and his staff devised a very detailed attack against a smaller British force, but the plan was overly complicated and did not go off as intended. The British were able to fight off the disorganized American advance as some American units in the disarray on the battlefield fired on their own troops. Howe and the British were able to claim victory as the Americans suffered many casualties and withdrew. The loss was not as devastating to the Americans as it could have been. If not for ill timing and inexperience they very well could have carried the day. The Americans and Washington still had lessons to learn about military discipline tactics and strategy to more effectively bring the fight to the British. Some of those lessons would be worked out over the winter of 1777 and 1778 at Valley Forge under the direction of another foreigner, Baron Friedrich Wilhelm von Steuben.

A group of disgruntled senior American officers at the time wished to have Washington replaced as Commander-in-Chief of the American Army. The plot was known as "The Conway Cabal." Brigadier General Thomas Conway wrote letters criticizing Washington's leadership and the direction the war was going. The suggestion was that Washington be replaced by Horatio Gates, the victorious commanding general at Saratoga, who was part of the letter-writing interaction with Conway. Some in Congress, including Samuel Adams and Richard Henry Lee, had also lost faith in Washington, though they were in the minority. Some of the letters were forwarded to the Continental Congress, and the issue was made public. Washington's supporters, including Generals Nathanael Greene, Lafayette, and Lord Stirling (William Alexander) who informed Washington of the initial conspiracy against him, sprang to his defense. Washington was supported also by other important officers, including Alexander Hamilton and John Lawrence. The campaign against Washington never gained traction and came to an end in early 1778 as Conway offered his resignation from the army and Gates offered an apology to Washington.

The winter of 1777-1778 was a particularly cold and challenging ordeal for Washington and his army at Valley Forge. The army spent six months in the encampment, and supplies of all goods, including food and warm clothing, became increasingly scarce. Congress, then in exile in York, Pennsylvania, failed to support the army with sufficient materials and left it to its own devices. Once again, sickness, including influenza, typhus, dysentery, and malnutrition, along with exposure afflicted Washington's army. More of the army died from disease than from combat against the British. For Washington's army, surviving Valley Forge that winter was as arduous as any of the battles the Americans fought during the course of the war. Things for the army began to improve in the spring of 1778 as warmer weather arrived. New recruits joined the American camp, and the ranks of the army received instruction in the finer art of military regimentation and discipline from Baron Friedrich Wilhelm von Steuben. Von Steuben was born in 1730 in Magdeburg, which is now Germany. He was a former officer in the Prussian Army and served under Frederick the Great. As a Prussian officer, he fought in the War of 1744 (siege of Prague) and the Seven Years' War. He was a devotee of classical military science as devised and implemented in the eighteenth century. He brought order and discipline and improved morale

among the American ranks. Washington came to trust von Steuben
and made him a Major General as well as Inspector General of the
army.

Other profound events were happening that winter of 1778
as Washington's army struggled through the cold and snow at
Valley Forge. The American cause was reinvigorated when, after
more than two years of diplomatic maneuvers by Benjamin Franklin
with support from Arthur Lee and Silas Deane, France was won
over. The American victory at Saratoga coupled with Franklin's
persuasion finally convinced King Louis XVI and the French
government to commit to the Americans. On February 6th, 1778,
France and America signed the Treaty of Amity and Commerce and
the Treaty of Alliance in Paris. The treaties recognized the United
States as an independent nation and opened up new and important
channels of financial and material support to the American war
effort.

In March, France declared war on Britain – "the Bourbon
War" – and ended the 15-year period of peace between the two
European powers. Starting in June, the French and British Navies
fought battles in the English Channel, the Mediterranean, the
Caribbean, and Asia. As renewed hostility commenced, England
was forced to defend the expanse of the British Empire that it had
won at the end of the Seven Years' War in 1763. The British could
no longer exclusively focus their resources and military forces
against the rebellion in North America. France and her allies were

once again challenging British supremacy on the high seas and across the globe.

As events were unfolding in Europe, all was not well in the British camp that spring. British General Howe and his army had won two victories over the Americans in the fall of 1777 at Brandywine and Germantown. Additionally, they were able to take Philadelphia unopposed, and Congress was forced to flee to York. However, the main objective of the British Army was the capitulation of Washington's army and the end of the rebellion. To that end, Howe and his army were unsuccessful, and with the defeat of Burgoyne's army at Saratoga the American cause for independence had been greatly advanced. Howe received considerable blame for Burgoyne's fate, and Parliament, British newspapers, and ministerial officials in London under Prime Minister Lord North cast dubious eyes on Howe's strategy. As the pressure mounted, Howe resigned his post as Commander-in-Chief of British land forces in America and left for England on May 24, 1778. Sir Henry Clinton, Howe's number two, assumed the role of British Commander for the rest of the war.

In June of 1778, Washington's army left its encampment and training ground at Valley Forge. The army was different: the 14,000 soldiers who left their winter encampment were a more disciplined group of soldiers. In previous campaigns, the American Army was not much more than a disorganized gathering of local militias with a somewhat common purpose. After the long encampment and training at Valley Forge, the Continental Army resembled a more cohesive and disciplined military force with a mission. Baron von Steuben had brought regimentation to the ranks. Von Steuben developed a manual titled *Regulations for the Order and Discipline of the Troops of the United States.* It became the blueprint that the army used to train soldiers in the skills required to make an effective fighting force. The army soon tested its new skills against its adversary in the fields around a courthouse in the New Jersey town of Monmouth.

In the same month, Britain's new commander, Lt. General Sir Henry Clinton, was ordered to abandon Philadelphia and return the main body of the British/Hessian forces to New York. The orders were due to concerns over the French fleet potentially blocking British movement by sea. The British were adopting a more defensive strategy in light of France's entry into the conflict. A defensive posture was somewhat more consistent with the military philosophy of their new commander, Henry Clinton. It also shed light on the futility and strategic failure of Britain's previous year's campaign. Burgoyne's effort to separate New England from the rest of the colonies ended in a humiliating defeat. In one respect, the Americans were swallowing up the British and forcing them to exert great efforts in futile attempts to end the war. It may not have been obvious at the time, and hardships still lay ahead, but Washington and the Americans were winning.

On June 18th, General Henry Clinton evacuated approximately 17,000 British and Hessian troops from Philadelphia. Once again, the British Army marched across northern New Jersey on its way back to New York, and once again it was harassed by local New Jersey militias en route. The movement by the British presented an opportunity for Washington; the long British supply train had more than 1,500 wagons as well as military supplies including heavy articles like cannons. The caravan also included a large contingent of Philadelphia loyalists and dependents. Clinton's destination was Sandy Hook on the New Jersey coast where he and his army would embark on ships for the rest of the journey to New York City. The caravan had traveled two thirds of the way from Philadelphia when it arrived near the town of Monmouth on June 28th. It was a sweltering hot summer day as the dawn broke, and the temperature rose to near 100 degrees Fahrenheit.

A young American soldier, Joseph Plum Martin, was in nearly every campaign for the Americans since his enlistment in the Connecticut Militia in 1775 at the age of fifteen. He later joined the Continental Army in 1777 and served until June of 1783. He authored *A Narrative of Some of the Adventures, Dangers and Sufferings of a Revolutionary Soldier*, a diary of his personal experiences while serving. In it, he described the sweltering heat as his unit approached the Battle of Monmouth on June 28. "... the sun shining full upon the field...the mouth of a heated oven seemed to me to be but a trifle hotter than this ploughed field; it was almost impossible to breathe."[5]

In the build up to the American action against the British Army's movement across New Jersey, Washington's supporting generals, including his second-in-command, Major General Charles Lee, voiced objections to an attack against the British column. Charles Lee had come to Virginia in 1773 and served as a Lt. Colonel in the British Army during the Seven Years' War. He also volunteered as a senior officer in the Polish Army under King Stanislaus II Augustus. Lee was ambitious and coveted Washington's position as Commander-in-Chief, believing he was the superior and more experienced officer. Lee and others thought Washington should wait for the French to arrive before conducting any major assault against the main body of the British Army. Washington had waited long enough and wanted to test his new army after the training it had received at Valley Forge under von Steuben. He decided on a half measure of attack against the rear elements of the British column. He preferred Lafayette's division to lead the attack on the rear of the British column, but military protocol and rank considerations dictated that the attack should be led by Charles Lee, to which Washington acquiesced. Assigning command to a general who was against the plan of attack proved to be a mistake.

As Washington's army followed the British withdrawal across northern New Jersey, Lee was in command of approximately one third of the American force out in front. The plan was to launch an attack on the morning of June 28th against an exposed British rear guard of approximately 1,500 redcoats at the Monmouth Court House. The information the Americans gathered about the size of the British force in front of them was faulty. A much larger British force of approximately 9,000 under Cornwallis was closer than the Americans realized as Lee's units began the engagement.

As more British regiments entered the battle, the Americans required a readjustment of strategy and commitment. British resistance stiffened, and American units began to fall back. Lee, instead of rallying his command into action and a determined initiative, ordered a retreat from the battle. As the morning progressed, Cornwallis' division was joined by other British regiments under the command of Clinton, and they continued to take control of the field. Some of the American units had a greater awareness of their soldierly duties than General Lee did, and they stood fast and resisted the British advance, allowing Washington and the rest of the American Army to arrive on the scene. Washington was outraged as he witnessed American soldiers under Lee's command retreating in the face of the enemy. Washington and Lee had a heated exchange, and Washington relieved Lee and took personal command of the action as more American soldiers arrived to reverse the tide of the early stage of the battle.

Washington immediately assessed the situation and ordered the retreating units from Lee's command to form a defensive line along a hedge row and an adjoining wooded area. As more American units arrived under Generals Nathanael Greene and William Alexander (Lord Stirling), the line held and reversed the negative momentum orchestrated by General Lee's ill-conceived plan. Washington's battlefield command instincts had taken control at the right moment for the Americans. He rode through the ranks conveying support and encouragement for his men to stand fast as the day wore on. Nathanael Greene noted of Washington's actions: "The Commander-in-Chief was everywhere, his presence gives spirit and confidence and his command soon brought everything into order and regularity."[6]

Washington was up against Cornwallis once again, and Clinton ordered more cannons to be brought into the battle. The newly forming British line of advance was nearly one mile long. It was a closely held formation that had worked time and time again against the Americans, making militias flee from the field once the British bayonet became the decisive weapon of the battle. In this new battle, the results would be no different, or so the British thought. As the rest of Washington's army came up, he placed Greene's division on the right of the American line. Additionally, Greene was able to install cannons on high ground, which put the British line in a cannonade crossfire. Stirling's unit was placed on the American left, and General Anthony Wayne was in the center while Lafayette took command of Lee's remaining men. It was the first time in the war that the Americans successfully stood man to man and held their ground against British regulars in a conventional line engagement. As the day wore on, a three-hour artillery slugfest evolved between American and British field pieces. The Americans were in a more advantageous tactical position thanks to Greene's initiative, and after more than twelve hours of hard fighting in the hot summer sun, Clinton realized that the American position was too strong. He ordered a withdrawal and ceded the field and the victory to the Americans. Washington launched two additional attacks against the retreating British as well as probing movements at the British flanks, but those efforts were halted as darkness approached. Both sides camped the night of the 28th in close proximity to each other. Washington was prepared to take up the battle the next day, but Clinton slipped away in the early morning hours of the 29th, and the British continued their way toward Sandy Hook and the evacuation to New York. Washington did not pursue Clinton, partially because the ground between Monmouth and Sandy Hook would mostly likely favor the British, and partially because the area around Sandy Hook was believed to be occupied by a strong contingent of loyalists who could provide support to Clinton as his army moved through the area.

The Americans held their ground at the Battle of Monmouth and were on the offensive as the day's action came to a close. It is estimated that the British suffered approximately 1,100 killed, wounded, or missing while the American casualties were in the range of 500. The idea of forcing the Americans into that elusive and conclusive battle must have vanished from the minds of Clinton and Cornwallis from that point forward. It was no longer the "old fox" that was slipping away in the dead of night.

Washington's Military Family

Washington was supported by several dynamic and courageous young officers who looked up to him and who admired his personal attributes as a general and a leader. Some of them served as Washington's aides-de-camp. The most notable was a young immigrant from the West Indies — Alexander Hamilton. He was born on the island of Nevis, most likely in 1757. His parents were not married. In 1766, his father, a Scottish trader named James Hamilton, abandoned his mother, Rachel Faucette Lavien, who was married to another man. Hamilton's mother died in 1768, leaving him an orphan at a young age. The young Hamilton worked as a clerk on the island of St. Croix where his intelligence was noticed. As his talents became obvious, he gained the support of wealthy merchants who, in 1772, sent him to America to attend King's College in New York City (now Columbia University). From the onset, Hamilton was recognized for his brilliant mind and organizational skills. He put those skills to use when he joined the New York Militia as an artillery officer in 1775. He later joined the Continental Army and participated in many of the early battles, including Harlem Heights, White Plains, Trenton, Princeton, the Philadelphia campaign, and Monmouth. Washington recognized the exceptional talents of his young officer and requisitioned him to his staff as a senior aide-de-camp on March 1, 1777, assigning him the rank of Lt. Colonel.

As the war progressed, Hamilton became indispensable to Washington. He attended meetings for the Commander and drafted letters and notices. It was almost as if Hamilton was Washington's alter ego with a sixth sense of anticipating what Washington wanted to say in his letters and correspondences. Of major importance was Hamilton's role in constructing cogent arguments in letters to Congress and others throughout the states. Those letters argued the case for increases in supplies and support for the army as the soldiers struggled through the harshest of times and circumstances. Hamilton provided a vital role for American independence, and he held his post in support of Washington for four years until the spring of 1781. Like his friends the Marquis de Lafayette and John Laurens, Hamilton wanted to be in the center of the action on the field of battle. He finally got his wish as the final stages of America's war for independence played out.

The Marquis de Lafayette was a close friend of Hamilton, and an unlikely one due to the very different circumstances of their births. Lafayette was born into French nobility in 1757 to a family with a rich military history that went back to the Middle Ages and Joan of Arc. From the beginning of the American experience, having a meritorious skill set always trumped a highbrow dilettante pedigree. That was true of the relationship between Hamilton and

Lafayette. What mattered was not their nobility or lack thereof, but their integrity, courage, and contributions to the cause of freedom, liberty, and American independence. Intellectually, Hamilton was superior to all the young officers who surrounded Washington's inner circle or, as Washington called it, his "military family." Lafayette was a superior and instinctive military field tactician, which he demonstrated during his first engagement at Brandywine when he rallied the retreating American soldiers, even after being wounded. He became a valued friend of Washington and a trusted officer and field commander despite his youth and relative inexperience. Lafayette served Washington throughout the war and returned home only to use his connections to advance the American cause.

As the Philadelphia campaign came to an end in the summer of 1778, the main British Army under Clinton left New Jersey and settled into a protracted occupation of New York City. Washington agreed to Lafayette's request to go back to France in February of 1779. Lafayette's mission was to strengthen ties between America and the French king, and his efforts were successful. He received commitments from the French to send an army under General Rochambeau and assistance from the French fleet to America. That support proved vital as the last phase of the war moved to the southern states.

As Lafayette worked his connections with Franklin and the other American diplomats, the French nobility and public alike were fervently embracing the cause of their new friends across the ocean. There were many reasons why France supported American independence. The first and most obvious was that it was an opportunity to turn the tables on its principal rival — Great Britain. France's loss in the Seven Years' War still invoked a bitter response and blow to French national pride. That was in addition to France's loss of Canada and other holdings. Additionally, the French widely viewed America as the embodiment of Enlightenment philosophy in practice. French intellectuals like Voltaire and Montesquieu and others played an important part in conceptualizing man's relationship with God, natural rights, and our place in the universe. America was going to revive and implement the ideas of republicanism and representative government. French writings and newspapers idolized Americans as robust individuals who were standing up for themselves (the citizen farmer) and the rights of man in the formation of a new society.

John Laurens was another one of Washington's aides-de-camp and a close friend of Hamilton and Lafayette. Born in 1754, his upbringing, like Lafayette's, could not have been more different than Hamilton's. Laurens was born into wealth and privilege in South Carolina. His father, Henry Laurens, was a planter, politician, and slave merchant, and he was one of the wealthiest men in the colonies. Back when the Revolutionary War was just looming on the horizon, Laurens' father sent him to be educated in Europe in an effort to shield him from the conflict. When the war started, Laurens petitioned his farther to let him return home and join in the struggle for American independence. In a letter to his father, Laurens wrote, "Let us not look with fond regret upon what we were, or what we expected to have been, but act with courage the most laudable part that can be taken in present circumstances…We can die but once, and when more gloriously then in defence of our Liberties?"[7] Laurens returned home in December of 1776 and later joined with Hamilton on Washington's staff. Laurens was brave and was even considered reckless. At Brandywine, his first battle, he took a musket ball to his foot, and later that year at Germantown he was wounded in his shoulder. A close bond developed between Laurens, Hamilton, and Lafayette as the young men aided Washington and shared in the trials and dangers of the conflict.

In December of 1778, Lee, still unable to recover from the insult of being relieved of command at the Battle of Monmouth, slandered Washington. Laurens took offense to the calumnies against his commander and challenged Lee to a duel, in which Laurens wounded Lee in his side. After the first two shots were fired, the duel was halted by none other than Alexander Hamilton, who was Laurens' second and Lee's second. Lafayette had noted about Laurens and his conduct in action, "it was not his fault that he was not killed or wounded, he did everything that was necessary to procure one or t'other."[8]

Laurens was an early abolitionist in his home state. On several occasions he tried to convince his fellow South Carolinians to allow slaves to take up arms and join the ranks of the Continental Army. He was able to get conditional approval from Congress, but his efforts were unsuccessful as many South Carolinians felt more threatened by armed slaves than they did by the British. Laurens was ahead of his time, at least as a young man of wealth and privilege from the South was concerned. He had an enlightened view on the status of Blacks and their sharing in the fruits of freedom and liberty. Henry Laurens supported his son's efforts for partial emancipation of Black slaves and their entrance into the army, a surprising position for a one-time slave merchant. It appears that even the elder Laurens was reconsidering the slavery issue, but that's in consideration of the fact that he never freed his personal slaves during his lifetime.

Henry Laurens also served his country during the war period. He became a delegate to the Second Continental Congress and succeeded John Hancock as the president of the Congress. Later, he became minister to the Netherlands. Unfortunately, he was captured by the British at sea and imprisoned in the Tower of London in October of 1780. He suffered ill health during his imprisonment, and after nearly two years he was released in a prisoner exchange. John Laurens also entered into diplomatic service, though briefly and with apparent influence from his father. He was appointed as a special emissary to France, a post he thought was better suited for Hamilton, but in the end he accepted the position. Laurens sailed to France with Thomas Paine in February 1781. Benjamin Franklin introduced Laurens to various French officials and King Louis XVI, and the American delegation was able to secure a promise of French naval support and additional money and supplies for the American cause. How much Laurens actually contributed to those efforts is somewhat in question. It became apparent that diplomatic service was not for him. In that same year, he returned to America and the army in time for the final major campaign of the Continental Army.

Washington's Spies and the Culper Ring

Washington, from the early days of the war, valued intelligence about British movements, troop strengths, supplies, and intentions. Prior to him taking command of the army, spies in Boston tipped off Samuel Adams and the Sons of Liberty that the British were about to march on Lexington and Concord and later assault Bunker and Breed's Hills. As the New York campaign developed in the summer and fall of 1776, the British captured and occupied New York City. As those events unfolded, the need for accurate intelligence became critical for Washington and his army. Washington's first Spy Master was Nathaniel Sackett, a civilian from Duchess County, north of the city. Sackett was good at organizing and worked with William Duer, a Continental Congressman, who was helping Washington set up a spy ring in the city. Despite Sackett's ability as a good organizer, his spies yielded little valuable information, and Washington replaced him with Major Benjamin Tallmadge. Tallmadge, then the Director of

Military Intelligence for the Continental Army, built on Sackett's work and recruited others to the spy mission. As the British captured New York City in the fall of 1776, Washington, in a somewhat capricious move, looked for a volunteer to take on a dangerous mission to spy on the British inside the city. Nathan Hale, a young teacher and Yale graduate and friend of Tallmadge, stepped forward and volunteered for the dangerous mission.

As Hale was deciding on which direction to take as the revolutionary struggle began, he was teaching in New London, Connecticut. He joined the state's militia and within a short time became a 2nd Lieutenant. He was motivated to join the cause at the coaxing of a letter written to him by Tallmadge: "Was I in your condition, I think the more extensive service would be my choice. Our holy religion, the honor of our God, a glorious country, & a happy constitution is what we have to defend."[9] Hale was sold and later in the spring of 1776 became part of Thomas Knowlton's Rangers, America's first intelligence-gathering unit. Volunteering for the spy mission in New York City might have been somewhat impetuous on Hale's part, but there was some logic to his decision about getting involved with Thomas Knowlton and the Rangers, if only on the surface.

Hale's plan as a spy was to pretend to be a Dutch teacher looking for work as he moved about the city on his intelligence-gathering efforts. Hale traveled across Long Island Sound to the town of Huntington on September 12th, 1776, to begin his mission, but his deception didn't last long before he was discovered. He was recognized by Robert Rogers of the Queen's Rangers and pretended to be a fellow patriot, but he naively revealed his loyalties. Evidence was found on him, and he was implicated as a spy. There is also a conflicting story that Hale was revealed to the British by a relative. On the morning of September 22nd, just ten days after arriving on Long Island, Hale was hanged as a spy in Manhattan near current day 66th Street and Third Avenue. Hale was reported to have taken his fate with great dignity and courage. A British officer, Frederick Mackenzie, a witness to the hanging, wrote in his diary that Hale "behaved with great composure and resolution."[10] Hale is also reported to have said, "I only regret that I have but one life to lose for my country,"[11] a quote that was also reported by another British officer who was present, John Montresor.[12] Washington lamented that he had sent young Nathan Hale, a young man who was ill prepared for his mission, into a dangerous situation. The death of Hale convinced Washington that he needed to rely more on civilian patriots for the spy mission. They could more effectively blend into the background and not raise suspicions from the British as they went about their work. Later in the war, Washington would remember the British military's judgement and fate of Nathan Hale when he was deciding the fate of a young British officer under similar circumstances.

Benjamin Tallmadge grew up on Long Island in the town of Setauket, and his family later moved to Connecticut. Tallmadge's father, Rev. Benjamin Tallmadge, had prepared his young son well in traditional classical studies, and Benjamin entered Yale College in 1769 at the age of fifteen. After the Battles of Lexington and Concord, Tallmadge was offered a position as a Lieutenant in the Connecticut Regiment of the Continental Army, which he accepted. He first saw action at the Battle of Long Island in September of 1776. His older brother also served at the battle and was taken prisoner and died in British captivity. Tallmadge served with distinction throughout the war in both the Second Continental Dragoons and as Washington's Director of Military Intelligence. Tallmadge maintained connections with several childhood friends with whom he grew up in New York and on Long Island. They were people he believed he could trust. One of those friends was a farmer from Setauket, Abraham Woodhull.

Tallmadge and Woodhull, along with a New York City innkeeper named Robert Townsend, became the centerpieces of the most effective spying operation of the war. The Culper Spy Ring organized in 1778 and continued until the end of the war in 1783. Washington named the spy organization after a county that was near his home in Virginia: Culpeper County. The Culper Spy Ring also included Caleb Brewster, an experienced boatman who ferried messages across Long Island Sound by whaleboat from predetermined covers to Fairfield, Connecticut. The strategy was to avoid capture by British and loyalist frigates and gunboats that were trying to intercept the clandestine crossings. Brewster would know from which cove to receive the messages based on instructions from Anna Smith Strong, a neighbor of Woodhull. Anna would organize the wash on her clothesline in plain sight in discrete arrangements that indicated the location of the materials Brewster was to transport. Once the messages arrived to Tallmadge in Connecticut, he would add additional intelligence about British shipping activities in the city and send a report to Washington.

Woodhull went by the code name Samuel Culper Sr., and Tallmadge went by John Bolton. Tallmadge also developed a sophisticated numerical code book of several hundred numbers denoting names and places. The Culper Code Book was constructed to protect the integrity of the spies and the messages they passed on to Washington and the army. Washington's number was 711, but not every member of the ring has been identified by history. That includes Agent 355 who was a mysterious woman associated with Robert Townsend. It is thought that she played an important role in uncovering some of the most sensitive information gathered by the Culper Spy Ring during operations. That might have included the plot of turning over West Point to the British and the defection of Benedict Arnold. The Culper Spy Ring also used invisible ink to write messages between the lines of ordinary correspondences. The recipient would apply a reagent, and the message would be revealed.

Alexander Hamilton also assisted with the New York spying mission. Upon Hamilton's arrival in New York City in 1772, he was taken in by an Irish immigrant, resident Hercules Mulligan.

Hamilton and Mulligan developed a close relationship, and Hamilton recruited Mulligan into the clandestine spying mission as the British occupied New York after the Battle of Long Island. Mulligan was connected with other members of the Culper Spy Ring and worked with them as circumstances dictated, but for apparent security reasons he acted on his own initiatives as he went about his mission.

Woodhull was always in fear of being discovered. When he was eventually suspected by the British, a raiding party of Queen's Rangers under British Lt. Colonel John Simcoe was organized. The raiding party arrived at Woodhull's house in Setauket to arrest him. Fortunately for Woodhull, he was away in New York City, but the British severely beat his father. In 1779, Woodhull, to lessen his exposure and facilitate the intelligence-gathering effort, recruited another member to the spy ring. The addition was Robert Townsend, an established New York City merchant who went by the code name of Samuel Culper Jr. He became a vital link of important information about British activities, supplies, troop strength, and future intentions. Along with being a trusted merchant to the British, Townsend also wrote articles for a loyalist paper, *Rivington's Gazette,* to further enhance his cover. Townsend might have been aided in his intelligence-gathering activities by the publisher, James Rivington, who was likely also a member of the Culper Spy Ring. Once Townsend had important information for Washington, another member of the spy ring, Austin Roe, would transport the message out of Manhattan past British sentries to Setauket (a journey of approximately fifty miles). Roe ran a tavern in Setauket, which gave him cover and a reason to periodically travel to Manhattan for supplies.

Intelligence information is only valuable if it is received in time for the recipient to act on it. That was Washington's and Tallmadge's predicament. The Culper Spy Ring was very effective at gathering information that was valuable to the cause, but the path of the package was complicated. First the information was gathered in Manhattan by Townsend and associates. Next it was passed to Roe to be couriered to Setauket and hidden in a secret location. Subsequently the package was picked up by Brewster and transported across Long Island Sound to Tallmadge in Connecticut. Then an express rider was dispatched to Washington at his headquarters in the Lower Hudson Valley of New York. Tallmadge was always trying to speed up the process.

In 1780, three important pieces of intelligence were uncovered by the Culper Spy Ring. First, the British were attempting to destroy the value of American currency by a counterfeit effort. Measures were put in place to mitigate the effects of that effort. Second, traitor Benedict Arnold was plotting with British Spy Master Major John Andre to surrender West Point to the British. Andre was captured and, like Nathan Hale, was hanged as a spy. Arnold was able to escape. Third and possibly most important of all, the Culper Spy Ring discovered that the British Army under Clinton was going to march from New York to Rhode Island and attack the newly arriving French Army before it had an opportunity to construct defensives and establish itself. Washington, acting on the information, orchestrated a feint against New York City, compelling Henry Clinton and the British to stay in place and abandon their plan of attacking the French.

The War Moves to the South

In the early days of the Revolutionary War, in 1775 and 1776, patriot militias in South Carolina and Georgia resisted loyalists' and British soldiers' attempts to subdue and control the region and were successful in driving Georgia's Royal Governor from Savannah. In December of 1775, the Battle of Great Bridge was fought in Virginia at the Chesapeake where the Continental Army defeated a British contingent and ended British control of the state. South Carolina's low country along the coast was a patriot stronghold where the patriots defeated a British force under Henry Clinton at the Battle of Sullivan's Island in June of 1776. The engagement was an attempt by Clinton to take the deep-water port of Charleston, but the Carolina patriots forced the British to withdraw and return by sea to New York. For the next two years, the war played out in the northern colonies where Washington's army sparred first with William Howe and then with Henry Clinton and Charles Cornwallis.

As the war in the North entered a period of stalemate, Washington and his army stood guard in nearby White Plains as the British were entrenched in New York City. In December of 1778, the British, in a renewed and dedicated commitment, started a campaign in the South by attacking and capturing Savannah, Georgia, from the sea. The British strategy was to build on the loyalist element they believed existed in the South. They also hoped to raise passions among the slaves and have them join the ranks on the British side. The British hoped to cultivate dissent among Blacks and dangled the carrot of better treatment and freedom under British rule. To that end, the British did have some success in recruiting Blacks into their ranks, but Blacks also fought alongside their fellow Americans, complementing the forces of Francis Marion. The term "Tories" is a term from Parliament and refers to those loyal to the king and the monarchy. The "Whigs" were those of a liberal persuasion, and they opposed absolutism and the king's unchallenged authority. More often than not, the phrase Tory is synonymous with loyalist, and, in the context of the American revolutionary struggle, Whigs are rebels and are also referred to as patriots.

The British believed that if they were not successful in subduing the northern colonies and were compelled to negotiate a separate peace with them, they could hold onto the four southern colonies of Virginia, North Carolina, South Carolina, and Georgia. The South was a rich agricultural region of valuable cash crops: rice, cotton, indigo, and tobacco, which were not grown in Britain and could not easily be acquired from other sources. The half measure of success made some sense from a British perspective in light of the British evacuation from Philadelphia, the Battle of Monmouth, and France's entry into the war. The British had not given up on winning back all the colonies, but they were looking for alternative solutions to the dilemma they found themselves in. The war effort was becoming an extraordinarily costly event in terms of soldiers and financial resources. Washington and the Americans were more resourceful and committed than the British had originally imagined. From the British perspective, securing the South still provided the riches of the region and allowed them to stay, at least in part, in the American colonies.

In an effort to counter the British attempt to capture Savannah in the South, a joint American and French force began an assault on the city in June of 1779. The American Army in the South was led by Major General Benjamin Lincoln and a French combined naval and land force under the command of the Count d'Estaing. The combined force attempted to remove the British from the port city. The siege of Savannah did not go well for the allies. The allies outnumbered the British, but the British prevailed, and the engagement was over by October 1779. The British held onto Savannah until July 1782.

During the siege of Savannah, Brigadier General Casimir Pulaski conducted a cavalry charge against a British position.

Pulaski was critically wounded by grapeshot and succumbed to his wounds on October 11, 1779. Pulaski's actions cemented his legacy as another immigrant hero of the American war for independence. It also memorialized his status as a champion of liberty and self-determination in his nation of birth, Poland. In a letter to Washington, he wrote about the American cause for freedom and his intention "to serve it and live or die for it."[13] Pulaski did live and die for the universal cause of human freedom and dignity, not just in the country of his birth but in his new home in America. Pulaski is an example of a brave crusader who exemplified the human spirit and the desire to live free of the dictates of elites and authoritarian rule.

The British undertaking in the South was a significant expenditure of personnel resources. It utilized approximately 25% (8,000-10,000 soldiers) of the total troops that were available to Clinton. The bulk of the British Army remained in New York City where it could maintain the ocean link to the mother country and be near the major population centers in the colonies. Clinton led the early campaign in the South after the British gained control of Savannah. Clinton's next move, for the second time in the war, was to orchestrate an assault on Charleston.

During the Revolutionary War period, Charleston was the fourth largest city in America and contained approximately 12,000 inhabitants. Along with New York, Boston, and Philadelphia, Charleston was among the most important ports in North America.

It was by all measures a suitable entry port for British military operations because it sustained their ocean links to New York and Britain. Once the British intentions to move against Charleston were clear, the Americans reinforced the city with additional Continentals and militias. In April of 1780, the British moved a major part of their force of redcoats under both Clinton and Cornwallis and began a siege of Charleston. Charleston's defense was once again under the command of Benjamin Lincoln who brought his force of Continentals south to confront the British. The British took Charleston by mid-May, forcing the surrender of 2,500 American defenders and seizing a large cache of badly needed American supplies comprised of more than three hundred cannons, six thousand muskets, and a large store of powder. The American defeat at Charleston was a stunning setback and one of the worst losses of the war for the Americans. After Charleston, Clinton returned to New York and gave command of the British southern campaign to General Lord Charles Cornwallis.

After Charleston fell to the British on May 12, 1780, and as part of a regional strategy, the British attempted to rally local loyalist support in the Carolinas, which inflamed animosity and violence between the loyalists and the patriots in the region. There were a considerable number of Tories in the South, especially in North Carolina, who were willing to join with the British in re-establishing control. Additionally, many newly arrived immigrants, including some Scotch-Irish, resented the treatment they had received from the local gentry class throughout the Carolinas. A minority of the Scotch-Irish immigrants set aside their traditional animist toward the British Crown and joined the struggle against the ruling class in the region. Hatred and vengeance rose to new levels of carnage as the two factions waged war against each other. A partisan war erupted in the South as the British and Cornwallis forced those on the fence to choose sides. Farms were pillaged and burned, and complete families were murdered. Many British officers were appalled by the level of violence their allies inflicted on the civilian population. Cornwallis' position was that the locals were either with the re-establishment of royal authority and control or they were against His Majesty's Armed Forces and would be treated as such.

The Scotch-Irish originally came from the lowlands of southern Scotland and had waged war against the English Crown for centuries. English King James I, in 1610, frustrated with the troublesome group, offered them land to settle in Northern Ireland's Ulster County. Tens of thousands left their ancestral homeland in Scotland and relocated in Northern Ireland. In Ireland, the Scots fought and intermingled with the Irish, and over generations they developed a unique culture and identity. Beginning around 1710 and running through the Revolutionary War period, upwards of 250,000 Scotch-Irish left Ireland for a new future in the American colonies. It was one of the largest waves of immigration to America at that time. They landed in Boston, Philadelphia, and New York, and many of them made their way south. For the most part, they settled in the Carolinas and Virginia's back country (the region west of the Appalachian Mountains). The region west of the mountains was attractive to the Scotch-Irish, as well as to German and other English settlers, due to the frontier nature of the area and the absence of British authority and control. It was Indian land, controlled by the Cherokee and Iroquois, and hostility continued to rage between the indigenous people and the new settlers for generations. The Scotch-Irish became experts at hunting, trapping, and the Indian methods of stealth warfare and close-in fighting. Many of the Scotch-Irish settlers, especially in the Overmountain region, staked their futures with the cause of American independence.

The American position in the South was reaching a critical point. The Americans had just lost the better part of their southern army at Charleston, and the British had a free hand in the southern region. The British under Cornwallis hoped to build on the partisan divide. Their main strategy was to fight larger-scale battles against the Continentals and use loyalist militias as a pacification force once the main American Army was defeated. If the British were successful in their plan, it would have profoundly complicated the situation in the South for the Americans. During the campaigns in the North, there were always loyalist elements for the patriots to deal with. In the South, the issue was compounded due to the population being spread out over greater distances and the agrarian nature of the region. Approximately one third of the population in the South was made up of patriots. Another third was made up of loyalists, and the last third was not committed to either side. The British hoped to bring as many of the loyalists and those still on the fence to their side.

To that end, Cornwallis appointed a Scotsman, Major Patrick Ferguson, known as "The Bull Dog," to the mission of recruiting loyalists and converting and training militias in the Carolina back country. Ferguson was known for his advocacy of light infantry tactics and the use of rifles over smooth-bore muskets. He was a charismatic leader and was looked up to by his loyalist forces. It was reported that at the Battle of Brandywine Ferguson had a high-ranking American officer in the sights of his rifle. The officer turned his back to Ferguson who decided not to fire due to eighteenth-century sentiments of gallantry and protocols of gentlemanly behavior. It was thought that the officer was either Pulaski or Washington himself. Later, Ferguson received a musket ball to his right elbow, crippling his arm.

Ferguson trained his loyalist militia in light infantry tactics and had his partisan force employ intimidation measures against its fellow Carolina countrymen. He advanced a proclamation that threatened to implement a "scorched-earth policy" to punish the inhabitants and to hang the back-country leaders who were partial to the patriot cause. The conduct of the British military had an effect opposite of what was intended. That was especially true in the Overmountain region where Scotch-Irish militias were forming in support of the patriot cause for independence.

The next action by the British was led by an aggressive and resourceful cavalry officer, Lt. Colonel Banastre Tarleton. The Americans attempted to send a reinforcement contingent of approximately 400 men under the command of Colonel Abraham Buford, but the force didn't arrive in time to assist in the defense of Charleston and withdrew to the north. Cornwallis became aware of the force and dispatched Tarleton to engage Buford and his men. Tarleton caught up to Buford at a place called Waxhaws on the border between North Carolina and South Carolina. Tarleton and his men made quick work of the Americans. It was reported that Tarleton's men murdered many American soldiers who were trying to surrender. The incident became known as "Buford's Massacre," and Tarleton was branded a butcher. The war in the South had devolved into a bloody affair the likes of which had not been experienced by either side in prior engagements of the war. The Americans used the incident for propaganda purposes, much as they had with the slaying of Jane McCrea during the Saratoga campaign in the fall of 1777. The events at Waxhaws galvanized American resistance to British control as men throughout the South took up arms and joined the fight against the invaders in the coming months.

A partisan war broke out, and the patriots once again employed hit-and-run tactics as their main strategy. Francis Marion led the patriot side. Prior to the Revolution, Marion ran his family's plantation in Berkley County, South Carolina. He was also a veteran of the French and Indian War in which he fought with the British.

Marion, also known as the "Swamp Fox," along with Thomas Sumter, Andrew Pickens, and other patriots, disappeared into the back woods and swamps of South Carolina to avoid discovery. Patriots knew the marsh areas well, and it was difficult for the British to follow and organize assaults and countermeasures. In those back areas, Marion's men regrouped, garnered supplies, and planned their next attack. The "Swamp Fox" and his contingent hit the British along their lines of supply, employing what has become known in conventional lexicon as guerilla warfare. The U.S. Army Rangers of today take inspiration from Marion's irregular methods of fighting. The tactic depleted British morale, causing them to commit great exertions to maintain their occupation of the region. Marion led a determined campaign against the loyalists and British forces and rose to the rank of general in the Continental Army.

The Americans' humiliation and defeat at Charleston continued at the next major encounter with Lord Charles Cornwallis and the British Army. In the summer of 1780, Congress appointed Major General Horatio Gates to take command of the southern department without consulting Washington. Gates marched his army south into South Carolina where, on August 16th, he was met by the British Army at their back-country supply depot in Camden. Gates made a critical tactical mistake in the Battle of Camden Court House; he installed the inexperienced militia at the most vulnerable position for the redcoats to exploit on the American left flank, which in turn brought about the collapse of the American line. At that important moment in the fight, the militia, along with Gates and the Continentals, fled the battle and headed to North Carolina, abandoning part of the army still fighting in the field. The Americans suffered upwards of nine hundred men killed or wounded and one thousand captured. It was another devastating blow to the Americans, and the second American Army to be destroyed by the British and Cornwallis in less than four months.

Horatio Gates never again held a major battlefield command during the war. At that moment, it was left to the efforts of Francis Marion and others to bring the fight to the enemy. Their mission was to wear down the British along their lines of supply across the expanse of North and South Carolina. After Camden, the Continental Army obviously needed new leadership and a new strategy in the South. Once again, the Americans regrouped and formed a new strategy to fight another day.

Vive la France

Other more positive events were happening for the American cause that summer of 1780. An allied fleet had finally arrived in American waters, and it brought a French Army of nearly six thousand soldiers under the command of Lt. General Jean-Baptiste Donatien de Vimeur, comte de Rochambeau. The French landed in Newport, Rhode Island, unopposed by the British. The landing was assisted by intelligence gathered by the Culper Spy Ring, which detected British intentions to confront the French fleet.

In September of that year, Washington and Rochambeau met in Hartford, Connecticut, to discuss strategy. Washington continued to stress his desire to attack the British in New York City, but at that point it was already late in the year to plan a large-scale attack on the British main force under Clinton. Moreover, neither army was ready for such a risky enterprise against the formidable defenses the British had erected at their main base in New York City. For the timebeing, holding the main British Army in place in a protracted stalemate was the best the beleaguered Continental Army could achieve, even with the arrival of Rochambeau and the French.

Nathanael Greene: Washington's Fighting Quaker

> We are soldiers who devote ourselves to arms not for the invasion of other countries but for the defense of our own, not for the gratification of our private interest, but for public security.[14]

On October 22, 1780, Washington removed Horatio Gates and appointed his most reliable and trusted subordinate, Major General Nathanael Greene, to take command of the battered southern department. It proved to be one of the wisest decisions Washington made during the war. Greene was born in Warwick, Rhode Island, in 1742, and his family settled early in the state. Greene and his family were Quakers, and his father was a preacher. The Quakers, like other "non-Puritan" Protestant faiths, were not welcomed when they first arrived in America and were subject to religious intolerance in Puritan Massachusetts Bay colony. Greene's family therefore decided to settle in Rhode Island in the 1630s. His family had a mill in Coventry, which the young Nathanael ran. He was a consummate reader, particularly with regards to military science. As the struggle for independence drew near, Greene's interest in military issues caused him to have a rift with the pacifist Quaker Church. He did, however, remain a devout Quaker his entire life.

Greene became an early advocate for independence and was elected to the Rhode Island Legislature in 1770. He served as an officer in the state militia, of which he helped establish a unit in 1774. After Lexington and Concord, he participated in the siege of Boston. During the siege, he joined the Continental Army under Washington, serving first as a Brigadier and then rising to the rank of Major General. Greene demonstrated many admirable personal traits and was a loyal and devoted soldier. He embraced the principles of the Declaration of Independence and conducted his efforts and behavior to advance the cause of American independence and individual rights. He is quoted as saying, "I am determined to defend my rights and maintain my freedom or sell my life in the attempt."[15]

Because of his organizational skills and business experience in running a mill back in Rhode Island, Greene was appointed Quartermaster General of the Continental Army in 1778. He developed into a skillful tactician and understood the larger strategic picture he shared with Washington. The strategy was to wear the

British down, exhaust them, frustrate their plans, and create doubt in the success of their mission. In the South, Greene fought when the enemy presented opportunities, but he didn't allow them a complete or decisive victory. Washington is quoted as saying to Greene, "In my absence the command of the army devolves upon you. I have such entire confidence in your prudence and abilities, that I leave the conduct of it to your discretion..."[16]

By October of 1780, the Continental Army had little success against the British Army and Lord Charles Cornwallis in the renewed southern campaign. Cornwallis and his army were advancing into North Carolina toward Charlotte from their base at Camden. On the west wing of Cornwallis was Major Patrick Ferguson and his loyalist force. The British strategy was to eliminate all major patriot resistance as they moved north. Ferguson had trained more than one thousand loyalist militiamen. To confront the force, a motivated contingent of Overmountain Men (mostly Scotch-Irish), led by Colonel William Campbell, John Sevier, and Isaac Shelby, crossed the Blue Ridge Mountains. Ferguson and the loyalist force were camped in western South Carolina on a low-lying rocky ridge called Kings Mountain. Ferguson knew the Overmountain Men were coming but decided to stay on top of the ridge. He believed the upward slope and the approach to the mountains would protect his forces, even though British reinforcements were not far away.

On October 7th, approximately nine hundred Overmountain Men organized an assault up all the sides of the ridge, eliminating the prospects of escape for Ferguson and his men. Once again for the Americans, it was the Kentucky/Pennsylvania Rifle that was the decisive implement of the struggle. At the Battle of Kings Mountain, the Overmountain Men inflicted a heavy toll on the loyalists, killing or wounding nearly five hundred and capturing more than six hundred and fifty. The victory was complete for the Americans. Legend puts forth that Ferguson said "God himself" could not remove him from the mountain. Ironically, Ferguson was hit by rifle fire and fell from his horse and died. He was buried in an unmarked grave on top of Kings Mountain, fulfilling his own prophecy. With the death of Ferguson and the destruction of his loyalist force, the partisan fight moved in favor of the Americans. Legend has it that after Kings Mountain, Washington said that if he ever had to make a last stand, he would want to stand with the Overmountain Men, "who know how to stand and fight."

Benedict Arnold, Peggy, and Andre

The major fighting at that time focused on the actions of Lord Charles Cornwallis and the British Southern Army's campaign to subdue the South. Other events were playing out in the North as Clinton and the main British Army occupied New York City and Long Island while Washington and the Continentals monitored their activities from the Lower Hudson Valley to the north. One of the

Revolutionary War's and American history's most notorious, complicated, and conflicted characters was Benedict Arnold. He was born in 1741 in Norwich, Connecticut, and he operated a shipping business in his early life. He joined the American Army during the siege of Boston in 1775, the same year his wife died, causing him to leave his three young sons to be raised by his sister. Financial difficulties and the death of his wife caused hardships and complications in his personal life. Notwithstanding, he still had the resolve to lead several important early actions against the British, including the capture of Fort Ticonderoga in May of 1775 with Ethan Allen and the Green Mountain Boys, and an invasion of Canada later that year.

Arnold was a colonel at that point and had suggested the idea of invading Canada to Washington and sent a letter to Congress. Arnold had some experience in Canada prior to the war through his shipping business, and he believed the French Canadians could be cajoled into joining with the Americans and the cause for independence. Arnold got the go-ahead in September and was joined by eleven hundred Continentals and General Richard Montgomery. The planned invasion of Canada was a two-pronged advance to capture the Canadian Provincial capital of Quebec. Arnold was to advance toward Quebec from the east through the wilderness of what is now Maine while the second prong, by Montgomery, was to head north through Lake Champlain. From the outset, the Canadian mission went awry. Arnold and his men were hampered by logistics, the wilderness, and the winter elements. He arrived with only a portion of his force, as many of the men had turned back or were greatly weakened by inadequate supplies, hunger, and the winter cold.

When Montgomery arrived with his force, he and Arnold launched and assault against the British at Quebec on December 31, 1775. The entire campaign initiated by Arnold was a valiant and creative effort. In many ways the idea of bringing Canada to the American side was brilliant, but the assault by the Americans was unsuccessful, and the campaign ended in failure. During the fight, Arnold received a wound to his left leg, the first of two crippling injuries he received in that leg during the war. For his efforts during the Canadian expedition, Arnold rose to the rank of Brigadier General.

In the early phase of the war, part of the British strategy was centered around dividing the American colonies along the natural line that separated the Hudson River and the two main lakes reaching toward Canada, Lake George and Lake Champlain. By October of 1776, Arnold and other American officers who were positioned in Upstate New York realized the dire position they would be in if the British were successful in separating New England from the rest of the colonies. Moreover, the British were building a large fleet that would include four galleys and several schooners and gunboats on Lake Champlain. Additionally, they assembled an army of nine thousand redcoats under the command of General Guy

Carleton. The British plan was to push down the lake and move towards Albany. As Arnold and the remnant of his army withdrew south from Canada earlier in the year, they were able to commandeer most of the available boats on the lake, an action that delayed the British plans to move south. Though it was late in the season, the British constructed their new fleet and were ready to advance south in October 1776.

After the failed attempt to win over Canada, the Americans under Arnold withdrew back to Fort Ticonderoga and the fortifications at Crown Point, south of Lake Champlain. To counter the British, the Americans under Arnold also constructed a small fleet of their own on Lake Champlain. A battle took place near Valcour Island, one of the first battles in U.S. naval history. The British fleet far outgunned the Americans, but Arnold hid the American fleet and was able to lure the British into battle where prevailing winds favored the Americans. The two fleets fought a fierce battle, and the outnumbered Americans inflicted many casualties on the British, including the sinking of several British gunboats. The actions by Arnold and the Americans further delayed the British advance south, and the remnant of the American fleet was able to slip past Carleton and move toward Crown Point. Arnold was forced to destroy what remained of his small navy once he arrived at the southern end of the lake. He also destroyed much of the fortifications and structures at Crown Point so as not to leave them to the British. Arnold and his men then moved further south to the fortifications at Fort Ticonderoga.

The British landed at Crown Point and held the position for two weeks, but supply lines were stretched and snow had already started to fall, so Carleton decided to withdraw up the lake to winter quarters. The British had achieved control of the entire lake, and they believed they could exploit that advantage in the coming year when they would have more favorable conditions. Arnold's intuitive battlefield/naval strategy and delaying tactics prevented the British from accomplishing their overall plans at the end of 1776. It was a brilliant effort led by Arnold and the Americans, and it would be another year before the British attempted to move south from Lake Champlain. It would involve John Burgoyne and a rendezvous with Arnold and the American militia at Saratoga.

Along with his heroics, fearlessness, and battlefield instincts, Arnold was a jealous, vengeful, and a conflicted person. He became disgruntled and believed other officers received credit for his actions. He was accused of corruption during his tenure as Military Governor of Philadelphia after the British occupation ended in the summer of in 1778. Washington appointed him to the Philadelphia post later that year and stood by him during his difficulties. Arnold had been wounded twice in his left leg and was a cripple when he received the Philadelphia post, but Washington believed that Arnold still had value to the war effort and the American cause. It was in Philadelphia that Arnold met his second wife, Peggy Shippen, when she was only eighteen years old. Peggy was a dilettante socialite whose wealthy family had loyalist leanings. She was twenty years younger than Arnold and apparently beguiled him with her youthful beauty and feminine persuasions. Peggy was noted to be the most beautiful woman in Philadelphia. They were married after a short courtship in April of 1779.

In the previous year, while the British occupied Philadelphia, Peggy developed a friendship with a young and charismatic British officer, Major John Andre. Andre was also Adjutant General for the Army and part of British Commanding General Henry Clinton's staff. He was also appointed as Head of Secret Service for the British Army in America. Apparently due to Peggy's family's leanings, the British occupation, and her relationship with Andre, her commitment to the British cause deepened. Peggy and Andre continued their correspondence as the main British Army evacuated Philadelphia in June of 1778 to once again direct the British war effort from New York City. It is not known how exactly the idea of treason first took root in Arnold's consciousness. The interesting question is: Was it his idea from the start or did Peggy plant the seed and cultivate its development? That causation appears lost to history. What is known is that Peggy must have been the conduit between Andre and her husband once the idea of betrayal had firmly established itself in Arnold's mind. Historians Mark Jacob and Stephen Case, in their book *Treacherous Beauty*," which tells the story of Peggy Shippen Arnold, describe her as "the most dangerous teenage girl in American history."[17] Arnold and Andre entered into negotiations, and Arnold put the high price of twenty thousand pounds on his loyalty and honor.

In July of 1780, Washington appointed Arnold, at Arnold's request, to a new post as Commander of West Point. At that point in the war, West Point was a strategic fortification that protected the approach to the north along the Hudson River. It was during that time that the Culper Spy Ring uncovered the fact that a high-ranking American officer was going to defect to the British. In September, Arnold and Andre had a clandestine meeting at Stoney Point near West Point. The plan was to work out the details of Arnold's defection. Most important to Andre and the British was Arnold's plan for surrendering West Point. Unfortunately for Washington, standing by Arnold during his difficulties and placing trust in him fell under the category of "no good deed goes unpunished."

For the meeting with Arnold, Andre traveled up the Hudson River via a British warship called the Vulture. After Andre left the ship, American forces observed the Vulture and moved a cannon into position from high ground along the river and fired on it. The Vulture was forced to relocate down river, and Andre, once his meeting with Arnold was concluded, was forced to head south by horseback along the Hudson toward New York City. During the meeting between Arnold and Andre, a price for Arnold's defection was agreed to and plans of West Point's defensives were handed over to Andre. As Andre left the meeting, he discovered that the

Vulture had moved, and he was forced to travel through an area controlled mostly by American militias, some of which might also have been part-time highwaymen. Three of those militiamen came upon Andre and detained and questioned him. Andre originally thought they were loyalist militias and addressed them as such, which caused suspicion among the men. The men were John Paulding, Isaac Van Ward, and Davis Williams. Andre then offered them a pass signed by Arnold for a "John Anderson," and he also offered them a bribe. The men decided to search Andre and discovered in his boots the plans for West Point and other documents signed by Arnold, implicating him in treason.

The militiamen turned Andre over to their Commander, Lt. Colonel John Jameson, who was at the army post in Tappan, New York. Jameson intended to send Andre back to Arnold at West Point, somewhat surprisingly, not suspecting anything amiss at that point. Benjamin Tallmadge was the first to arrive on the scene and put the pieces together. Tallmadge convinced Jameson that Andre was working for the other side and that Arnold was the high-ranking officer with dubious intentions and loyalties. Jameson had already sent Andre to Arnold but was able to call him back. Additionally, Jameson, before becoming aware of the nefarious events, sent a note to Arnold that John Anderson (Andre) had been captured. The note tipped Arnold off that his treasonous plot had been foiled. Jameson also sent the materials confiscated from Andre to Washington.

Tallmadge supervised the custody of Andre for the next eight days until final disposition.

Back at Tappan, Andre was interrogated at an inn, now called the 76 House, and came clean to Tallmadge. Andre asked Tallmadge what his fate might be under Washington's command. Tallmadge was a classmate of Nathan Hale and played a role in Hale's joining the army and lamented the fate of his one-time friend. He reminded Andre of the judgement Hale received as a spy when he was hanged by the British under General William Howe four years earlier. Tallmadge's assessment to Andre was that he would receive the same fate as Hale. Washington and Tallmadge both had the young Nathan Hale on their minds when considering what should be done with Andre. The same was true for other American officers who were charged with rendering a verdict for Andre.

Washington and his staff, which included Hamilton and Lafayette, arrived at West Point. To Washington's dismay, Arnold was not there to greet him, which was a breach of protocol. Arnold had already been tipped off that his plot had been discovered and had fled down river to the Vulture. Washington and his staff further discovered that the fortification's defensives were in disrepair. It was in the afternoon of September 23, 1780, that Washington, upon meeting with Tallmadge and viewing the evidence, became aware of Arnold's treason. It was the only time that Washington was reported to have been emotionally moved to tears.

Washington eventually offered Andre for Arnold in a swap. The British Commander Henry Clinton had fond feelings for his Adjutant General and Aid John Andre. Moreover, Clinton was reported to loath Arnold, but eighteenth-century notions of honor and commitment, as well as the circumstances, dictated that Clinton refuse the offer. Andre stood trial as a spy. The tribunal consisted of fourteen American generals, and the Board of Inquiry was headed by Nathanael Greene shortly before Greene left to take command of the southern department. During the trial, both Hamilton and Lafayette conversed with Andre and, as odd as it might seem, socialized with him. At the end of the trial, Andre was sentenced to death as a spy. The British sent a new uniform for Andre who requested to meet his fate by firing squad. That request was denied. Both Hamilton and Lafayette believed that Andre should not receive the death sentence and disagreed with the verdict. John Andre found the courage to put the noose around his own neck and was hanged on October 2, 1780, in Tappan, New York.

Andre fought for his king and country. Hamilton, Lafayette, and Tallmadge fought for American independence. Notwithstanding the fact that they fought on different sides, the young men shared in the personal risks of the conflict. They bore fidelity and loyalty to their causes, however different they might have been. As soldiers and young men of conscience, they shared in similar duties and services. In the end, they were eternal brothers in arms. Tallmadge gained respect for Andre and shook his hand on the way to the gallows. Lafayette cried at the hanging, and Hamilton wrote of Andre that "never perhaps did any man suffer death with more justice or deserve it less."[18]

In Arnold's haste to flee capture, he left Peggy behind with their new baby. Peggy, recognizing the difficulty of her situation with her husband gone and Washington's staff mulling through her house and possessions, pulled off a great deception. She feigned a mental breakdown and delusions for Washington and his staff to witness. She was reported to decry that Washington was going to kill her baby, and she moved about in an inappropriate and scantily clad state. Her actions drew sympathy from all, especially the young men in the group, including Hamilton and Lafayette who were more than happy to render her any assistance she required. It appears that once again, Peggy relied on her feminine charms and beauty to advance her interest. Washington allowed Peggy and the baby to join her husband in New York. It was in New York that Arnold began new military responsibilities as a Brigadier General, discarding his blue uniform for a red one with British epaulets.

Morgan Joins Greene in the South

In November of 1780, Washington sent Brigadier General Daniel Morgan to support Greene in the South and to reverse the tide of the struggle. Morgan's family was Welsh. They originally immigrated to New Jersey, where Morgan was born in 1735/36, and eventually settled in Winchester, Virginia. Morgan was with Arnold at the failed assault on Quebec in 1775. He also fought with the British in the French and Indian War and received a musket ball through his cheek, giving him a lifelong disfigurement. He also received three hundred and ninety-nine lashes as punishment for assaulting a British officer. He was supposed to receive four hundred, but the British solider lost count. It became a running joke that he was owed one more lash by the British. Morgan, like Washington and several other American officers, gained experience in military affairs during the French and Indian War. As the Revolutionary War loomed, he became an officer in the state militia, and he went on to raise a rifle company at the start of the conflict. His Virginia/Maryland Riflemen made an important contribution to winning the Battle of Saratoga in September of 1777. They knew the importance the British placed on their officers on the battlefield, so they targeted those officers during engagements, causing disorder and dislocation in the British ranks.

Morgan and Greene both recognized that to win against the British Army in the Carolinas they would need to adopt unconventional tactics. Greene divided his force and gave Morgan command of a contingent of the army. Morgan and his contingent headed west while Greene's force stayed near Cornwallis' main section of the British Southern Army. Part of the British plan for subduing the South was a dependency on loyalists coming to their side, but since the Overmountain Men defeated Ferguson's loyalists,

Cornwallis' left flank was exposed. It was a fatal flaw in the British strategy.

The Americans suffered several major defeats, including Savannah, Charleston, and Camden, during the first phase of the fighting in the South. The part of the American Army that was originally commanded by Generals Benjamin Lincoln and Horatio Gates had become substantially depleted. The Americans lost thousands of soldiers to either casualty or capture during the fighting in 1779 and 1780. The difference between the Americans and the British was that the Americans were continually able to replace their losses with a seemingly endless supply of new fighters. Conversely, the British had great limitations in their ability to replace their losses. They needed to rely on their ocean supply line to New York or direct from Britain for additional reinforcements. It was a great logistical problem for the British, especially as the war debt mounted. For Clinton in New York, he needed to consider the issue of sending greater numbers of regulars south and the consequences it could have in degrading the main army in New York. Further depletions of the main garrison would hinder his ability to fight Washington. Furthermore, the arrival of the French Army had boosted Washington's force, creating the potential for a new front to materialize in the North. There was also a growing dislike for each other between the two principal British officers — Clinton in the North and Cornwallis in the South. Clinton would send orders to Cornwallis with regards to movement and deployment. Sometimes

Cornwallis complied with his superior's orders and sometimes he ignored them.

After the losses at Charleston and Camden, Greene, supported by Morgan, organized a new southern army using militiamen to replace those lost in the encounters. Morgan's force of approximately two thousand men moved to western South Carolina toward an area and town known as Ninety Six. The plan was to secure the area since Ferguson and his loyalist force had been defeated by the Overmountain Men. Morgan and his men stopped at an open-range cattle-grazing area known as the Cowpens. It was there, on January 17, 1781, that Morgan and the Americans met up with Tarleton and his division of the British Southern Army and engaged in a decisive action.

At that point in the war, Morgan had learned important lessons about how best to fight the British on America's terms. The British soldiers were experienced, well trained, and brave, and they were led by an excellent core of officers. Inherently, the British were aggressive and accustomed to employing frontal assaults on their enemy. Once the enemy was held in place by the frontal attack, the British would charge with bayonets, which were often a decisive element of the battles. The British would then orchestrate a flanking maneuver to envelop their enemy. It was a tactic that had worked several times for the British against the much less experienced Americans. Additionally, the British learned by 1781 that the American militias would flee the action if a determined frontal assault was bearing down on them with fixed bayonets. It was only the more experienced and better trained Continentals who would stand when confronted face to face with British regulars.

Morgan's division of the army was swelling with additional groups of militias from Virginia and the Carolinas. His challenge was how best to utilize the forces he had to their best advantage. He picked the place of engagement at the Cowpens: an open rising field where he could conceal the disposition of his battle lines. There were also wooded areas on either side, providing additional concealment. Tarleton's redcoats would be forced to advance toward the American lines and into concealed higher ground. Tarleton had been tracking Morgan's army since the 12th, and he arrived in the area ready for battle in the early morning hours of January 17th. Thinking he had Morgan trapped with his back against the Broad River, Tarleton pushed his men all night, arrogantly confident that he could achieve a decisive victory against the Americans.

Morgan, knowing that Tarleton's force was upon him, moved about his men the night before the battle. He imbued confidence and reminded them of the value their efforts would bring to the cause and to their personal reputations. He then devised a brilliant battle plan that considered all the relevant elements of the coming action. He picked the location of the encounter, which allowed him the freedom of concealment and movement, and organized his forces into three lines: a "defense-in-depth" that was designed to absorb the initial British attack. An important element of the defense was Morgan's Georgia and Carolina sharpshooters, who fired from concealed positions and forward in the first line. As the battle began, Tarleton advanced a frontal assault, but the move was anticipated by Morgan. Morgan's riflemen focused their attention on the officers, but they also targeted the British Dragoons who were on horseback and attempting to advance on both flanks. When the precise rifle fire of the sharpshooters caused the dragoons to withdraw, the riflemen moved to behind the second line. The second line was composed of militias from the Carolinas and Virginia, and they were under the command of Andrew Pickens. The militias were the least experienced men on the field, and Morgan knew not to ask too much of them. He knew that an unrealistic reliance on militias had caused problems for the Americans in previous battles. The militia was asked to get off two volleys and then withdraw behind the third line. When the militia withdrew, it presented the over aggressive Tarleton and the British with the illusion of a break in the American line. Morgan's strategy was working as the Battle of the Cowpens developed. The British had become exhausted, and Morgan's plan drew them deeper into the trap that was about to be sprung on them.

As the militia withdrew, they were harassed by other advancing British Dragoons, but the American Cavalry under William Washington entered the battle and got the better of them. All the while, Morgan rode along the line of battle, encouraging his men and yelling, "Form, form, my brave fellows! Give them one more fire and the day is ours. Old Morgan was never beaten."[19] After less than an hour into the battle, the British had casualties and were exhausted. The third American line, comprised of Continentals, held the British in place. It was then that the larger American force that had withdrawn earlier appeared on both sides of the British and orchestrated a double envelopment of Tarleton's force. The British assault collapsed, and the remaining British regulars surrendered. Tarleton retreated and was chased by American Cavalry but was able to escape with a small number of his force. It was a clear and decisive victory for the Americans. The British force suffered approximately three hundred casualties with more the one hundred killed, and the Americans took nearly six hundred and fifty of them as prisoners. On the American side, twenty-five were killed and one hundred and twenty-five were wounded. The loss of nearly one thousand regulars was a severe blow for the British. They were experienced regulars that could not be easily replaced. The Battle of Cowpens was the most decisive American victory since Saratoga in the fall of 1777, and it was the most important American success of the southern campaign up to that point in the war.

After the Battle of Cowpens, Cornwallis moved the main British Southern Army into North Carolina to pursue Greene and the Americans. The two armies skirmished with each other during the advance north. The British bested the Americans in most of those engagements but, to Cornwallis' distress, continued to suffer casualties. On January 18th, Cornwallis' army was augmented by an additional twelve hundred regulars from Charleston under the command of Major General Alexander Lesley, which brought the size of his force to approximately twenty-five hundred men. Greene withdrew north across North Carolina in February, and Cornwallis and his army pursued him in a race to the Dan River, which separated North Carolina and Virginia.

Cornwallis hoped to catch up to the American column that was escorting the British prisoners taken at Cowpens. To speed up his advance, he ordered non-essential parts of his wagon train to be set ablaze. Greene, with assistance from Morgan and his men, skillfully placed obstructions in Cornwallis' path to delay his movement north. The two divisions of the American Southern Army had joined near Guilford Court House on February 8th, bringing Morgan and his men together with Greene.

Greene won the race to the Dan River. On February 14th he crossed over into Virginia where he and his men rested and resupplied. The movement north pulled Cornwallis and his army further away from their supply base in Camden, South Carolina, exposing their supply lines to American militias. Cornwallis never caught up to the prisoner column, and he withdrew in frustration toward Hillsborough, North Carolina. He never returned to South Carolina where he had spent the last two years implementing various tactics and strategies to end the American resistance. Cornwallis begrudgingly complimented Greene when he wrote, "Greene is as dangerous as Washington; he is vigilant, enterprising, and full of resources. With but little hope of gaining an advantage over him, I never feel secure when encamped in his neighborhood."[20]

Greene then re-crossed the Dan River back into North Carolina and met Cornwallis at Guilford Court House in Greensboro in the middle of March 1781. Greene's army was made up of approximately four thousand men — a mix of Continentals from Virginia and Maryland and local militias from Virginia, North Carolina, and Delaware. Additionally, the force was supplemented by cannons and cavalry under William Washington and General Henry Lee ("Light Horse Harry Lee"), the father of Robert E. Lee. Greene's battle plan was to copy the successful strategy that Morgan had implemented at Cowpens several weeks earlier. He would draw Cornwallis into battle at Guilford Court House on ground that he believed would provide his army with an advantage. Then he would organize a defense-in-depth, keeping his most experienced Continentals in the third and final line.

On March 15th, Greene deployed his force and waited for Cornwallis to attack him. Greene positioned his militias from North Carolina and Delaware along a fence row with sharpshooters from Virginia in the first line. Light Horse Harry Lee and William Washington's dragoons were positioned on each flank. Approximately three hundred to four hundred yards behind the first line was the second line, made up of Virginia militiamen with two-pound batteries (artillery pieces). Continentals from Virginia, Maryland, and Delaware, with two additional six-pound batteries, made up the third and final line. Going into the battle, the British had some disadvantages. They did not have intelligence on the disposition of Greene's army, and Cornwallis and his staff were not adequately apprised of the terrain on which they would be fighting. Nonetheless, Cornwallis went forward with his attack against Greene. Cornwallis' force was approximately twenty-one hundred men including Royal Welsh Fusiliers, grenadiers, Hessian Jaegers, Fraser's Highlanders, and Tarleton's British legion. The battle commenced, and the Virginia militia fired an effective volley into the advancing British. Despite taking heavy casualties, the British pushed forward against the first line of American militia. As the action progressed, firefights broke out in the wooded area on the periphery of the battlefield. The British continued to push through, causing a break in the first two lines, and the American militia withdrew from the battle.

To halt the forward momentum, William Washington's cavalry charged the British units. Once through, he turned around and charged again. The 1st and 2nd Maryland Continentals followed that up by launching a bayonet charge. It was once again the British regulars fighting against the American Continentals. Cornwallis, in an indiscriminate action, then ordered cannon grapeshot to be fired into the middle of the fighting, killing both American and British soldiers. The British then advanced into the breach and secured the battlefield. The British had achieved another tactical victory, and Greene ordered a withdrawal.

The Battle of Guilford Court House was the largest battle in the southern campaign. Once again, the cagey Cornwallis had bettered the Americans. He entered the battle with less than half the men Greene had. The experience and discipline of the British regulars had won the day, but the American Continentals had distinguished themselves. Cornwallis paid a compliment, saying that "the Americans fought like demons."[21] The list of casualties validates Cornwallis' statement. The British suffered more than five hundred casualties with approximately one hundred killed. The American losses were around three hundred and fifty casualties with a similar number of approximately one hundred killed. Unlike the action at Cowpens where Morgan won a decisive victory against Tarleton's force, Greene's lines were spread too far apart from each other, which caused disorder and confusion in the ranks. Once the militia withdrew from the first two lines, it did not fully reinforce the third line of Continentals. Additionally, as many as one thousand of Greene's militiamen slipped away after the battle and went back home.

Cornwallis briefly chased Greene but then decided to move the remnants of his battered force to Wilmington on the coast of North Carolina where he received supplies and reinforced his army. Greene moved his army back to South Carolina to fill the void left by Cornwallis, effectively ending British efforts to recruit additional loyalists in North and South Carolina.

Greene moved toward Camden in South Carolina where the British continued to maintain a supply base. On April 25th, he and his men were attacked at Hobkirk's Hill by a British force under Lord Francis Rawdon. After a highly contested fight, the British achieved victory and Greene's small force withdrew. Once again, the British sustained more casualties than Greene's force. Shortly after the battle, the British abandoned Camden to consolidate their forces and moved back to Charleston, virtually ceding the majority of South Carolina to Greene and the Americans. Greene then moved his army further west where, from May 22nd to June 18th, he conducted a siege on the loyalist Star Fort at the town of Ninety Six. Greene abandoned the siege after a final and unsuccessful assault. He was technically losing a majority of the battles he fought, but his overall strategy of depleting the British and wearing them down was working. Greene summed up his strategy: "We fight, get beat, rise and fight again."[22]

The final encounter between Greene's army and the British in the Carolinas occurred on September 8th at Eutaw Springs. The Americans moved on a British force led by Colonel Alexander Steward that was foraging for supplies. Light Horse Harry Lee captured more than four hundred of them. Greene then moved on the main force of British regulars under Steward. In the end, both sides claimed victory as they both held a portion of the battlefield. Greene lost approximately six hundred men. Around one hundred and twenty were killed and the remainder were wounded or taken as prisoners. The British lost nearly nine hundred with approximately four hundred taken as prisoners. Once again, the British withdrew back toward Charleston and abandoned all other outposts in Georgia, North Carolina, and South Carolina with the exceptions of Savannah, Charleston, and Wilmington.

The British were never able to stop Greene's calculated and measured offensive strategy. Moreover, the American partisan militias under Marion and Pickens in South Carolina and William Davie in North Carolina fought and harassed the British at every turn and wore them down. The loyalist and Tory support first promised by the southern royal governors and royalist sympathizers back in 1778 never came out in sufficient numbers. Greene's army was able to absorb defeat after defeat and quickly rebounded as new militia recruits continually replenished the American ranks. Moreover, British actions became increasingly desperate and punitive toward the local inhabitants.

The Return of the Turncoat

In January of 1781, Brigadier General Benedict Arnold, newly of the British Army, along with John Graves Simcoe of the Queen's Rangers and sixteen hundred assorted loyalists and British regulars, traveled up the James River in Virginia. The British surprise initiative was courtesy of the Royal Navy, which had brought the force to Virginia from New York City. Arnold's plan was to take the Virginia capital of Richmond and create havoc in the

Virginia countryside. Thomas Jefferson, who was then the governor, had recently moved the capital from Williamsburg to Richmond because he thought it would be easier to defend, but Arnold's assault was consequential enough to convince Jefferson to leave the city. Arnold's force burned and pillaged much of the city and the plantations surrounding it. Jefferson and Washington were appalled by the conduct and placed a bounty on Arnold's head. The attack took all of Virginia by surprise. After skirmishes with local militias, Arnold moved his force down the James River to Portsmouth where he built defensive positions and waited for reinforcements. Arnold's raid was a success, and he received praise from Virginia loyalists and the British command for his daring exploits.

Washington attempted to counter the Virginia raiding parties by Arnold and other British commanders by sending General Marquis de Lafayette to Yorktown in March of 1781. Lafayette had recently returned to America after his brief diplomatic mission to France. When Lafayette returned to the military side of the contest, he was given unequivocal orders from Washington to capture Arnold. Lafayette's army of approximately twelve hundred soldiers eventually moved to Richmond to protect the city from further British incursions. Lafayette was supported by a small French fleet. On March 16th, that fleet battled a larger British fleet that was bringing supplies and reinforcements to Arnold. The British prevailed in that first Chesapeake Bay engagement, and the French fleet returned to Rhode Island. The British landed a force of two thousand additional soldiers under Major General William Phillips to reinforce Arnold. Phillips assumed command of the combined forces. The British under Phillips went on to take Petersburg in late April. Phillips died from illness in May, and Arnold briefly took command of the force. Of greater consequence was a more senior British officer who was on his way to Virginia for an eventual rendezvous with Washington and Rochambeau at the tobacco port town of Yorktown.

Cornwallis Advances into Virginia

After the Battle of Guilford Court House, Cornwallis withdrew his army to the coast and the city of Wilmington to rest his men. He was encouraged by the success of Arnold's raids and was on the move again by April. His new target was Virginia, the region's center of patriot resistance and resources and manpower for the American cause. As his army advanced north, they plundered and ravaged farms, took livestock, requisitioned horses, and freed slaves.

In New York, Clinton disagreed with Cornwallis' new offensive in Virginia and issued orders for him to move back to South Carolina and consolidate the British position. Clinton was concerned about a drain on available manpower and resources and was becoming increasingly conservative and mindful of the potential that Washington posed to New York. He also had to deal with the new French contingency and its navy, which was giving

Washington a freedom of movement greater than he had earlier in the war.

Cornwallis believed there were opportunities to exploit further north and ignored Clinton's orders. That being noted, Virginia was closer to New York than Charleston or Savannah was, and it would be easier to receive supplies and additional manpower. Once the advance into Virginia was committed, Clinton sent additional men and supplies to Cornwallis. Cornwallis arrived in Petersburg, Virginia, on May 20th, 1781, and shortly thereafter absorbed Arnold's force as well, putting approximately 7,200 combined British/Hessian forces under his command. Cornwallis then moved west and waged a political, military, and economic campaign against the locals in the Virginia countryside. Lafayette and his American force followed Cornwallis during the late spring and early summer and adopted the same strategy as Washington's in the North and Greene's in the South. They would wait until their enemy was vulnerable and then strike a blow that would not commit them to a full-scale engagement that played to the strengths of the British and Cornwallis.

In June, Lafayette was becoming increasingly aggressive against Cornwallis and would conduct small scale attacks against British patrols and foraging parties. He thought he found an opportunity to strike a real blow against the British on July 6th at a plantation called Green Springs near the James River. Cornwallis was moving his army from Williamsburg to cross the James River and head toward Portsmouth where they could again link up with the Royal Navy. During a river crossing, an army is vulnerable with a portion of the army on one side and the other portion either crossing or preparing to cross. Cornwallis was aware that Lafayette was close behind him and mindful of the American battle philosophy of looking for the opportunity to strike a quick blow. Moreover, Lafayette's force had recently been augmented by a contingent of Continentals under General Anthony Wayne. Wayne had often been referred to as "Mad Anthony Wayne," a moniker he earned for his fearlessness and sometimes reckless approach against the British from the early engagements in 1776 up to and including the Virginia campaigns in 1781. The addition of Wayne's Continentals raised the size of Lafayette's army to approximately four thousand men.

Cornwallis' movements across the river and the additional forces under Wayne provided the necessary encouragement for Lafayette to plan a strike against the British. Wayne's force was in the front for the initial attack in the Battle of Green Springs. Lafayette ordered them to advance against what he thought was a rear guard, but the ever-savvy Cornwallis anticipated the move and set a trap for the Americans. Cornwallis sent only a small portion of his army across the James River and kept a major part of his army in the vicinity of the staging area. The attacking Continentals were successful against the British defending force at first, but then Cornwallis directed a counterattack with the bulk of his army from a concealed position behind a hill and overwhelmed the Americans. Wayne ordered a bayonet charge that temporarily stopped the British advance. Lafayette recognized the trap and sent additional Americans into the fight to allow time for Wayne's force to retreat. The British had won another victory, but Lafayette and the Americans averted a disaster.

Cornwallis did not chase Lafayette. He continued on to Portsmouth and then chose to comply with Clinton's orders to move his army to the deep-water tobacco port of Yorktown where he and his army of approximately eight thousand arrived on August 2nd. The town overlooks the York River and is across from Gloucester Point, which Cornwallis reinforced subsequent to his arrival. For the British, Yorktown was a more conducive location for receiving supplies from the Royal Navy. The deep-water port also advanced the possibility of evacuating Cornwallis' army and sending it back to New York if the Franco-American alliance chose to attack the British there. It was a contingency for which the British had to prepare given the reputation that Washington and the Americans had developed for being resourceful and unpredictable. The British built fortifications around the perimeter of Yorktown and secured defensive positions should they be attacked by the ever-vigilant Americans. Lafayette and his men kept track of the British and kept them in place and were just beyond the newly constructed positions.

A Message to Rochambeau from Admiral de Grasse

In 1781, a large French fleet under the command of Admiral Francois Joseph Paul de Grasse was operating in the Caribbean waters around the island of Hispaniola in support of French interests and France's Spanish ally. De Grasse had twenty-eight ships of the line at his command and had been in communications with General Rochambeau. In June, Rochambeau would move his French Army from Newport to the Lower Hudson to join with Washington. De Grasse and Rochambeau had reviewed the possibility of de Grasse's French fleet providing support to the joint Franco-American effort against the British in North America. On August 14th, Rochambeau received a message that de Grasse's fleet had departed for the Chesapeake on August 3rd. Unlike Washington who wanted the French fleet to assist in an assault on the main British base of operations in New York, Rochambeau thought the British were too strong in New York and wanted the fleet to go to the Chesapeake to attack Cornwallis.

De Grasse made his fleet available to assist the American war effort through October of 1781. On his own initiative and without orders from Paris, he was also able to borrow three regiments of approximately thirty-five hundred troops who were under the control of France's Spanish allies. De Grasse was also able to raise a loan of one point two million livres (six million dollars) so Washington could pay his army. The news that a large French fleet was going to be operational in American waters and at the disposal of the Franco-American alliance's land forces was what Washington had been waiting and hoping to hear.

Rochambeau's original order from King Louis XVI was that he was to be subordinate to Washington. One of Washington's strengths as a commander was his willingness to take council from officers who were part of his command. That was certainly the case when it came to Lt. General Rochambeau, one of the most experienced senior officers in the French Army. On hearing the news of the movement and destination of the French fleet, Washington and his French allies began to put a plan in place. Understanding the reality of the circumstances, Washington acquiesced to Rochambeau and discarded the notion of attacking New York. He fully embraced the new opportunity in Virginia presented by the French Navy and the prospects of exploiting the vulnerability of Cornwallis and his southern army.

Part of Washington's quickly evolving plan was to create another feint that would keep Clinton and his army in New York. The Continental Army was positioned in the Lower Hudson and was monitoring the British Army's movements. Washington ordered the construction of new encampments and sent correspondences with the intention of the British intercepting them. These messages conveyed the idea of an imminent attack by the Continental Army against the British in New York. Washington left a force behind to support his guise that the Americans were preparing an attack.

By July, Rochambeau had finished moving the bulk of his French Army to the Lower Hudson where they joined with Washington's Continentals. On August 19th, less than a week after receiving the news that de Grasse and the French Navy were heading for the Chesapeake, the Franco-American Armies were on the move south to Virginia and a meeting with Cornwallis and history. The combined force operated in secrecy as much as possible to avoid revealing its eventual destination. The Continentals under Washington amounted to thirty-five hundred, and Rochambeau's force was upwards of forty-five hundred, totaling approximately eight thousand. Many soldiers, too, remained behind to facilitate the New York attack deception so Clinton and the British garrison in New York would stay vigilant preparing for an assault that would never come.

The Battle of the Virginia Capes

On August 30, the French fleet under de Grasse arrived at the Chesapeake and began offloading supplies and French troops borrowed from the Spanish. It was usually the case in the eighteenth century, especially in contested waters, that it would not be long before the Royal Navy appeared on the horizon to advance His Majesty's interest. The British received word that the French fleet left the West Indies for America. Suspecting something was up, Clinton sent Admiral Sir Thomas Graves with nineteen ships of the line to aid Cornwallis at Yorktown with orders to evacuate his army if necessary. Much to Graves' chagrin as his ships arrived at the mouth of the Chesapeake was that the French fleet had already arrived. Moreover, the French fleet was larger and was blocking his passage to Yorktown and Cornwallis.

On September 5th, de Grasse quickly organized his warships and ventured into Chesapeake Bay to battle Graves and the Royal Navy. It had been nearly one hundred years since the French Navy defeated a British fleet on the high seas, and the pride of the French nation was again on the line. The two fleets engaged each other in a traditional line of battle, battering each other for two-plus hours. As the struggle for regional sea supremacy commenced, the battle lines of warships were unable to fully engage in the action. Only the forward and middle sections of the battle lines fired on the opposing fleet's warships. The sea battle was somewhat inconclusive, but momentous consequences would develop as a result of the Battle of the Virginia Capes and the culminating and decisive battle that would soon take place at Yorktown. It would be there that the fate of a new and great nation would be decided in fire and blood.

Graves broke off the battle as the day and sunlight were diminishing in the evening sky. He received criticism for his decisions and tactics in the aftermath of the battle. The French had two ships damaged but got the better of the British. Graves' fleet had five ships hit with cannon fire and was forced to scuttle one of his vessels. The two fleets shadowed each other for the next two days with Graves returning to New York to secure additional reinforcements and de Grasse returning to the Chesapeake. The Battle of the Virginia Capes (also known as the Battle of the Chesapeake) turned out to be one of the most important naval engagements in American history. Cornwallis' sea link to New York was cut, and more French ships arrived from Newport with additional supplies to isolate the British Commander and his soon-to-be beleaguered southern army. Professor and historian Russell Weigley of Temple University notes, "The Battle of the Chesapeake was a tactical victory for the French by no clearcut margin, but it was a strategic victory for the French and Americans that sealed the principal outcome of the war."[23]

Yorktown

In a coordinated move, French Admiral de Barras sailed south from Newport with another French fleet to join de Grasse at the Chesapeake, making a total of thirty-six French ships of the line to seal off the bay from the British. De Barras also brought heavy siege guns that the Franco-American Armies would employ against Yorktown's British defensives. Washington rode ahead of the army and arrived at his home in Mount Vernon on September 9th. He had been away for more than six years since his departure for the Second Continental Congress in the spring of 1775. Rochambeau arrived at Mount Vernon the following day, and the two generals planned the coming engagement against the British Southern Army. The stay was brief. The two men left on September 12th to join with the rest of their combined armies and to move first to Fredericksburg and then to Williamsburg, which is thirteen miles from Yorktown. The American hope at Yorktown was that Cornwallis would finally meet the "old fox."

The combined armies under Washington and Rochambeau assembled at Williamsburg on September 25th. The force also included the French Army contingent delivered by Admiral de Grasse from the West Indies under Marquis de Saint-Simon. The two armies arrived at Yorktown and met up with Lafayette's force on September 28th. The allied army, including militias, was upwards of eighteen thousand men and was double the size of Cornwallis' army, which numbered approximately eight thousand. Additionally, the allies offloaded supplies and the all-important siege guns, including some seventy-three heavy pieces from the French ships. Part of the pending cannonade would comprise one- and two-hundred-pound Parrotts (muzzle-loaded artillery) focused at Cornwallis and his southern army trapped in Yorktown.

When the allied armies arrived at Yorktown, they set in motion the mechanisms to close the issue with Cornwallis and his army. The French had become experts in siege warfare, and as Rochambeau noted, the siege and victory had become "reducible to calculation."[24] Washington's and Rochambeau's engineers laid out the first parallel trench line. The trenches extended two thousand yards in a semi-circle in front of the British positions and were constructed with cannons in thirteen artillery batteries and concealed firing positions for infantry. This first line was approximately one thousand yards from the British defensive positions around the town. It was started on October 6th with Washington laying the first pickax in the ground. It was completed by the 9th, and the cannonade began when Washington lit the first cannon that afternoon.

Over the next few days, many thousands of cannon rounds crashed into the British positions. The French occupied the position on the left of the line while the Americans held the position of honor on the right. The British attempted to disrupt the construction of the allied positions with cannon fire of their own, but the British cannon fire was eventually overwhelmed by the allied onslaught. In anticipation of the battle, the British had constructed ten forward redoubt positions. Recognizing the very large force he was up against, Cornwallis, in an effort to consolidate his position, ordered the abandonment of most of his forward redoubts. He left redoubts #9 and #10 fully manned with cannons on the right side of the allied perimeter, which blocked access to the York River. The French extended the line and installed gun installations to fire on British supply ships, some of which Cornwallis ordered to be scuttled so as not to fall into the hands of the allies. Cornwallis realized he would need additional supplies of food and materials. He ordered the infamous Banastre Tarleton and his dragoons to forage for supplies across the river near their fortified position at Gloucester Point. Tarleton encountered French Dragoons and Virginia militiamen during the movement. The subsequent battle came to be known as the Battle of the Hook. The allied forces defeated Tarleton's dragoons and forced them to retreat to their fortified position.

The allies began construction of a second parallel line on the 11th, seven hundred and fifty yards in length and three hundred and fifty yards from the British perimeter. The British launched an attack on the allies' new position, but it did not have much effect. Additionally, Cornwallis attempted to escape from the trap by having his army cross over the York River, but the effort failed due to bad weather and lack of boats. Like General John Burgoyne at the Battle of Saratoga in the fall of 1777, Cornwallis held out hope that his army would receive salvation from Clinton in New York. Also like Burgoyne, Cornwallis was assigned to his fate; Clinton's reinforcement did not arrive in time. As the final stage of the battle unfolded, the full weight of the Franco-American force began to tighten the band it had on Cornwallis and his army.

As the cannonade continued to rain fire on the British inside the perimeter at Yorktown, conditions for Cornwallis and his army grew dire. Supplies grew low, and they were forced to slaughter more than four hundred horses for food, the carcasses of which were left to lie about the town. To escape the bombardment, Cornwallis and the British force took to sheltering underground. On the evening of the 14th, the allies made plans for the two remaining British redoubts #9 and #10 on the right side of their parallel. Washington ordered that the two redoubts be taken, and an assault commenced that evening. Lt. Colonel Alexander Hamilton, Washington's most trusted aid, understanding the significance of the pending engagement, prevailed upon Washington to appoint him the leader of the American assault party. Hamilton had asked Washington on several other occasions during the war to give him a battlefield command, but Washington had refused. However, in recognition of Hamilton's skills and his importance to him on his staff, Washington finally acquiesced. Hamilton was appointed to command the assault on redoubt #10, the closest to the river and the farthest position away from the American line. Hamilton was joined by his second-in-command, his friend Lt. Colonel John Laurens, in the attack.

Lafayette was in command of the overall assault on the two British redoubts. The French, under the command of Major General Baron de Viomenil, would assault redoubt #9. Each of the assaulting allied contingents had four hundred soldiers including sappers (soldiers responsible for building and repairing structures) to dislodge the abatements (defensive positions with sharpened tree branches). Both the American and French troops attacked with unloaded muskets so the bayonet would be the decisive weapon in determining the outcome of the engagement. On the opposite side of the parallel, in the French section, they initiated a feint and cannonade against the fusilier redoubt as a diversion, and the two assault contingents made ready the attack.

Flares were sent into the night sky to signal the commencement of the assault. Hamilton's force had to traverse nearly a quarter mile of open field to reach redoubt #10 and received heavy musket fire from the British. As the Americans reached the redoubt, the sappers broke through the front of the obstructions, and Hamilton's men entered the redoubt. Laurens led eighty men around the back of the redoubt. They forced their way over the battlements and, along with Hamilton's men, engaged in hand-to-hand combat with the British. The Americans quickly secured the redoubt and subdued the defenders, taking upwards of one hundred prisoners. Likewise, the French overcame the British and German defenders at redoubt #9, but they suffered more casualties in the assault due to musket fire from the enemy defenders. In the end, the French also took more than one hundred prisoners. With the two redoubts captured, the allies were able to complete the second parallel.

The bombardment of Cornwallis' forces intensified with the allied cannons in very close proximity to the British positions. The bombardment continued for the next two days until, on the 17th, a drummer appeared with a British officer waving a white flag atop the battlements of Yorktown. For Washington and the Americans, it was the event they had been waiting to witness for more than six long and painful years. It was the unimaginable event of an entire British Army about to surrender. It must have been a moment when time, in its endless and regimented march, seemed to pause, even if just for an imaginary instant. It was a reflection point in the course of human history that only occurs under the rarest of circumstances. It was the moment a new nation took its first unencumbered breath, the boot of British oppression having been lifted from America's chest. The world was about to change, and a new one was about to be born. America was going to have life, and the ideas of the Declaration of Independence would be consecrated and validated by the blood of freedom-aspiring patriots. Men were not sacrificing themselves for a nation but for the ideals of freedom, liberty, and justice. Those concepts, righteously rooted in faith in a divine and benevolent creator, were not just noble platitudes. They were the bedrock of a new civilization and a moral guiderail by which people would be able to live their lives.

The surrender negotiations lasted for two days, and an agreement was signed on the 19th after Cornwallis finally accepted Washington's terms. Washington played hardball and didn't allow the British to unfurl their regimental flags on the surrender field. He also rejected the British position that Cornwallis' army would be pardoned and allowed to return to Britain. Washington had not forgotten about the thousands of American prisoners the British had taken over the course of the war and the conditions they had to face in royal captivity. More than eight thousand British and German soldiers along with many British sailors surrendered. It has been lionized in American poetic folklore that the British band on the surrender field played a toon called "The World Turned Upside Down," but that is unconfirmed. The American cache of weapons and materials included some eight thousand muskets, more than one hundred and fifty cannons, and many British naval vessels, but the deepest wound the British were forced to accept was the devastating blow to their pride, morale, and ambitions in America.

The dubious honor of surrender fell to Brigadier General Charles O'Hara, the second-in-command. O'Hara was appointed by Cornwallis to surrender his sword to the allies at the head of the British line. Cornwallis claimed to be ill and did not attend the surrender ceremony. The American and French forces flanked the surrendering British column. At the head of the column was O'Hara, who first offered the sword of surrender to Rochambeau as a slight to Washington and the Americans. Rochambeau, in one of history's most courteously deferential moments, rejected the sword from O'Hara and pointed across the line to Washington. O'Hara then offered it to Washington who also rejected the gesture and pointed to his second-in-command, General Benjamin Lincoln. Lincoln had suffered the indignity of surrendering his army to the British at Charleston and was then part of the momentous event at Yorktown. After receiving the sword, Lincoln returned it to O'Hara.

It was done! The British Southern Army marched off to a prisoner-of-war encampment. Washington wrote to Congress regarding the conclusion of the events at Yorktown. "I have the honor to inform Congress, that a reduction of the British army, under the Command of Lord Cornwallis, is most happily effected."[25] The war was not over quite yet as in the South the British maintained a force in Savannah and Charleston. New York remained a British stronghold with a large fleet and upwards of twenty-five thousand troops. On the day of Cornwallis' surrender at Yorktown, Clinton dispatched a fleet from New York with an additional five thousand soldiers to rescue their battered southern army. It appears to have been a last-grasp effort by Clinton to keep the fire of reunification of the American colonies within the British Empire. After Yorktown, that fire turned into a flicker and eventually burned out.

News traveled slowly in the eighteenth century. It wasn't until November 25th that the dispatch about Cornwallis' surrender reached London. On hearing the news, British Prime Minister Lord North was reported to say, "Oh God! It is all over!"[26] On December 8th, Parliament voted not to send any more troops to America and on February 17, 1782, voted to end the war. King George was slower to accept the facts of the situation and desired to continue the effort. Lamenting the turn of events, the king eventually came face to face with the reality that the war was lost and the American colonies were gone.

It's hard to see how America would have achieved independence without the French. The French supplied money, military equipment, soldiers, and men like Lafayette and Rochambeau. They went the distance with their American allies and helped shepherd through the birth of a nation conceived in a new social order. It was, in reality, an investment in the ideals of the Enlightenment, but King Louis XVI's support for American independence did not turn out well for the French monarchy. He allowed the French treasury to fall further into debt to support the

American cause, which further complicated an already difficult situation for him. In less than six years after the American Revolution, the allure of the ideas of liberty and fraternity swept across France, ending with the French Revolution and a subsequent meeting for poor Louie with the guillotine.

Nearly a century and a half after the French commitment to American independence, American Doughboys piled out of transport ships in French harbors to join with their French and British allies to defeat the German Hun. In Paris on the 4th of July, 1917, a U.S. Army detachment proceeded to Picpus Cemetery and at Lafayette's tomb voiced the phrase, "Lafayette, nous voila" (Lafayette, we are here.). The Americans joined the fight to save the French nation. Young American soldiers returned to France again in 1944, landing in Normandy at beaches code named Omaha and Utah. They went not just to free France but to liberate the continent from Nazi oppression and tyranny. The debt to France for American independence had finally been repaid.

Cornwallis did not stay long as an American prisoner. In a particular note of irony, Lt. Cornel John Laurens, with Alexander Hamilton, assaulted and captured redoubt #10 at Yorktown, which advanced the demise of Cornwallis and his army and facilitated their ultimate surrender. At that time, John Laurens' father, Henry Laurens, was being held in the Tower of London, the only American ever to hold that dubious distinction. On December 31, 1781, Henry Laurens was part of a prisoner exchange for none other than Lord

Charles Cornwallis. After the prisoner exchange, Cornwallis returned to Britain in January of 1782. Joining Cornwallis on his voyage home was one-time American hero then infamous traitor, Benedict Arnold, and his wife Peggy.

The reunion of John and Henry Laurens on American soil did not last long. The young Laurens was brave, headstrong, and reckless, and he returned to South Carolina in August of 1782 and joined the American forces outside of Charleston. In July, the British evacuated their forces from Savannah, Georgia, but they still held a garrison in Charleston and sent parties out to forage for food. Laurens was assigned a detachment of troops and attempted to cut one of them off. On the morning of August 27 at the Combahee River, Laurens' men fell into an ambush. He then led an ill-conceived charge at the British and in the first British volley was hit by musket fire and fell from his horse. He died from his wounds. The Battle of Combahee River was an inconsequential fight; the British were no longer on the offensive. Laurens was one of the last American soldiers to die during the American Revolutionary War. He was twenty-six years old, and his death is especially sad in light of the contributions some of his peers went on to make to advance the causes of liberty and freedom. Laurens was also a committed abolitionist. It's interesting to ponder what courageous young Laurens' abolitionist efforts might have been able to advance in his home state should he have lived. On December 14th, less than four months after Laurens' death, the British finally evacuated Charleston.

The British High Command in North America was reeling from the events in Virginia. Sir Henry Clinton received the lion's share of the blame for the loss of Cornwallis' army and resigned his post as commander and chief of British forces in North America and returned to Britain. He was replaced by General Guy Carlton. Except for a few localized skirmishes, such as the one in South Carolina that took the life of John Laurens, major fighting was over. British Ministers approached the American delegation in Paris in the Spring of 1782 to begin peace negotiations. The American delegation consisted of Benjamin Franklin, John Adams, and John Jay, and the talks continued into the fall. The peace deliberations were paused for a time as the British refused to recognize the United States as a free and independent nation. The British wanted to end the very expensive war with America, but pride and indignity made it difficult for them to accept the fact that their one-time colonies were going to be an independent nation. A draft of a treaty was developed on November 30th, 1783. In the end, the British had to swallow their pride and accept America as a nation.

The Articles of Confederation, under which Congress and the American government were operating, didn't grant Congress power of taxation. The power of taxation resided with the thirteen individual states. That made it very difficult for Congress to conduct a war. It was particularly arduous since the management of national affairs and the execution of financial obligations required unanimous consent of the states. Such was the case when it came to providing supplies and materials, including pay, to the army. Payment to the officers became a critical dilemma in Philadelphia, and hints of a potential rebellion by the officers against Congress became a pressing issue.

Newburgh Conspiracy

Horatio Gates had continuously petitioned Congress for a new post during the final phase of the war. Earlier in the conflict, Gates had been given high accolades for the stunning victory at Saratoga in the fall of 1777. After Saratoga, many of Gates' supporters wanted to see him replace Washington as commander and chief of the army. The political environment during the war period, both inside and outside of Congress, was marked by deception. That was particularly true with regards to Gates and the "Conway Cabal," which attempted to replace Washington. In the end, the cabal collapsed and Gates had to apologize to Washington for his part in the affair. Washington and many officers on his staff didn't like Gates; however, Congress appointed Gates as commander of the southern army in the summer of 1780 in an attempt to reverse the tide of battle there. Once again, Congress interceded in military affairs without consulting Washington. Gates' command of the southern army turned into a debacle and a consequential loss at the Battle of Camden that summer. His battlefield acumen and performance were severely questioned. Gates' reputation was at a low point. Surprisingly, he still had supporters in Congress, and in the waning months of the war Congress appointed him as second-in-command of the army under Washington. Gates took up residence at the army encampment in Newburgh, New York.

The failures of Congress and its inability to independently raise revenue under the constraints of the Articles of Confederation boiled over into a potential crisis. In section 8 of the Articles, it noted that Congress could not raise taxes on its own but was required to requisition funds from the states. At that point in the war, with peace on the horizon, many of the states were already in debt. The various states were not interested in providing any additional money to Congress no matter how justified Congress' obligations were. Many of the army's officers had not been paid in more than nine months. Moreover, they had been promised a pension of half pay for life in recognition of their service. During the winter of 1783, rumors of a mutiny abounded. A radical element among the officers was becoming more vocal, and it received encouragement from members of Gates' staff. Gates' involvement was never confirmed, but he most likely contributed to the agitation.

Alexander Hamilton left his post alongside Washington in the army and was elected by the New York delegation to the Continental Congress in 1782. Hamilton wrote several essays denouncing the weakness of the Articles of Confederation and proposed a stronger federal system in which Congress would have, among other powers, taxing authority. He created a draft outline of how a new federal governing system would work, but his plan was rejected by Congress. In December, as the crisis of debt mounted and the officers in Newburgh grew increasingly discouraged, Hamilton joined efforts with James Madison and Robert Morris (the Superintendent of Finance of the United States) to exert pressure on Congress. The newly formed group believed it could use the threat of a mutiny in the army to shock Congress into action. The threat was further emphasized on January 6th, 1783, when General Alexander McDougal testified to Congress on the grievances of the army officers and the fearful consequences if their petitions were ignored.

The Hamilton/Morris-led group allied with other like-minded nationalists called the Federalists and proposed a modification to the Articles that would allow Congress to impose tax on imported goods. The Federalists believed it would provide revenue to pay the army and funds for other obligations the government had accumulated during the war. The amendment to the Articles required all thirteen states to agree to the change. Rhode Island rejected the amendment, and other states reversed their affirmative votes. Recognizing the futility of the circumstances, Robert Morris resigned his post as Superintendent of Finance. The crisis grew worse as the more radical contingent among the officers drafted a letter to Congress. In the letter, they criticized Congress and Washington who they viewed along with Henry Knox as being too moderate in their dealings and positions towards Congress' lack of action. Rumors existed that the army might march on Philadelphia and Congress. Hamilton and many of the other Federalists thought the crisis among the army officers presented an opportunity to force Congress to adopt stronger centralized governmental powers. Hamilton wrote a letter to Washington outlining his position with respect to the crisis with the officers. Washington disagreed with his one-time valued aide and noted that it was very dangerous to use the army in that manner. He further believed that it was a threat to the accomplishments of the Revolution and republican ideals.

Newburgh Address

In Newburgh, an anonymous meeting was called among the officers on March 11, 1783. It was at that critical moment that Washington stepped into the drama unfolding within his army. He first noted that the meeting on the 11th was illegitimate and called his own meeting for the 15th in an effort to reaffirm his leadership authority and to assuage concerns. Washington was not anticipated to attend the meeting on the 15th, and Gates was prepared to address the group. It was then that Washington appeared at a side doorway of the hall and requested of Gates that he be permitted to address the officers. Gates had no choice but to acquiesce to his superior officer — superior in every measure of the phrase. Washington spoke:

A grateful sense of the confidence you have ever placed in me, a recollection of the cheerful assistance and prompt obedience I have experienced from you...and the sincere affection I feel for an army I have so long had the honor to command, will oblige me to declare... the great duty I owe my country, and those powers we are bound to respect...[27]

In his comments, Washington reminded the men of their patriotism to the country and that a mutiny would bring discredit to the army. It would also undermine the foundation of the new republic. Most importantly, it could adversely affect the achievements they had fought so hard to secure. He also noted that he was with them in their cause and conveyed that Congress would eventually pay them what they were owed. It was reported that near the end of the speech Washington reached into his pocket and took out a pair of spectacles. Most of the men present had never seen their commander using a vision aid. Washington's measured display of his mortal fragility dispensed with the aura of his invincibility. He was attempting to reach his men, not only as their commander, but as a fellow soldier and man who had suffered alongside them and who had also paid the price for his service. He was about to read a letter from Congress, but first, in dramatic fashion, he said, "Gentlemen, you will permit me to put on my spectacles, for I have not only grown gray but almost blind in the service of my country."[28] It was reported that many of the officers openly wept. The conspiracy was over. Washington had once again stepped forward and provided a lasting and invaluable service to his country. A service that he alone could have provided to end a rebellion that could have sent the new nation down a very different path. The officers were eventually paid a one-time lump sum of five years' pay. A portion of the money was personal funds provided by Robert Morris (the wealthiest man in America at the time), a true American patriot and founding father.

It was announced on April 19th, 1783, exactly eight years to the day of Lexington and Concord, that an agreement had been reached in Paris that put an end to hostilities between Great Britain and her one-time colonies in America. Two months later, the American Continental Army, which had fought the greatest military power of the day and struggled through the harshest of ordeals, disbanded on June 20th. Washington rode his trusted horse, Blueskin, with his military entourage into New York City on November 25th, 1783 — Evacuation Day. Simultaneously, the last British soldiers were departing from the docks of the city and heading back to England. Within less than a month, Washington traveled to Annapolis, Maryland, which at that time was the temporary seat of Congress, and on December 23, 1783, he resigned his commission as the Commander-in-Chief of the American Army. His desire was to return to his home in Mount Vernon and spend a peaceful retirement with his wife, Martha, and their family.

Washington was following the example of the famed Roman leader Cincinnatus who "laid down the scroll" and returned power back to the Roman Senate. Washington was surrendering his power and authority back to Congress and civilian leadership. That act by Washington, who could have been king, is one of history's greatest examples of living up to the true ideals of republicanism, self-sacrifice, and service to country. King George III, upon hearing from artist Benjamin West of Washington's resignation, was reported to say, "If he did, he would be the greatest man in the world."[29]

Part Three

The Bands of Connection

Chapter Seven

A More Perfect Union

America had won its war for independence. Benjamin Franklin, John Adams, and John Jay made up the American delegation to the Treaty of Paris, and they were very skillful in their diplomatic negotiations with the various powers represented, including England, France, Spain, and the Netherlands. The British, in adherence to part of the treaty's terms, relinquished control of the northwest territory to America. That region included what is currently Ohio, Indiana, Illinois, Michigan, Wisconsin, and parts of Minnesota east of the Mississippi. Spain, to whom France had ceded its remaining territorial holdings in North America after the Seven Years' War, received the endorsement to negotiate with the Americans the regions west of the Mississippi River, including the port of New Orleans. The Spanish attempted to limit the westward expansion of the United States, but John Jay drove a hard bargain and rejected the constraining limitations. The United States territory expanded beyond any reasonable expectation, and the Treaty of Paris was signed on September 3, 1783.

The United States had grown to more than double the size of the original thirteen colonies and had more land mass than England, France, and Spain combined. The country stretched from the Northeast south of the St. Lawrence (current day Maine), west to the

Great Lakes and all territory east of the Mississippi, and to the border region of northwestern Florida, which was still held by Spain. Part of the success of America's expansion and new territorial claims was assisted by what seems to be an unlikely source: Great Britain. Looking to the future, the English realized that America had great potential to grow into an important trading partner. Moreover, the Americans were English-speaking and shared many customs and traditions with their former mother country. Over time, the bitter memories and losses from the war would fade, and America could become a valued ally. That visionary perspective has come to fruition. Despite another bitter fight between the two nations in the War of 1812, as well as disputes over territories in the Northwest and on the high seas, America and Great Britain have evolved into vital allies against the international forces of world tyranny.

In the years following the treaty, America went through growing pains. New settlers moved west to farm and populate the new lands west of the Appalachian Mountains and up to the east bank of the Mississippi River. That put the new settlers in greater contact with the indigenous people who pushed back against continuous American encroachment into what were ancestral lands. Hostility with the native tribes boiled over into Indian wars for the next one hundred years. Congress was unable to keep pace with the rapid changes taking place in the new nation, and the weakness of the Articles of Confederation as a loosely binding document was becoming more apparent. Additionally, the fledgling American economy was suffering due to a lack of a unified monetary policy and an effective mechanism to manage foreign and interstate commerce. The Articles didn't provide for a national court system to settle disputes between the various states, and the absence of an executive branch provided no plausible enforcement of congressional acts. American unity and cohesion suffered in the years following the Revolution.

To address the lack of cohesion the nation was experiencing under the Articles of Confederation, Congress, at the suggestion of Charles Pinckney of South Carolina, proposed that changes be made. In May of 1786, Congress appointed a committee with Pinckney as the chairman. The group spent the next few months developing changes that would overcome the most glaring weaknesses of the Articles. The committee proposed several important changes, including giving Congress authority over commerce. Despite the efforts of Pinckney and his committee, those changes were never acted upon by Congress. Even though the changes were quite ambitious, they were not enough to significantly alter the current state of affairs.

The Constitution

By 1787, it was clear that more changes to the Articles of Confederation were needed to keep the states together and provide an effective national governing system. George Washington, James Madison, Alexander Hamilton, Roger Sherman, and others were at the center of proposing a new convention. At the convention it was first proposed that the Articles simply be modified to address the needs of the growing nation, but that idea changed as many of the delegates soon realized that the Articles could not be adequately amended and something more was required.

That spring, as the glaring shortcomings of the Articles became increasingly apparent, the intellectual genesis of a new governing system was being formulated. The principal architect of the new system was James Madison. The ideas that he and the other Founders proposed were gathered from the teachings of antiquity and the history of Western civilization. The new system was an amalgamation of man's experience with governance. The Federalists, comprised of James Madison from Virginia, Alexander Hamilton and Gouverneur Morris from New York (Morris was serving as a delegate from Pennsylvania), Roger Sherman from Connecticut, James Wilson from Pennsylvania, and George Washington, believed that what the nation needed was a strong federal government. They, especially Madison, were all influenced by the ideas of Enlightenment political philosophers like Locke, Montesquieu, and others. The result was a completely new structure of government that was believed to address the needs of the new nation.

On May 25, 1787, the Convention convened at the Pennsylvania State House in Philadelphia. The deliberations were held in secret to prevent the direction of the debates from leaking out. The concern was that negative discourse would emerge among the population and produce skeptics before the document was completed. It would also allow the delegates to discuss the issues in full candor without scrutiny from the public. Among the skeptics was one-time Governor of Virginia and influential figure Patrick Henry. Henry suspected that something more than suggesting amendments to the Articles was afoot, and he chose not to participate in the Convention. He was quoted as saying that he "smelt a rat."[1] In addition, other prominent Founders, including Samuel Adams from Massachusetts, did not attend the Convention because they believed it was illegitimate and that the results would be a potential threat to liberty. John Hancock also did not attend later during the ratification process. He, like Mason, wanted a Bill of Rights to be included in the document. John Adams was away in Europe serving as the American Ambassador to England during the Convention.

The Convention commenced, and the Federalists, with the concurrence of Washington, early on dispensed with the formalities of modifying the Articles and began discussing the details of a new governing system. The direction of the discussion surprised many of the delegates from the twelve states in attendance. Rhode Island failed to send a delegation. Madison analyzed the views of the fifty-five attending delegates and surmised that they fell into three groups. The first group was made up of Federalists, like himself and Washington, who wanted a new stronger federal government. The second group was made up of moderates, who at first were surprised by the new direction of the Convention but were open to the possibility of a new Constitution.

The third group was a contingent of Anti-Federalists who were opposed to the concept of a strong central government and preferred the loose association under the Articles of Confederation. The Anti-Federalists wanted the major power to reside with the separate states and were very wary of a strong central government with dictatorial powers over the states. Their concern was that a strong central government would lead to political corruption. Some of the more noted members of the group included George Mason of Virginia, Eldridge Gerry of Massachusetts, and Luther Martin of Maryland. Two of the three delegates from New York were also part of the Anti-Federalist group. They abandoned the Convention and left Alexander Hamilton as the sole delegate from their state. Their departure nullified New York as a voting member at the Convention and reduced the number of participating states to eleven.

Madison's thinking was that many of the delegates had sufficient experiences with the shortcomings of the Articles of Confederation since their adoption in November 1777. Those experiences would allow most of the delegates to have open minds to the idea of a new Constitution. The glaring weaknesses of the Articles were very evident during the war, especially to the officers in the army as Congress struggled to fulfill its commitments to them and delayed vital war supplies, provisions, and salary payments.

Twenty-two of the delegates to the Convention had served in the army during the war, and almost all of the delegates had some personal and direct experience with the failures of the Articles.

James Madison played the key role in the construction of the new Constitution, and he developed many of the document's inspirational ideas. Gouverneur Morris, Benjamin Franklin, Roger Sherman, and Alexander Hamilton played important supporting roles, and Washington's preeminence among the supporting members provided great value to the cause. During the deliberations, Hamilton proposed ideas that were viewed as extreme. In a speech he made on June 18th on the floor of the Convention, he railed against the over-reliance on the whims of the people. He referred to them as the mob. He also proposed life-long terms for senators and the president, to whom he referred as a monarch. He further proposed that the president have overriding veto power, a bridge too far for most of the delegates to cross. Hamilton's proposals revitalized concerns about an all-powerful king-like executive, but they furnished value to Madison and the eventual adoption of a new Constitution. Madison's proposal appeared to be the middle ground between Hamiltonian autocracy and the anarchy of the Articles. In the end, it was decided that the president would have veto power over legislation, but as a compromise Congress would be able to override a presidential veto. The compromise on the limitations of presidential power is an example of the principles of checks and balances.

   While developing his plan for the new government, Madison received aid from his mentor, Thomas Jefferson, who was in Europe serving as American Ambassador to France. In the months leading up to the Convention, Madison corresponded with Jefferson and reviewed contemporary European ideas of many of the period's great thinkers on governance. Jefferson sent crates of books on political philosophy to him, and Madison made his way through several languages to understand the thoughts of some of the best minds from the Enlightenment period and antiquity. No political philosopher was more influential in shaping Madison's thinking than the French Judge Charles Louis Baron de Montesquieu. Montesquieu originated the concept of the separation of powers, a legacy that the great French Judge made to Western democratic political thought. Madison referred to Montesquieu as the "Great Sage." Montesquieu's concepts on checks and balances and the diffusion of powers among the different branches of government was believed to be the most advantageous way of preserving liberty.

   Madison was also concerned about factionalism within the growing nation and the adverse effects that special interest groups and political parties posed for republicanism. He believed his plan provided protections to mitigate the ill effects of those groups. Additionally, the new system provided safeguards against the ever-present lurkings of tyrannical rule. Madison believed that the new governing system should take into consideration the duality of the human condition to be both self-gratifying and virtuous.

Madison arrived at the Convention in May well prepared for the debates and to move the discussion from simply modifying the Articles to the creation of a new Constitution. The Convention, known at that time as the Federal Convention or the Philadelphia Convention, dramatically changed the shape of the United States governing system. George Washington was elected president of the Convention. He used his prestige and influence to advocate for a strong central government. It was not long into the debates that many of the attendees realized that a new Constitution and a remedy for repairing the growing disconnection between the states was in the making.

Madison developed the Virginia Plan, which was proposed to the Convention by his fellow delegate from Virginia, Edmond Randolph. The Virginia Plan proposed that power be broken up among three separate branches — a legislative branch, an executive branch, and a judicial branch. Each branch would have enumerated powers that counter-balanced the other branches and provided protections against one element of government becoming too powerful. Congress would act as the legislative branch and would be the branch most closely aligned with the people due to direct elections. Congress would be slightly more powerful than the other two branches. The president would act as the executive branch and would have separate and distinct authorities including enforcement of rulings made by the judiciary. The judicial branch would be the interpreter of the provisions of the Constitution and federal law and would act as the arbiter of disputes.

As the Convention progressed through the summer, disputes arose. One of the most highly charged issues was the apportionment of Congress. The dispute was between large and small states and how those states would be represented. The Virginia Plan proposed a bicameral legislature in which the number of members representing each state would be based on that state's population, but that would give the larger states like Virginia, Pennsylvania, and Massachusetts an advantage in representation. Smaller states like New Jersey and Delaware wanted equal representation, so William Patterson proposed the New Jersey Plan, which suggested a unicameral legislative body that provided equality by giving each state one vote. The concept of one vote for each state was a holdover from the Articles of Confederation. The dispute became so heated that it threatened to end the Convention.

In an effort to break the deadlock, Ben Franklin worked with Roger Sherman and Oliver Ellsworth of Connecticut to hash out a position that would be acceptable to both the large and small states. The resulting proposal was the Connecticut Plan, which has come to be known as the "Great Compromise." The plan proposed a bicameral legislature similar to the Virginia Plan with a House of Representatives where the number of delegates for each state would be based on each state's population. In deference to the New Jersey Plan, there would also be a Senate where each state would have

equal representation. The Connecticut Plan was accepted. The crisis was averted, and a precedent for compromise in American governance was established. The new Constitution would also reserve certain powers not enumerated to the federal government. Those powers would be reserved for the states.

There were also other contentious issues that needed to be worked out. The original Virginia Plan worked up by Madison did not have a Bill of Rights. George Mason, Madison's fellow Virginian who had developed the Virginia State Bill of Rights, wanted one included in the new Constitution. The issue of the Bill of Rights was deferred for several years, and Mason became a vocal opponent to the new Constitution. He, along with his fellow Virginian Edmond Randolph and Elbridge Gerry of Massachusetts, refused to sign the final document. At the conclusion of the Convention, Mason created a list of issues he had with the document. He circulated the list to Anti-Federalists in other states and formed opposition to the Constitution's ratification.

Another contentious issue was how much power the president would have and how he would be elected. It was decided that the president would be elected through an electoral college and not through a direct election by popular vote. The electoral college would bring the state legislatures into the process and give the smaller states equal input into selecting the president. The debate also centered around whether the office should be held by one person or several. Two proposals were offered. One proposed that the president serve one seven-year term. The other proposed that each section of the country have a representative president. Both of those ideas were rejected. Washington was in favor of a single president and preferred a limited tenure of service. It was ultimately decided that one person would serve a four-year term with no limit on the number of times he could be reelected. The president would also be given executive law enforcement power; veto power over legislation; authority to grant pardons; control over the armed forces; and control over foreign policy, which included receiving ambassadors. The president would be given more power than many of the delegates desired, and there was a fear that the president would be a king by another name.

As the Convention proceeded through the summer, it had become clear that there was one issue on which a compromise could not be reached. That was the issue of slavery. It was believed that the southern states would walk out of the Convention if the new constitution tried to end slavery. By the time of the Convention in 1787, slavery had become embedded in the region's economic and social fabric. One of history's cruel ironies is that many of the leaders and delegates from the southern states recognized slavery as an evil institution. It was a duplicitous position held by many slave owners, including Washington, Madison, Jefferson, and Mason. They might have personally recognized the evils of slavery, but due to the institution's economic importance to the agrarian South, they

didn't have the will or the moral or financial resolve to try abolishing it at that time.

Some southern delegates rationalized that slavery had been thrust upon them and that they had inherited the evil system. For those southern delegates, there did not appear to be a near-term solution. Some of the southern delegates, especially George Mason, suggested that slavery would hold the southern states back from economic development. He believed that "Slavery discourages arts and manufactures" and that "Every master of slaves is born a petty tyrant."[2] He also spoke about the judgement of God and seemed almost to be making a foreboding prediction of future misfortune that would grip the nation: "As nations cannot be rewarded or punished in the next world they must be in this. By an inevitable chain of causes and effects providence punishes national sins, by national calamities."[3] George Washington described slavery as his life's "only unavoidable subject of regret."[4] He, however, unlike most of his southern peers, freed his slaves upon his death.

Congress would be divided into two houses. The upper house, called the Senate, would allow two senators for each state regardless of the size of that state's population. The individual senators would be elected by the state legislature. The lower house, called the House of Representatives, would be proportional, and each state would have a number of representatives based on the size of its population. It was during the debate on representation and population size that the issue of slavery again emerged. The southern slave-holding states of Virginia, North Carolina, South Carolina, and Georgia wanted the slave population to be counted to increase their representation in Congress. Representatives from the northern anti-slave states contended that if slaves were property they should not be counted when determining the number of the southern states' representatives in Congress. An agreement was eventually reached in the Three-Fifths Compromise. Each slave would be counted as three-fifths of a person. It is important to note that the anti-slave delegates were not denigrating slaves as less than whole people but were attempting to limit the slave-holding states' power and representation in Congress.

The more mercantile states in the North, like New York and Massachusetts, were advancing due to trade and commercial activities and didn't have an economic dependence on slavery. There was a strong anti-slavery contingency among the Convention's fifty-five attending delegates. It included Franklin, Hamilton, Oliver Ellsworth, Roger Sherman, and others. Most of the delegates attempted to steer clear of the slavery issue, but one member did not shy away from it — Gouverneur Morris. Morris thought slavery was "a nefarious institution" and "the curse of heaven on the States where it prevailed."[5] On his wooden leg, Morris rose and spoke a recorded 173 speeches, more than anyone else at the Convention, and was one of the Constitution's leading advocates. He was born in 1752 in New York City and, like Hamilton, attended King's College, now Columbia University.

Morris was one of the most dynamic and colorful characters among the Founding generation. In addition to signing the Articles of Confederation and the Constitution and serving as a U.S. Ambassador to France, he was also known for certain human frailties. Morris had a weakness for the ladies, particularly married ones. He recounted his exploits in his personal diary. Morris lost his leg in a carriage accident, reportedly while fleeing from an angry husband who had caught Morris in the clutches of romance with his wife.

In late July, a group was appointed to organize the points agreed to by the delegates as the Convention adjourned for more than a week. The Committee of Detail was appointed and chaired by John Rutledge of South Carolina. Other members included Edmond Randolph, Oliver Ellsworth, and James Wilson. The group was a cross section of both large and small states, and it developed a draft roughly based on the deliberation agreements and general parameters of Madison's Virginia Plan. The exception was an attempt by Rutledge to add measures to protect the slave trade. Those measures were rejected when the entire delegation reconvened.

During the later phase of the Convention, there were several issues on which there seemed no compromise to be had among the delegates. To help break the deadlock on those issues, Benjamin Franklin offered a prayer "imploring the assistance of Heaven and its Blessing on our Deliberations."[6] Franklin was a Deist and believed that God does not intercede in human events, yet, at that critical moment, he, the American sage of the eighteenth century, offered a divine appeal to God to lighten the way forward for the soon-to-be new American Republic at the Constitutional Convention. Offering the prayer was a departure from his beliefs and signified the seriousness and precariousness of the events. For the Republic to survive, it would need to call upon the inner resources and resolve of the American people and implore guidance from Providence.

By the time of the Convention, Franklin was eighty-one years old. He was born in 1706 in Boston and lived a full life as a successful businessman, printer, and publisher from his shop in Philadelphia. He also attained worldwide notoriety as a scientist experimenting with electricity. He was self-educated and renowned for his clever home-spun witticisms and artful writing skills. He put those skills to work during the Second Continental Congress as he, Jefferson, and Adams worked on the draft of the Declaration of Independence. Arguably, his most important contribution to the American cause for independence was as a leading diplomat to France during the Revolutionary War.

The delegates completed their work by early September and advanced the document for approval. Several additional changes were made in the final weeks of the Convention, and a final copy was prepared. Of the remaining forty-two delegates, thirty-nine signed the new Constitution on September 17, 1787. Many of the

leading advocates of the Constitution, including Washington, Madison, and Hamilton, were not completely happy with the final document. In retrospect and in consideration of the diversity of interests represented by the delegates, it was a document as strong as could conceivably be advanced at that time. It provided a strong federal government; the regulation of commerce; a taxing authority; an arbiter of legal grievances; and supreme laws of the land. The new system would guard against the fracturing of the new nation.

The Convention sent the new Constitution to New York to receive the concurrence of the Articles-of-Confederation Congress. The Constitution called for ratification by nine states for the document to become the law in those states. The Articles Congress received the new Constitution and waited for many of the representatives to return from Philadelphia where they were serving as delegates at the Constitutional Convention. When the delegates returned to New York on September 28th, 1787, twelve of the thirteen states present unanimously voted to send the Constitution to their state legislatures for ratification. Adoption of the new Constitution required each state to hold a convention "by the people" to agree to the provisions of the document. The ratification process began. It took ten months before the required nine states completed their reviews and discussions in state conventions.

As Benjamin Franklin was leaving the convention in Philadelphia, a woman on the street asked him, "Mr. Franklin so what kind of government do we have? A Monarchy or Republic?"

Franklin's answer was, "A Republic madam if you can keep it."[7]
Franklin understood that the American venture in republican
government, though firmly rooted in equality and the unalienable
rights of the individual, was still a fragile experiment. Franklin's
retort to the woman in the street of Philadelphia that day in the fall
of 1787 was a cautionary message to future generations of
Americans. America's visionary republican experiment would
require continuous validation of its principles and ideas from a
proactive and informed citizenry. American republicanism is not for
an agnostic or ambivalent people. Our American governing system
has the best opportunity for success when we the people are involved
and mindful of our history, faith-based institutions, customs, and
traditions. It requires a well-informed, educated, religious, and
morally centered people. Unlike other dubious forms of authority,
such as despotic totalitarianism in the form of Marxism/Socialism,
or the corruption of unelected self-absorbed bureaucrats, or the
power of privileged celebrities and corporate elitist, American
government receives its legitimacy from the inspired initiatives and
involvement of the people.

In the end, the delegates adopted seven Articles of the
Constitution and appointed a new committee called the Committee
of Style and Arrangement to create a final draft. The committee
principally included James Madison, Alexander Hamilton, and
Gouverneur Morris. Morris is credited with authoring the Preamble

to the Constitution. His words in the Preamble set the tempo for the
rest of the document with their simplicity, elegance, and symmetry:

> We the People of the United States, in Order to form a
> more perfect Union, Establish Justice, Insure Domestic
> Tranquility, Provide for the Common Defense, Promote the
> general Welfare, and secure the Blessings of Liberty to
> ourselves and our Posterity, do ordain and establish this
> Constitution for the United States of America.[8]

By connecting the Constitution directly to the power and authority
of the American people, Morris' Preamble validated the
preeminence of the document and the new federal government. The
Constitution established six core principles under which the new
nation would operate: 1) popular sovereignty; 2) Federalism; 3)
separation of powers; 4) checks and balances; 5) judicial review; 6)
limited government.

The seven Articles of the Constitution outlined the structure
and operations of the new government. The first three articles
outline the three separate branches of government, and the last four
are process articles. Article 1 describes the legislature, which is a
congress comprised of two houses, the House of Representatives
and the Senate. Congress is designated with making laws. Article 2
describes the vested powers of the president and the authority to
enforce laws. Article 3 describes the powers of the judiciary, the
Supreme Court and lower courts, and the interpretation of laws.
Article 4 describes the relationship between the various states and
the federal government and Congress' authority to administer the

addition of new states. Article 5 describes the method of amending
the Constitution through state legislatures. Article 6, referred to as
the "Supremacy Clause," establishes that federal laws take
precedence over state and local laws. Article 7 describes the process
of ratification, by which nine state legislatures, in convention,
approve the Constitution and it becomes the law in those states. The
Constitution became the law of the land when New Hampshire, the
ninth state, on June 21, 1788, approved its adoption. The original
Constitution did not include a Bill of Rights. The adoption of a
Bill of Rights happened during George Washington's first
administration in 1791. The Bill of Rights became law on December
15, 1791, and are the first ten amendments to the Constitution.

1. Freedom of speech, religion, and press.
2. Right to bear arms
3. Limitations on quartering of soldiers
4. Limitations on search and seizures and arrests
5. Rights in criminal cases
6. Rights to a fair trial
7. Rights in civil cases
8. Limitations on bail, fines, and punishment
9. Rights retained by the people
10. States' rights

The Constitution codified the inspiration of the Declaration
of Independence: the preeminent rights of the individual and that
God created all men equal. The Declaration and the Constitution
were to work together. The Declaration was the covenant document,

and the Constitution represented the laws by which the country would function. The Declaration contends: "We hold these truths to be self-evident, that all men are created equal, that they are endowed by their Creator with certain unalienable rights, that among these are life, liberty and the pursuit of happiness."[9] The Declaration proclaims an unbreakable connection between God, the American people, and the nation's founding. The acceptance of God and His Natural Law is the fundamental building block of the American nation. As G.K. Chesterton, an early twentieth-century English philosopher, writer, and lay theologian put it, "The Declaration of Independence dogmatically bases all rights on the fact that God created all men equal...There is no basis for democracy except in a dogma about the divine origin of man."[10]

The emphasis of the Constitution was the limitation of government over the governed. The one glaring shortcoming of the Constitution was that it did not end slavery. That would be left for another generation of Americans to sort out in the fields across the nation at places call Shiloh, Antietam, Chancellorsville, and Gettysburg.

The Federalist Papers

As part of their effort to pass the new Constitution in late 1787 and early 1788 at the beginning of the states' ratification processes, Hamilton, Madison, and John Jay authored *The Federalist Papers*, a series of anonymous articles written under the pen name of "Publius," which means "the people" or "of the people." They were written anonymously because the authors had pledged secrecy about the details of the proceedings during the Convention. The articles were first published in New York newspapers to urge the state to ratify the Constitution. In the months after the Convention, New York had become a focal point for the Anti-Federalist movement. Eighty-five essays were written in total, and they ranged from October 1787 to May 1788. Hamilton, a prodigious writer and thinker, wrote fifty-one of the essays. Madison wrote twenty-nine. Jay wrote five.

The purpose of the essays was to justify the new Constitution and the new government system that was to follow. The essays were a mental exercise on contemporary thinking on government. They laid out an inspired blueprint for a government that would have limited power over the people.

The question was how to most effectively give government enough power to act in the interest of the people while providing safeguards to prevent government from usurping the people's natural rights. It is a profound and nuanced balance. Madison artfully addressed the issue in *Federalist Paper* No. 51:

> If angels were to govern, neither external nor internal controls on government would be necessary. In framing a government which is to be administered by men over men, the great difficulty lies in this: you must first enable the government to control the governed; and in the next place obligate it to control itself.[11]

The success or failure of the American constitutional republic hinges on the government operating responsibly and in the interest of the people. The people will then be free to conduct themselves without unnecessary government intrusion into their private lives and business enterprises.

One of the major successes of the Constitution is its understanding of the fallibility of man in his basic nature. Madison understood it well. Every human being has his own self-interest and, under the right circumstances, might use his designated powers to serve himself rather than the people. That is the reason for checks and balances and controls over government. Man, by nature, is neither a benevolent creature nor a beast. We are born into nature able to be shaped and guided by our parents, faith, mentors, and teachers to progress past our primal survival instincts. We are educated to act rationally and morally and to cooperate with others to develop and thrive in a civil society that is protected by a constrained and diligent government. Governments are created by men to facilitate the development and well-being of the people and to act in all cases to protect the people's best interests.

During the Convention, some of the southern delegates expressed deep concerns about the morality of slavery and the corrosive effects it has on society. Two and a half centuries later, one could speculate that if the anti-slavery contingent mounted a more forceful attempt, it might have been able to end slavery; however, it's arbitrary to contemplate the question without an in-depth understanding of the circumstances of the time and the conditions under which the participants were operating. The Founders at the Convention understood that their primary mission was to reinvigorate the governing system and to bring order and cohesiveness to the states of the nation. When the issue of slavery arose, the delegates steered away from the topic to avoid derailing the Convention and the new Constitution. The purpose of the Convention was to find the middle ground in the struggle between states' rights and the power of the newly proposed federal government and arrive at a consensus. At that time, there was no consensus to be found on the issue of slavery and the toxic nature of the southern states' social and economic reliance on it. The Founders certainly understood that there would be a future reckoning over the issue.

****

In the decades that followed the founding period, slavery and racial animus towards Blacks remained the great paradox of American history. The great accomplishments of the eighteenth century founding period have been so important to the progress of man that they should not be diminished by that generation's inability to deal with the issue. However gifted the Founders were, they were still just mortal men subject to all of the frailties and weaknesses of any group of men from any period back to antiquity. America's entry as a new governing system set a new standard for future countries to emulate and has had great meaning not just for America but for all of humanity. Many contemporary Leftists fail to recognize the proper historical context and the value that America has advanced for mankind. The Leftists contend that slavery and racism should be the defining issue of the founding period and America's legitimacy as a nation. Their perspective is a catastrophic injustice and fails to consider the panoply of benefits the American system has provided.

Extoling the virtues and dignity of the individual and leaving out the enslaved population is obviously contradictory. The Founding generation and the anti-slave movement were thinking past the issue to a more enlightened future. They left the resolution of the issue to a future time when demographic shifts, social change, and a moral imperative would drive the nation to confront it head on. The American generation of the mid-nineteenth century was given a chance to correct the blight on our nation's history. The Founders wanted to set a national course that was guided by a providential moral compass. Slavery and racial prejudice were obstacles on that path and would need to be corrected so the nation could achieve a brighter future.

After the adoption of the Constitution and during Washington's first term as president, Alexander Hamilton, who was the Secretary of the Treasury at the time, proposed that the new federal government assume all the war debt from the states. The plan would add value and establish the viability of the federal government moving forward. Virginia, unlike many of the other states, did not have major debt from the war. Virginia's acceptance of the Assumption Plan was a major concession that Hamilton was able to work out with Jefferson, who was the Secretary of State and represented Virginia and the southern position. With that, if Virginia also moved on the abolishment of slavery, it would have compounded the economic impact on the state and disrupted the economic and social fabric of the South. Even during Washington's term as president (1789 to 1797), the slavery issue was still a bridge too far for the nation to meaningfully cross.

Moreover, some omissions in the final draft were viewed by many as fatal flaws in the document, and major changes or a complete overhaul were thought by many to be the only path forward. Fortunately, that was not to be the case, and the broadness of the text in the Constitution proved over time to be a major strength of the document. If the Constitution evolved into something more specific, it would lose its relevance as time passed and the document could become outdated. The beauty is in its broadness and reaffirmation of individual prerogatives, Western legal traditions, and moral principles that give it a lasting value. It leaves specific details for reflection and interpretation. The Constitution was be adopted on June 21, 1788, when New Hampshire, the ninth of the thirteen states, ratified the document. Shortly thereafter in 1791,

Congress adopted a Bill of Rights with the first ten amendments to the Constitution.

A House Divided

In 1858 at the Republican State Convention in Springfield Illinois, Abraham Lincoln noted, "A house divided against itself cannot stand."[12] That invocation of Matthew 12:25 was how Lincoln described the period leading up to the Civil War when American society was ripped apart by feelings of extreme passion over the issue of slavery. The divide fueled angry and bitter emotions on both sides of the issue, and those passions manifested in violence across the fields of the nation. The conflict thrust the American society into a conflagration that in the end took the lives of more than half a million soldiers. American history can be viewed as two halves: before the Civil War and after it. The Civil War was a crucible that the nation had to endure for redemption. It was a metaphorical cleansing in the blood of young men before healing and a new social order would emerge. During the Civil War, approximately four million Black slaves lived in the South. It is estimated that 350,000 Union soldiers' lives were, as Lincoln noted, sacrificed "upon the altar of freedom."[13] They gave their lives to preserve the union and our constitutional republic so that Americans of all races and nationalities could live in freedom.

After the Civil War, the nation could claim that it would forever move on the path of true justice for all of its people. Lincoln noted in the Gettysburg address:

> It is for us the living, rather, to be dedicated here to the unfinished work which they who fought here have thus far so nobly advanced. It is rather for us to be here dedicated to the great task remaining before us –that from these honored dead we take increased devotion to that cause for which they gave the last full measure of devotion—that we here highly resolve that these dead shall not have died in vain—that this nation under God, shall have a new birth of freedom—and that government of the people, by the people, for the people, shall not perish from the earth.[14]

Lincoln was reaffirming the promise of America through a rebirth and commitment to the values that drove the nation's inception. That promise can be seen in the sacrifices of the nation's young men on the battlefields of the Civil War.

Chapter Eight

"A City upon a Hill"

(A Quote from Jesus' Sermon on the Mount,
Used as a Reference to America Exceptionalism)

Humans are motivated by self-interest. This is not to be judged as bad or good; it's simply a condition of human nature. For people to accept personal allegiance to a new national credo, the credo must be consistent with basic human nature. The brilliance and creative thrust of the Constitution is that it outlines the limitations of government over the people. The people are the ultimate power over the government; however, to protect and maintain a civil society, necessary limitations on individual behavior, based on generally accepted principles, had to be established.

New immigrants to America have been attracted to the life-enriching values of freedom, liberty, justice, and self-determination that they haven't experienced in other places. America represents a new beginning, and the entry fee is the acceptance of these life-enriching values. Justice and due process secure liberty and freedom for all. The rights of the individual are sacrosanct and derive their legitimacy directly from God. One doesn't need to be a person of faith to benefit from this concept. The important thing is that the

Constitution protects all individuals and provides a check against the overreach of government authorities.

The nation has collectively struggled with the original sin of slavery; racial, ethnic, and religious discrimination; and the minimization and cultural exclusion of women and people with nontraditional orientations; however, despite all the shortcomings of human nature, new immigrants still yearn to come here and make America their home. It's a clear indicator that people from outside this country understand the promise of America far better than the pervasive Leftists and many of today's Progressives do. These new immigrants have lived experiences in different areas around the world where economic freedom and individual liberty are in short supply and not protected by a constitution. Unlike the "woke" Leftists and Progressives who have disdain for America, the new immigrants have life experiences that they can compare with the freedom and liberties that America offers. America is the country where immigrants are willing to risk their futures despite the imperfections of human nature that are exasperated by the hate-America contingent. For the new immigrants, America is still "a city upon a hill."

In society's ongoing march towards fairness, America, like every society that has ever existed, has struggled with unequal and sometimes heinous treatment of some of its citizens. America's greatness lies in this: while other societies have been slow or indifferent to inequities, America has set the standard for redressing social ills. The work continues, and the march toward a more perfect application of justice is ongoing.

There is a fragileness to the American experience. If we lose the essence of what makes us Americans, the binding force that holds us together can be dissolved. President Ronald Reagan noted in July of 1987 that "Freedom is a fragile thing and it's never more than one generation away from extinction. It is not ours by way of inheritance; it must be fought for and defended constantly by each generation…"[1] The great threat to the Republic, our Constitution, and our way of life is that we might become indifferent to our country's founding values, history, and legacy. The sacrifices of generations of patriots are discounted, forgotten, and not taught in schools. We see some of these concerning trends today when students in high school and on major college campuses can't answer basic questions about American history. Who was the first president? Which side won the Civil War? Who attacked the United States at Pearl Harbor?

Should this generation of Americans forget the lessons, advancements, and legacy of America, the nation will be destined for a bleak future. If we become indifferent to our history and the great accomplishments our society has achieved, it would have negative consequences not only for America but for the entire free world. If history has taught us one thing throughout the course of human experiences, it is that societies, even great ones, are always susceptible to falling into the clutches of the ever-lurking and diabolical grasp of authoritarianism.

If the aberrant philosophies of the Left take hold in our society and power structures, our freedom and self-determination will be abstract notions from the past. From that, something new will emerge, and it will not look like anything we have seen in our country's nearly two-hundred-and-fifty-year history. In the "woke" version of America, people will be divided along base primal lines. People will be defined by the group to which they belong and not by the value of their individuality. The measure of an individual's value will be based on his/her social grievance status. People will be defined intersectionally and grouped according to their race, gender, orientation, and political complicity. Any vocal thoughts that do not conform to Leftist dogma will be regarded as hate speech, and the casualty of hate speech is always free of speech.

Constraint on language deemed to be "hate speech" is the first step on the road to mind control. By limiting speech, the Leftists stop the free exchange of ideas, which is the basis of the intellectual development of the Western mind. Western philosophy and critical thinking along with provocative and even contentious exchanges are the root cause of human progress over the last two millennia. Without the liberty to freely express oneself, the ability to reason will be stifled.

In that bleak version of the future, the Leftists will get around to institutionally dismantling all other individual rights and freedoms outlined in the Bill of Rights, and they will usher in the dawn of a new dark age for America. They will separate people into groups and make dividing lines within society in order to break the cohesion of national identity. They will portray the national identity as the root cause and manifestation of all that is wrong with society. According to the Left, the only cure for the contrived ills of society is to replace the national community with Neo-Marxist ideology. The Left's contention is that they will provide a vast economic and social safety net for everyone. All you need to do is surrender your individuality and accept your role as part of a designated grievance group and everything will be fine. What the Left wants is capitulation to their will and for people to surrender their personal liberties and freedom for "the greater good." The greater good, from their perspective, is control by the intellectual elitist class schooled in the instructions of Marxism.

Nowhere in American society have Leftist principles been more destructive than on our college campuses. College is traditionally a place where young minds are encouraged to broaden their horizons and think for themselves in the immersion of study and knowledge. Today on the campuses of many universities and colleges, students are not encouraged to have open minds for learning new ideas and perspectives. Instead, they are coursed by "woke" Leftist faculties and administrators to be guided by feelings and sensitivities and to shut down debates and discussions that are contrary to progressive thinking. Speeches, statements, or

Michael Urtnowski

discussions that are deemed to be politically incorrect, insensitive to a group or race, or a violation of another's sensitivities are considered microaggressions and, again, are to be shut down. How does the free exchange of knowledge carry on in the Left's very asphyxiating and controlling academic environment?

The Left's mantra is that American society has been racist, misogynistic, and homophobic since its inception and that it should be uprooted and completely dismantled. They will attempt to "level the playing field" by restructuring all our institutions and implementing their ideas of "social justice." The long-established American economic system based on hard work, fair play, and justice under the law will be scrapped. Let it be known, however, that the Left only knows how to tear down civil societies and economic systems. Their utopian vision for the future has never been successful anywhere it has been tried. The old Soviet Union, Cuba, North Korea, Venezuela, and other socialist attempts are examples. Invariably, the forced implementation of a command economy, authoritarian rule, and false ideas of "social justice" have always led to tyranny, injustice, and the establishment of a ruling elite not obligated to report to anyone.

Misguided Notions and Linguistic Corruption

On the surface, the idea of social justice that is championed by the Left seems like a reasonable concept, but, like so many of the Left's concepts, it is a deception. The Left defines equity as all people being considered equal, but their idea of equity is actually the opposite of equality. They use equity as a tool for leveling the playing field and skewing results in favor of a grievance group. Likewise, they use the term "hate speech" to define any speech that disagrees with their Leftist dogma. The problem with social justice is that it isn't justice. Justice does not need any adjectives or qualifiers. Justice stands on its own. Including social in front of justice changes the meaning and describes something other than justice. It's clever how the Left attempts to alter the meanings of words and phrases to manipulate people. It's incumbent on us to push back against their distortions of our language and to expose them for what they are. Their deceptions are veiled attempts to deceive people and gain control.

America's foundational principles of liberty, freedom, and justice for all are under assault. These principles embody the most enlightened form of guidance for man to govern himself and prosper in a dynamic civil society. The proof of this assertion is the overall success of the American nation. America's success is manifested in its political, social, and faith-based institutions; economic strength; moral predication; and ascendency to a leadership position among nations. The American people are guided by a sense of fairness and have labored to overcome divides within society and to advance justice for all. So how, then, could this nation or any nation that exhibits such admirable and virtuous tendencies, be threatened by internal subversive forces? Unfortunately, the subversive elements of the Far Left's message have gained strength throughout the country in recent decades. The message has been advanced by the Lefts' collaborators in the mainstream media, progressive politicians, college professors and administrators, corporate elitists, and the cadre of privileged celebrities in Hollywood. These collaborators let the Neo-Marxist thought police do their thinking and dictate politically correct attitudes to have on a wide range of political, social, and economic issues. It is common to see many so-called reporters from different news networks regurgitating the same lines on specific topics from day to day. It appears they all receive their narratives and talking points from the same left-wing source. It is also common to see college professors and Liberal elitists accept and promote the idea of hate speech and limitations on freedom of speech. Freedom of speech is the most important liberty individuals have within a society. If individuals lose the ability to speak freely, all other liberties will be in jeopardy.

What keeps a civil society and nation state together? Nineteenth-century French scholar and writer Ernest Renan's work titled *What is a Nation?* defines the binding elements that keep a nation together.

"A nation is therefore a great solidarity constituted by the feeling of sacrifices made and those that one is still disposed to make. It presupposes a past but is reiterated in the present by a tangible fact: consent, the clearly expressed desire to continue a common life."[2] He also contends that "a nation is a soul, a spiritual principle."[3] There is no better example of this than America, where people with different orientations, religions, and cultures from all over the world have come to live, bound together by the spiritual ideas of liberty, freedom, and justice for all.

The Founders are often thought of as radical revolutionaries, which they partially were but not in the context of contemporary notions of radicalism or of twentieth-century revolutionary movements. Jefferson contended that the king had betrayed the people's basic rights and that a radical separation was the only recourse available. It is noted in the Declaration:

> Mankind are more disposed to suffer, while evils are sufferable, than to right themselves by abolishing the forms to which they are accustomed. But when a long train of abuses and usurpations, pursuing invariably to the same Object evinces a design to reduce them under absolute Despotism, it is their right, it is their duty, to throw off such government.[4]

The justifications for separating from England were evident.

America's founding was very different than the foundings of other countries. America is a nation of people drawn together by ideas of liberty and freedom. This makes Americans unique among the people of the world. It is disconcerting that so many Americans take their liberties for granted. We go about our daily activities enjoying the usual order of things, and it is inconceivable to most of us that our liberties could disappear without our continued reaffirmation and defense of them. A clear reflection of history shows that to secure and maintain our freedoms, exceptional individuals must rise to their defense and ultimately prevail over tyranny. Not recognizing the sacrifices of our brave patriots and the lasting effects of their efforts is today's greatest societal deficiency.

The Path to Tyranny

The American Revolution and later the French Revolution brought new and creative expressions of man's place in an ordered universe. The ideas of the natural rights of the individual received acceptance as Western democracies developed in the nineteenth and twentieth centuries. In tandem with the rise of democracy, the West underwent an industrial revolution that forever changed the workplace and the relationship that average workers have with industrialist owners/managers. Socialist ideology emerged as a new governing philosophy, and by the middle of the nineteenth century communism had taken hold as an accepted alternative doctrine in academic circles and coffee houses in Western European cities. It was believed by some academics in Germany, France, and England that communism was a better system to address the social ills brought on by industrialization. In the second half of the nineteenth century, socialist and communist theories developed into radical political parties, and in the early part of the twentieth century they developed into national governments, first in Russia in 1917.

Karl Marx and Communism

The father of communism, Karl Marx, was born in Trier, Prussia (later to become part of Germany), in 1818. Marx was a social and economic philosopher and was greatly affected by the teachings of Georg Hegel (1770-1831) and the political application of his theories on the dialectic. In the Hegelian dialectic on governance, an antagonism develops between a base thesis and an antithesis. Through that conflict, a synthesis develops, combining parts of both theses, and a higher level of truth is achieved from the process, at least according to the Hegelian dialectic. Marx applied the concept to his ideas on communism. In 1848, he collaborated with Fredric Engels to author the first of his major works, *The Communist Manifesto*, in which they state that capitalism will destroy itself and be replaced by socialism and later evolve into communism. Marx believed that the struggle between the working class, which he called the proletariat, and the ruling class, called the bourgeoisie, would end in revolution. The workers would then take over the means of production and a more benevolent socialist society would emerge and finally culminate in a communist state and society. As Marx's theory goes.

Marx believed religion was an anesthetic for the people as they struggled through their lives of hardship in nineteenth-century capitalist Europe. In 1844 he wrote that religion "is the *opium* for the people."[5] Religion, according to Marx, kept the working class in conformance and helped maintain the status quo. Marx was not an atheist, though future communist movements took on the trappings of atheism. He appeared to be somewhat ambivalent about the existence of God. He also never denounced the use of violence to bring about social change. Marx didn't live long enough to see the violent culmination of his philosophy in the Russian Revolution of 1917. He died in 1883.

Marx is recognized as one of the most important and influential thinkers of the last two centuries. His ideology took root in Russia and other countries during the twentieth century, but the societal utopia advanced by him and his followers never materialized in any of those places. Communism always falls short of expectations and descends into authoritarianism that causes despair, hunger, and death. Socialism and communism sound good in theory, but they always fail because they are antithetical to the human spirit, which yearns to be free and accountable to itself.

Some lessons of history never seem to take root. Millions who have come before us have paid an odious price for the calamity of communism, but it continues to be advanced as a viable alternative system. It is counterintuitive that communism always seems to resurrect itself from mankind's archive of bad ideas. Let us not deceive ourselves and give credence to the diluted notion that communism has anything to offer America or any other nation. For the sake of human wellbeing and progress, let communism die once and for all.

The American Left has taken a page from Karl Marx's playbook and his view on class struggle. Leftists substitute the class struggle from communism with conflict over race, and they look to group Americans as racists and antiracists. The Left points to *The 1619 Project* by Nicole Hannah Jones and the concept of critical race theory. It is a work that contends that America has been racist from its inception and was built upon the institutional preservation of slavery and that the trappings of racism have penetrated American society. Let it be noted that even *The Washington Times*, a left-leaning newspaper according to the Media Bias Rating, in an editorial dated May 24, 2020, wrote, "The '1619 Project' is bad history fueled by bad motives."[6] America is not a systemically racist society. Racism and slavery have been present since the beginning of civilization. Western societies were among the first to ban the institution of slavery. Great Britain ended the slave trade in 1807. France abolished slavery in 1848. The United States abolished slavery in 1865. As unbelievable as it seems, slavery still exists in parts of the world today, including regions of Asia and Africa.

Summer of Destruction

On May 25, 2020, America witnessed the killing of George Floyd by Minneapolis Police Officer Derek Chauvin. Americans viewed on national news and social media a nine-minute video taken by someone who witnessed Officer Chauvin kneeling on the neck of George Floyd who was handcuffed and lying prone on the

pavement. Several of Chauvin's fellow officers stood by and did not
intercede. Following the senseless killing of George Floyd, the
nation exploded with protests, which quickly devolved into riots in
several major cities, including New York, Washington, Los
Angeles, Chicago, Portland, Boston, Seattle, Atlanta, Minneapolis,
and others. The rioters destroyed many businesses, most of which
were already struggling due to the COVID-19 pandemic, and they
disregarded social distancing mandates that were put in place to
prevent the continued spread of the virus. The rioters also assaulted
residents and police officers; burned police vehicles; trashed private
and government property; disrupted transportation systems; blocked
traffic intersections; and caused havoc in the cities. The destruction
occurred mostly in Democrat-controlled cities and states where
years of Progressive Democrat policies helped to erode the harmony
and civic cooperation between the residents and the police. The
horrific death of George Floyd should not have been used to justify
the large-scale destruction of our cities and the breakdown of civility
across our nation.

       During the riots, several Democrat governors and mayors
prevented the police from protecting their cities and populations.
Progressive Democrats in New York, Los Angeles, and Minneapolis
went as far to urge reducing financial support for the police, and
other more extreme positions within the protest movement called for
the elimination of policing entirely. In Los Angeles, some
government officials voiced solidarity with the rioters as they

ransacked communities and tore through the streets of America's cities. At one event, officials actually kneeled before groups of demonstrators as if they were asking for penance for some sin. It was a stomach-turning obsequiousness shared by many in the Democrat party and white Liberals across the nation. When some Democrat politicians refused to augment their police forces with National Guard troops, they stated it was because the people had a legitimate right to protest. The majority of the Left-leaning news networks tried to portray the riots as "peaceful protests," all while Americans watched the destruction and burning of America's cities on their TVs. At least twenty-five Americans were killed in the riots.

The behavior of Progressive politicians in some cities emboldened the rioters and maximized the damage and carnage inflicted on local businesses and the civil population. The most noted acts of destruction include the burning of a police station in Minneapolis. In New York, rioters painted graffiti on St. Patrick's Cathedral and looted Macy's at Herald Square and countless other retail stores in Manhattan. In Washington, they painted graffiti on the Lincoln Memorial and other national monuments, and they burned a portion of historic St John's Church where presidents have prayed since the presidency of James Madison. It's hard to imagine that this kind of lawlessness would have been tolerated at any other time in American history.

Another excuse offered by the Left and the mainstream media was that the pandemic was contributing to the civil and political unrest. Progressive politicians used the pandemic to usurp authorities not granted to them under local and state law. They greatly restricted the movements and interactions of the people in their states, and they closed businesses, which had a severe effect on commerce. They closed schools and restricted access to public education, which has led to a regression of educational development among children and young adults. The Left points to recommendations from supposed experts in the public health sector to justify their mandates, many of which defied logic and scientific evidence. It's not hard to conclude that the Left had an underlying agenda that had little to do with the health crisis.

The protesters fell into three groups. The first was made of peaceful protesters expressing their legitimate rights to assemble and voice their outrage over the wrongful death of George Floyd. The second and third were made not of protesters but of rioters. The second contained mostly young locals with pent up energy and emotion, and they didn't necessarily have political agendas. They broke windows and looted stores and set fire to dumpsters. The third and most pernicious group was comprised of political agitators, anarchists, and members of Antifa, Black Lives Matter, and other left-wing groups. There is a secret hand at work in these groups: they are well funded and well organized. Their ultimate goal is to bring down America, its institutions, its government, and the civil society.

Using the George Floyd incident to condemn America as a racist society is void of any sense of history or honest perspective.

One needs only to review the progress the country has made in race relations over the last sixty years. Millions of Black Americans have joined the middle class and attended all of America's major institutions of higher learning. Black Americans have reached the highest levels in American society and industry, in entertainment, sports, the military, entrepreneurship, and all types of professions through their own hard work. They have reached the highest levels of politics, including both houses of Congress, mayorships, governorships, and the presidency. Barack Obama would not have become the 44th president of the United States if a majority of white voters had not chosen to cast their ballots for him rather than John McCain in 2008 and Mitt Romney in 2012, both white candidates. It's hard to make a case that America is a systemically racist society given that fact.

An Alternative Universe

Progressives on the left want the country to devolve into something very different from a constitutional republic. What protections will there be for individual liberty in the new world created by Leftists and anarchists? How will a vibrant economy exist and civil interaction be conducted when there is no structure to society? Who will provide for healthcare needs when the system collapses? How will justice, laws, and order be maintained without a police force? To say the Progressives have not thought this through is an understatement. Before we take another step towards their vision of America, let us remember Thomas Hobbes' view of what life would be like in a world void of civil constraints: "solitary, poor, nasty, brutish and short."[7]

Americans have always valued and relied on their freedom of speech, but the Left sees dialogue and debate as a threat to its control of the narrative. Conservatives, for the most part, welcome discussion on the issues, which is a testament to the confidence they have in the validity of their positions and their open-mindedness to evolve based on new information and perspectives. Today's Progressives, on the other hand, try to shut down dialogue and limit the exchange of views that are different from their own. It is a testament to the lack of confidence they have in the validity of their positions. Conservatives arrive at their positions based on their own thought processes, common sense analyses, and shared wisdom rooted in an understanding of historical precedent. Leftists arrive at their positions based on talking points from the supercilious intellectual class. If you disagree with their views, they will resort to personal attacks and verbal assaults against you. They will try to shame you by saying you're not woke enough or that you need sensitivity training to feel the pain of the grievance group that is currently fashionable. They will call you racist, homophobic, and misogynistic and accuse you of spouting hate speech. They are coercive and dishonest.

To all young Americans: don't be deceived by the Left's propaganda. If you work hard and educate yourself, you can achieve the American dream. It is attainable no matter your race, orientation, or place of origin or however humble your beginning might have been. It's there for everyone. Reach out and grab it. Shape your own destiny. It is the promise of America. Blaming America for your own shortcomings will constrain your personal development. Don't diminish your destiny by becoming part of a grievous group. Be honest with yourself. Take stock of your strengths and work to overcome weakness. Make a plan and stick to it. Don't become distracted. You will make mistakes and experience failure, but life is not a sprint; it's a marathon. You will need to go the distance for a successful and fruitful outcome.

Institutional Takeover

Most American parents send their children off to school to receive education for a more fulfilled future. Unfortunately, what parents too often get in return are classes taught by confused and angry zealots who have been coerced into believing that America and its institutions, including the institutions they attended to achieve their lofty professorships and the institutions that employ them, are evil, racist, and irredeemable. The zealots' religion is Wokism, and it is rooted in the methods of Neo-Marxism. America's colleges and universities have made it easy for the young and naive to be swayed by the misrepresented egalitarian notions of Marxist theory and the false promise of a happy and benevolent future. If colleges and universities educated students to think objectively using, say, the Socratic method of probative critical analysis and problem solving, America's young would not reach such radical conclusions about society, and they would not accept the radical Left's Neo-Marxist dogma. It is vitally important that America's young people understand the history of the eternal human struggle for liberty, freedom, justice, and self-determination.

How can it be that this great country has come to be so near the cliff of Marxism? At times it seems there are only a few brave patriots ready to push back against the ignorance, lies, and self-loathing of the Far Left. Have we ventured so far off course that we no longer have any convictions about who we are as a nation? Have the American people grown so complacent and indecisive... and has the spirit of '76 faded so far from memory, that we have lost our way and our resolve? Have we lost our will to stand up to the mob and for what we believe in? Has the hour grown so late that the light from the lantern in the Old North Church has gone out for America? America, which in its finest moments defeated Nazism, fascism, and communism and became the vanguard of freedom and liberty around the world? Has this great beacon of hope that stands for the rights of every individual come to its final chapter? Are we soon to be the most recent great civilization, like the Greeks and the Romans, to end up in the proverbial bonfire of history? Is it conceivable that this great country, the most noble venture in human history, will wither on the vine from apathy and indifference? Is this truly the end of our way of life, our creative human experiment, and our special place in time? I say no! Let us rally together and push

back against these bad ideas and reaffirm who we are as a people.

Abraham Lincoln had thoughts as to the challenges facing America:

> Our reliance is in the love of liberty which God has planted
> in our bosoms. Our defense is in the preservation of the spirit
> which prizes liberty as the heritage of all men, in all lands,
> everywhere. Destroy this sprit, and you have planted the
> seeds of despotism around your own doors. Familiarize
> yourself with the chains of bondage, and you are preparing
> your own limbs to wear them.[8]

To this generation of patriots: this is our moment. "These are

the times that try men's souls." Let us not be dissuaded from our

responsibility and sacred honor to defend this nation against all

enemies foreign and domestic. Let us not forget that America is a

great and noble country with a rich history of fairness and justice for

all. Let us not forget that this is a blessed place, graced by God with

a lauded heritage to defend freedom and defeat tyranny. Let us not

waver in our support for the dignity of all people. Let us not forget

that America is the iron shield against oppression. Let us not

question the merit of our cause. It is the most righteous of all causes

and is worthy of our greatest efforts. Let us not be discouraged by

the haters and the ignorant and coerced into accepting the lies that

America is an evil racist nation. Let us not forget those who forgot

their oath to protect the constitution and bent a knee with the mob to

beguile their wrath. As John Stuart Mill wrote, "Bad men need nothing more to compass their ends, than that good men should look on and do nothing."[9]

Without America's moral prerogative and dedication to the ideals of freedom, liberty, and justice for all, the world would be a very different place. Look to Hong Kong in the summer of 2020 as China's communist government cracked down on the people of the independent provincial city. The actions denied the residents their freedom of speech and liberty and violated an agreement with the British that established the city's relative autonomy. The world watched as the communists bullied their way into the city to crush the aspirations of the residents. And what did we see the protestors waving in defiance of the tyranny of communism? The American flag. Even to the people of Hong Kong, our flag represents liberty in the face of oppression.

All races and identities have added great value to American culture and the civil society. Asian Americans have made an important contribution and added to the context of the greater American family. Asian Americans have had great success in business, academia, the sciences, and social integration. The success of most Asian Americans can be traced directly to their strong nuclear family structures and their high regard for education and moral conduct. Moreover, most Asian Americans are either the first or second generation to immigrate to this country, and they made conscious choices to come here because of the opportunities America would allow them. It's a proud American story that needs to be told and pointed to as an example of conduct, perseverance, and achievement.

Enlightened Destination

Americans have a deep moral conscience and a continuous drive to do the right thing even if at great cost or consequence. The Civil War is one example of this. To shed the bindings of slavery from the nation's soul, the greater part of Americans willingly endured the turmoil of the great national divide. America, born in the fire of a revolution, inspired by Providence, and guided by the Constitution, is a nation of people who are constantly striving to do better. We are a community of individuals who constantly persevere to achieve a better way of life for our nation and, by our example, the world.

New American Awareness

Without God and a moral compass at the center of the American experience, the nation would not have marshaled the resolve to pursue justice. America, like all nations, is not perfect, but the country is on an eternal quest to better the human condition. America is passing through troubled times, and a minority of our people have been distracted into believing false claims about America. Those Americans need to come home to the truth about our country and discard the false ideas that are currently fashionable. America will endure, and our best days are still ahead. Let us remember these words from President Ronald Reagan's farewell address from January 11, 1989:

> I've spoken of the shining city all my political life, but I don't know if I ever quite communicated what I saw when I said it. But in my mind it was a tall proud city built on rocks stronger than oceans, wind swept. God blessed, and teeming with people of all kinds living in harmony and peace - a city with free ports that hummed with commerce and creativity, and if there had to be city walls, the walls had doors, and the doors were open to anyone with the will and the heart to get here. That's how I saw it, and see it still.[10]

At the heart of a new American awareness should be a rediscovery by many Americans of who we are as a people. All aspects of consciousness should be applied to the task of self-reflection, understanding history, spiritualty, and reason. It will coincide with a renewed commitment to God's moral teaching as the promise of America continues. These are vital components to guide the nation along the path of righteousness and truth. "Ye shall know the truth, and the truth shall make you free."[11] The truth will also set the American nation free. We Americans now need to use our collective faculties of wisdom and judgement to bring harmony to the nation. We need to come home to the truth and follow the vision that has brought millions of people from all parts of the globe to our shores, guided by the beacons of light to America, the North Star of humanity.

Notes

1. The Promise of America

1. History.com Editors, "Alexis de Tocqueville," HISTORY, November 9, 2009, last modified June 7, 2019, https://www.history .com/topics/france/alexis-de-tocqueville

2. de Tocqueville, Alexis, *Democracy in America*, trans. Henry Reeve, Esq. (New York: Edward Walker, 1847) https://archive.org/ details/democracyinameri00tocq_8/mode/2up. It is possible that this quote has been misattributed to Tocqueville and might instead have originated in a travel narrative written by Andrew Reed and James Matheson, two English ministers who traveled to America in 1834, three years after Tocqueville's journey. See Andrew Reed and James Matheson, *A Narrative of the Visit to the American Churches by the Deputation from the Congregational Union of England and Wales Volume II* (London: Jackson and Walford, 1836) 226, https://archive.org/details/anarrativevisit03mathgoog/mode/2up

3. Holloway, Carson, "Tocqueville on Christianity and American Democracy," Heritage.org, March 7, 2016, https://www.heritage .org/civil-society/report/tocqueville-christianity-and-american-dem ocracy

4. de Tocqueville, Alexis, *Democracy in America*, trans. Harvey C. Mansfield and Delba Winthrop (Chicago: University of Chicago Press, 2002) 279–280, 519, quoted in Carson Holloway, "Tocqueville on Christianity and American Democracy," Heritage.org, March 7, 2016, https://www.heritage.org/civil-society /report/tocqueville-christianity-and-american-democracy

5. Washington, George, *Washington's Farewell Address, Delivered September 17th, 1796* (New York: D. Appleton and Company, 1861) https://archive.org/details/washingtonsfa00wash/mode/2up. It is likely that "It is impossible to rightly govern the world without God and the bible" was not part of Washington's farewell address and instead derives from James K Paulding's 1835 biography of Washington. See James K Paulding, *A Life of Washington Volume II* (New York: Harper & Brothers, 1835) 209, https://archive.org/ details/lifeofwashington02paul/mode/2up

6. Adams, John, *The Works of John Adams, Volume 9 (Letters and State Papers 1799-1811)* (Boston: Little, Brown, and Company, 1854) https://oll.libertyfund.org/title/adams-the-works-of-john-ada ms-vol-9-letters-and-state-papers-1799-1811

7. Schlesinger, Arthur M Jr., *The Disuniting of America: Reflections on a Multicultural Society* (New York: W.W. Norton, 1998) 17,

https://books.google.com/books/about/The_Disuniting_of_Americ a.html?id=8zqPoZG2UYUC

8. Crèvecoeur, J. Hector St. John, *Letters from an American Farmer* (New York: Fox, Duffield, & Company, 1904) https://archive.org/ details/lettersfromameri01stjo/mode/2up

9. Lincoln, Abraham, *President Lincoln's Inaugural Address. March 4, 1861* (Printed at the Republican National Office, 1861) https://archive.org/details/presidentlincoln00linc/mode/2up

2. Western Civilization and the Roots of Democracy

1. Johnson, David M., "Herodotus' Storytelling Speeches: Socles (5.92) and Leotychides (6.86)," *The Classical Journal* 97, no. 1 (2001) 1–26, http://www.jstor.org/stable/3298431

2. Thucydides, "Funeral Oration of Pericles," in *The History of the Peloponnesian War*, trans. Richard Crawley (London: J.M. Dent & Sons, 1910) 75, https://archive.org/details/in.ernet.dli.2015.36976/ mode/2up

3. Lincoln, Abraham, "Gettysburg Address," *Century Magazine*, Volume 25, 1894, https://archive.org/details/century-1894-v-25/mode/2up

3. Age of Reason/Enlightenment

1. McInerny, Ralph and O'Callaghan, John, "Saint Thomas Aquinas," *The Stanford Encyclopedia of Philosophy* (Summer 2018 Edition) Last modified May 23, 2014, https://plato.stanford.edu/archives/sum2018/entries/aquinas

2. Westfall, Richard S, "Isaac Newton. English Physicist and Mathematician," *Encyclopedia Britannica*, last modified March 27, 2022, https://www.britannica.com/biography/Isaac-Newton

3. de Secondat, Charles (Baron de Montesquieu), *The Spirit of Laws*, trans. Thomas Nugent (New York: The Colonial Press, 1899) https://archive.org/details/spiritoflaws01montuoft

4. Hall, Evelyn Beatrice [pseud.], *The Friends of Voltaire* (London: John Murray, 1906) https://www.gutenberg.org/ebooks/56618

5. Shapiro, Ben, "If We Lose John Locke, We Lose America," PragerU, July 20, 2020, https://www.prageru.com/video/if-we-lose-john-locke-we-lose-america/

6. Smith, Adam, *An Inquiry into the Nature and Causes of the Wealth of Nations, Volume II*, 1778 (London: Printed for W. Strahan and T. Cadell, in the Strand, 1778) https://archive.org/details/inquiryintonaturx02smit/mode/2up

7. Burke, Edmund, *Reflections on the Revolution in France, and on the Proceedings in Certain Societies in London Relative to that Event* (London: J. Dodsley, 1790) https://archive.org/details/reflections00burkuoft/mode/2up

8. Burke, Edmund, *Thoughts on the Present Discontents, and Speeches* (London: Cassell & Company, 1886) https://www.gutenberg.org/ebooks/2173

9. Burke, Edmund, *Edmund Burke's Speech on Conciliation with the American Colonies, Delivered in the House of Commons March 22, 1775* (New York: D. Appleton and Company, 1900) https://archive.org/details/edmundburkesspee00burkiala

10. Rousseau, Jean Jacques, *The Social Contract and Discourses*, trans. G. D. H. Cole (London: J. M. Dent & Sons, 1913) https://archive.org/details/socialcontractdi0000rous/mode/2up

11. Ibid, Rousseau.

12. Jefferson, Thomas, et al., *Declaration of Independence, July 4, 1776*, https://www.loc.gov/item/mtjbib000159/

13. Ibid, Jefferson.

4. By the Rude Bridge

1. Lengel, Edward G., *General George Washington: A Military Life* (New York: Random House Trade Paperbacks, 2007).

2. Smith, Daniel A., *Tax Crusaders and the Politics of Direct Democracy* (Routledge, 1998) 21–23.

3. Adams, John, "John Adams Diary 22A, September - October 1774" [electronic edition], *Adams Family Papers: An Electronic Archive* (Massachusetts Historical Society) Retrieved on March 10, 2022 from http://www.masshist.org/digitaladams/

4. Fischer, David Hackett, *Paul Revere's Ride* (New York: Oxford University Press 1994) 214.

5. Rankin, Hugh F. (ed.), *Rebels and Redcoats: The American Revolution through the Eyes of Those Who Fought and Lived It* (Da Capo Press, 1987) 63.

6. Frothingham, Richard, *History of the Siege of Boston, and of the Battles of Lexington, Concord, and Bunker Hill. Also an Account of the Bunker Hill Monument. With Illustrative Documents* (Boston, C.C. Little & J. Brown, 1849).

7. Wirt, William, *Sketches of the Life and Character of Patrick Henry* (James Webster, 1817).

5. When in the Course of Human Events

1. Jefferson, Thomas, et al., *Declaration of Independence, July 4, 1776*, https://www.loc.gov/item/mtjbib000159/

2. Ibid, Jefferson.

3. Alexander, William (Lord Sterling), *The Papers of George Washington, Revolutionary War Series, Vol. 6, 13 August 1776–20*

October 1776, ed. Philander D. Chase and Frank E. Grizzard, Jr. (Charlottesville: University Press of Virginia, 1994) 159–162.

4. Tallmadge, Benjamin, *Memoir of Col. Benjamin Tallmadge* (New York: T. Holman, 1858) 10-11.

5. Churchill, Winston, *Never Give In! The Best of Winston Churchill's Speeches, Selected and Edited by His Grandson, Winston S. Churchill* (Pimlico, 2004) 214. https://archive.org/details /never-give-in-the-best-of-winston-churchills-speeches-2003/mode /2up. Accessed on September 26, 2022.

6. McCullough, David, *1776* (New York: Simon & Schuster, 2005)

7. The Connecticut Society of the Sons of the American Revolution, *Lt. Col. Thomas Knowlton, Connecticut's Forgotten Hero*, https:// www.sarconnecticut.org/lt-col-thomas-knowlton-connecticuts-forg otten-hero/, Accessed on September 26, 2022.

8. Paine, Thomas, *The Complete Writings of Thomas Paine* (New York: The Citadel Press, 1945) 49-57. https://archive.org/details/ TheCompleteWritings/mode/2up. Accessed on September 26, 2022.

9. Washington, George, *The Papers of George Washington, Revolutionary War Series, vol. 7, 21 October 1776–5 January 1777* (Charlottesville: University Press of Virginia, 1997) 490–491.

10. Ketchum, Richard, *The Winter Soldiers: The Battles for Trenton and Princeton* (New York: Holt Paperbacks, 1999) 291.

11. Ibid, Ketchum.

12. Smith, Page, *A New Age Now Begins: A People's History of the American Revolution* (New York: McGraw-Hill, 1976) 837.

6. A New Constellation Appears

1. *Journals of the Continental Congress*, 1774-1789, ed. Worthington C. Ford et al. (Washington, D.C., 1904-37) 19:137, https://memory.loc.gov/cgi-bin/ampage?collId=lljc&fileName=01 9/lljc019.db&recNum=148

2. 111th Congress, Public Law 94, Joint Resolution [H.J. Res. 26], Proclaiming Casimir Pulaski to be an honorary citizen of the United States posthumously, November 6, 2009, https://www.govinfo.gov/ content/pkg/PLAW-111publ94/html/PLAW-111publ94.htm

3. Burgoyne, John, "General Burgoyne's Proclamation," Public Paper, June 20, 1777, From: Teaching American History, https://teachingamericanhistory.org/document/general-burgoynes-proclamation/

4. Schenawolf, Harry, "General John Stark: Able and Defiant Leader of the American Revolution," *Revolutionary War Journal*, April 5, 2022, https://www.revolutionarywarjournal.com/general-john-stark-able-and-defiant-leader-of-the-american-revolution/#_edn30

5. Martin, Joseph Plumb, *A Narrative of Some of the Adventures, Dangers and Sufferings of a Revolutionary Soldier; Interspersed with Anecdotes of Incidents that Occurred within His Own Observation* (Hallowell ME, Glazier, Masters & Co., 1830) 92, https://archive.org/details/MartinTheAdventuresOfARevolutionary Soldier

6. Stewart, David O., *George Washington: The Political Rise of America's Founding Father* (Penguin, 2022) 264.

7. Massey, Gregory D., *John Laurens and the American Revolution* (University of South Carolina Press, 2016)

8. Editors of Encyclopedia Britannica, "John Laurens," *Encyclopedia Britannica*, https://www.britannica.com/biography/John-Laurens, Accessed August 23, 2022.

9. Carlisle, Rodney, *Encyclopedia of Intelligence and Counterintelligence*, (Routledge, 2015) 281.

10. Schellhammer, Michael, "Nathan Hale: A Hero's Fiasco," *Journal of the American Revolution*, March 19, 2013, https://allthingsliberty.com/2013/03/nathan-hale-heros-fiasco/, Accessed on August 23, 2022.

11. Campbell, Maria Hull and Clarke, James Freeman, *Revolutionary Services and Civil Life of General William Hull* (New York: D. Appleton & Co.; Philadelphia: G.S. Appleton, 1848) https://archive.org/details/revolutionaryse00camp/mode/2up

12. Seymour, George Dudley, *Documentary Life of Nathan Hale, Comprising All Available Official and Private Documents Bearing on the Life of the Patriot, Together with an Appendix, Showing the background of His Life* (New-Haven, The Tuttle, Morehouse, and Taylor Company, Privately printed for the author, 1941) https://archive.org/details/documentarylifeo00seym/mode/2up

13. 111th Congress, Public Law 94, Joint Resolution [H.J. Res. 26], Proclaiming Casimir Pulaski to be an honorary citizen of the United States posthumously, November 6, 2009, https://www.govinfo.gov/content/pkg/PLAW-111publ94/html/PLAW-111publ94.htm

14. McCullough, David, *David McCullough Library E-book Box Set: 1776, Brave Companions, The Great Bridge, John Adams, The Johnstown Flood, Mornings on Horseback, Path Between the Seas, Truman, The Course of Human Events* (Simon and Schuster, 2011)

15. Kashatus, William C. III, *Conflict of Conviction: A Reappraisal of Quaker Involvement in the American Revolution* (University Press of America, 1990), 45.

16. Washington, George, "From George Washington to Major General Nathanael Greene, 16 September 1780," *Founders Online*, National Archives, https://founders.archives.gov/documents/Washington/03-28-02-0151. [Original source: *The Papers of George Washington, Revolutionary War Series*, vol. 28, 28 August–27 October 1780, ed. William M. Ferraro and Jeffrey L. Zvengrowski (Charlottesville: University of Virginia Press, 2020) 210–211.

17. Jacob, Mark and Case, Stephen, *Treacherous Beauty* (Lyons Press, 2012)

18. Hamilton, Alexander, "From Alexander Hamilton to Lieutenant Colonel John Laurens, 11 October 1780," *Founders Online,* National Archives, https://founders.archives.gov/documents/Hamilton/01-02-02-0896. [Original source: *The Papers of Alexander Hamilton*, vol. 2, *1779–1781*, ed. Harold C. Syrett (New York: Columbia University Press, 1961) 460–470.

19. Lynch, Wayne, "Eyewitnesses at the Cowpens," *Journal of the American Revolution*, July 26, 2016. https://allthingsliberty.com/2016/07/eyewitnesses-at-the-cowpens/, Original source: Collins, James P., "Autobiography of a Revolutionary Soldier," reprinted in Commager & Morris, *The Spirit of Seventy-Six* (Cambridge, MA: Da Capo Press, 1958), 1156.

20. National Historical Society, Mabel Thacher Rosemary Washburn, *The Journal of American History*, Volume 7; Volume 13, Francis Trevelyan Miller ed. (Associated Publishers of American Records, 1913) 811.

21. Gunby, A. A. (Andrew Augustus), *Colonel John Gunby of the Maryland Line: Being Some Account of His Contribution to American Liberty* (Cincinnati: R. Clarke Co., 1902)

22. Greene, Francis Vinton, *General Greene* (New York: Appleton, 1913) 242, https://archive.org/details/generalgreene00greeuoft/mode/2up

23. Weigley, Russell, *The Age of Battles: The Quest for Decisive Warfare from Breitenfeld to Waterloo* (Indiana University Press, 1991)

24. Ferling, John, *Egotistic Brit General Turned the World Upside Down at Yorktown*, https://www.historynet.com/brit-blew-it-at-yorktown/

25. Washington, George, *The Writings of George Washington, Volume 9*, Worthington Chauncey Ford ed. (G.P. Putnam's Sons, 1891) 386.

26. Wraxall, Sir Nathaniel, "Memoirs of Sir Nathaniel Wraxall" (November 1781) From: Teaching American History, https://teachingamericanhistory.org/document/memoirs-of-sir-nathaniel-wraxall/, Accessed August 29, 2022.

27. Baldwin, John, *History and Guide to Newburgh and Washington's Headquarters, and a Catalogue of Manuscripts and Relics in Washington's Headquarters* (New York: N. Tibballs & Sons, 1883) https://archive.org/details/historyguidetone00bald

28. Head, David, *A Crisis of Peace: George Washington, the Newburgh Conspiracy, and the Fate of the American Revolution* (New York: Pegasus Books, 2019), 150.

29. Farington, Joseph, *The Farington Diary, Vol. 1, July 13, 1793 to August 24, 1802* (London: Hutchinson & Co., 1922-1928) https://archive.org/details/faringtondiary01fariuoft

7. A More Perfect Union

1. Kidd, Thomas S., *Patrick Henry: First among Patriots* (New York: Basic Books, 2011) 182-183.

2. Mason, George, "James Madison's Notes of the Constitutional Convention," *The Records of the Federal Convention of 1787. Vol. 2*, ed. Max Farrand (New Haven: Yale University Press, 1911) 504.

3. Ibid, Mason.

4. Wiencek, Henry, "George Washington and Slavery," *Encyclopedia Virginia* (June 15, 2022) https://encyclopediavirginia.org/entries/washington-george-and-slavery.

5. Phillips, Wendell, *The Constitution. A Pro-slavery Compact: & Extracts from the Madison Papers, Etc.* (New York: American Anti-Slavery Society, 1856) https://archive.org/details/constitutionapr00 madigoog/mode/2up

6. Smyth, Albert Henry, *The Writings of Benjamin Franklin, Volume IX* (London: The Macmillan Company, 1906) https://archive.org/ details/writingsofbenjam09franuoft/mode/2up

7. Farrand, Max, *The Records of the Federal Convention of 1787, Volume III* (New Haven: Yale University Press, 1911) 85.

8. U.S. Const. pmbl.

9. Jefferson, Thomas, et al., Declaration of Independence, July 4, 1776, https://www.loc.gov/item/mtjbib000159/

10. Chesterton, G.K., *What I saw in America* (New York: Dodd, Mead and Company, 1922) https://archive.org/details/whatisawin amer00chesrich/mode/2up

11. Madison, James, "The Federalist No. 51," Rpt. in *The Documentary History of the Ratification of the Constitution. Vol. 16.* Ed. Gaspare J. Saladino and John P. Kaminski (Madison: Wisconsin

Historical Society Press, 1986) 43-47, https://www.consource.org/
document/the-federalist-no-51-1788-2-6/20130122080331/

12. Lincoln, Abraham, *Proceedings of the Republican State
Convention Held at Springfield, Illinois, June 16, 1858* (Springfield:
Bailhache & Baker, 1858) https://archive.org/details/proceedings
ofrep7982repu

13. Lincoln, Abraham, *Three Letters from Lincoln: The Letter to
Horace Greeley, the Letter to J.C. Conkling, the Letter to Mrs. Bixby*
(Philadelphia: Printed by Benjamin F. Emery, 1908) https://archive
.org/details/threelettersfrom00linc

14. Lincoln, Abraham, "Gettysburg Address," *Century Magazine*,
Volume 25 (1894) https://archive.org/details/century-1894-v-25/
mode/2up

8. A City upon a Hill

1. Reagan, Ronald (Governor of California, 1967-1975), Inaugural
Address, January 5, 1967, https://www.reaganlibrary.gov/archives/
speech/january-5-1967-inaugural-address-public-ceremony

2. Renan, Ernest, "What is a Nation?" Text of a Conference
Delivered at the Sorbonne on March 11th, 1882, in Renan Ernest,

Qu'est-ce qu'une nation? Paris, Presses-Pocket, 1992 (translated by Ethan Rundell), http://ucparis.fr/files/9313/6549/9943/What_is_a_Nation.pdf

3. Ibid, Renan.

4. Jefferson, Thomas, et al., Declaration of Independence, July 4, 1776, https://www.loc.gov/item/mtjbib000159/

5. Marx, Karl, "Critique of Hegel's Philosophy of Right," *Marx on Religion* (Philadelphia: Temple University Press, 2002)171, https://archive.org/details/marxonreligion0000marx/mode/2up

6. The Washington Times, EDITORIAL: The '1619 Project' is bad history fueled by bad motives, Sunday, May 24, 2020, https://www.washingtontimes.com/news/2020/may/24/editorial-1619-project-bad-history-fueled-bad-moti/

7. Hobbes, Thomas, *Hobbes's Leviathan. Reprinted from the Edition of 1651* (Oxford: Clarendon Press, 1909)99, https://archive.org/details/hobbessleviathan00hobbuoft/mode/2up

8. Lincoln, Abraham, *Abraham Lincoln: His Speeches and Writings* (Cleveland, New York: The World Pub. Co., 1946)473, https://archive.orgdetails/abrahamlincolnhi00illinc

9. Mill, John Stuart, *Inaugural Address: Delivered to the University of St. Andrews February 1st, 1867* (London: Longmans, Gren, Reader, and Dyer, 1867)74, https://archive.org/details/fp-0143/mode/2up

10. Reagan, Ronald, "Transcript of Reagan's Farewell Address to American People," *The New York Times*, January 12, 1989, https://www.nytimes.com/1989/01/12/news/transcript-of-reagan-s-farewell-address-to-american-people.html

11. John 8:32 King James Bible Online, https://www.kingjamesbibleonline.org/John-8-32/

www.ingramcontent.com/pod-product-compliance
Lightning Source LLC
Chambersburg PA
CBHW071135130626
46553CB00004B/1381